Fields of Glory

The Extraordinary Lives of
16 Warrior Sportsmen

Fields of Glory

The Extraordinary Lives of 16 Warrior Sportsmen

Gavin Mortimer

ANDRE DEUTSCH

This edition first published in 2001

10 9 8 7 6 5 4 3 2 1

Text copyright © Gavin Mortimer 2001
Design copyright © André Deutsch 2001

André Deutsch is an imprint of
the Carlton Publishing Group
20 Mortimer Street
London W1T 3JW

A CIP catalogue record for this book is available from the British Library

ISBN 0 233 99990 6

Commissioning Editor: Martin Corteel
Project Editor: Kerrin Edwards
Picture Research: Debora Fioravanti
Project Art Direction: Mark Lloyd
Jacket Design: Steve Lynn
Plate Section Design: Michelle McConnochie
Production: Sarah Corteel

Printed and bound in Great Britain

The publisher would like to thank the sources credited in the plate sections for their
kind permission to reproduce the pictures in this book. Every effort has been made to
acknowledge correctly and contact the source and/ or copyright holder of each picture
and also for any other copyright material used in the book. The publisher apologizes for
any unintentional errors or omissions. Anyone who for any reason has not been contacted
is invited to write to the publisher so that a full acknowledgement may be made in
subsequent editions of this work

Contents

Foreword by Rory Underwood MBE

To represent one's country in one's chosen sport is the dream of supporters and followers up and down the land. If only they could grace the hallowed turf of Wembley, Twickenham, Lord's or Wimbledon; show off their skills in the ring; or experience the Olympic ideal.

To play sport at the highest level is what every serious sportsman aspires to. All the blood, sweat and tears seem inconsequential to the pride of representing your country as you run out to the acclaim of the crowd to pit your wits against the best of the rest of the world and relish the challenge it brings.

Those same aspirations fuelled generations of men to serve their country as soldiers, airmen and sailors. To carry that ambition from playground antics to reality requires drive and determination to overcome all the challenges and obstacles that lie in wait. The pride of completing their training and graduating or passing out makes all the sacrifices seem worthwhile.

And so, with great pride, I write the foreword to *Fields of Glory* as someone fortunate enough to have represented my country both at rugby football and as a pilot in the Royal Air Force. I have experienced what it takes to reach the top and I have seen many who have failed to realize their dreams; team-mates on the rugby pitch at school, who never carried it on into adult life; colleagues who failed to meet the required standard set by pilot training or who just felt 'a life in the RAF' was not for them.

All this, though, was without the personal experience of war. Despite the Gulf War and the many conflicts throughout the Balkans and the Middle East, I have never been in 'combat situations'. I knew that I could possibly be called upon to go to war and although I debated the thought many times I would not really know how I felt until the situation arose. The glamour of being a fast jet pilot is what drew me into the RAF, not the desire to go to war.

So despite the adoration that has been heaped on me, being a modern day 'hero', a sporting star and RAF pilot rolled into one, I feel somewhat humbled by the stories within this book. They were heroes at a time when war was pretty much a norm, when joining the services was acknowledging the fact that you would be going to war and risking your life. Having spent eighteen years in the

RAF I have an understanding of their psyche; I have seen friends and colleagues go to war and some not come home. Until I have to confront that situation I will never ever truly know and it is their bravery and courage to which I aspire should the need ever arise.

Introduction

'Life is a journey of self-discovery. I am curious to learn my strengths and weaknesses. But until they put cork on your face, a gun in your hand and point you in the direction of the beaches, you never really know what you're made of'

Tony O'Reilly, Ireland (29 caps) and the British Lions (10 caps)

None of the men in *Fields of Glory* were flawless. Some drank too much, others enjoyed a fight – in or out of uniform – and one or two pursued women with a singular determination. I dare say if you encountered them in a pub – a group outing doesn't bear thinking about – they might appear overbearing, opinionated and obstreperous as they stood at the bar holding sway.

In some ways they weren't very sympathetic characters, despite what they had all gone through on the battlefield. They never asked for sympathy and they didn't expect any in return. One suspects that they wouldn't know whether to laugh or cry if they returned today and discovered soldiers suing for stress. 'Stress,' they would say, 'I'll tell you what stress is.' But, of course, they wouldn't and things were different then. They saw what they did as their duty. If they had bad times in war they were balanced by the good times on the sports field. When they returned from the war they tried to get on with their lives as best they could – not all managed to readjust but none ever uttered a word of complaint.

Fields of Glory is a celebration of these sixteen extraordinary lives. I use the word 'celebration' with care; this book doesn't attempt to glorify what they did in the war – God knows, there is little glory to be found on the battlefield – but neither does it seek to portray them as victims by applying the attitudes of today to an earlier era when self-pity was anathema.

I have attempted to tell their stories through their own eyes and portray them as sixteen contrasting personalities. They all played hard and fought hard, and several of them lived hard. I hope that becomes apparent over the coming pages. To many of the sixteen, the war gave them the most exciting and enjoyable years of their lives, surpassing even what they achieved on the sports field. Of course there was fear, but there was also camaraderie, exhilaration and adventure.

Some people may find this book raucous or bellicose. I make no apology for that. It will appeal to a certain type of person, just like the men themselves.

Gavin Mortimer, Paris, 2001

CHAPTER ONE

Robert Johnston

Tall, upright and dignified, Robert Johnson was an establishment man who was born with an outstanding rugby talent. After winning caps for Ireland and the British Isles in the 1890s, the Dubliner proved himself a warrior in South Africa during the Boer War.

Robert Johnston and Tom Crean formed one of Ireland's earliest rugby double acts. Johnston, the son of a QC, was the straight man, trying to retain a semblance of sanity while the rambunctious Crean created havoc wherever he went. They played alongside each other for the Dublin Wanderers, Ireland and a British XV. When the Boer War broke out in 1899, they enlisted, trained and fought together. Johnston was awarded a Victoria Cross within the first month of the war. Crean had to wait a further two years for his. It was an extraordinary partnership.

Johnston was born in Laputa, County Donegal, on 13 August 1872 and educated at King William's College on the Isle of Man. He left school in 1890 and enlisted in the 5th Battalion, Royal Inniskilling Fusiliers. A short time later he had his first encounter with Crean at the Wanderers rugby club in Dublin.

It wasn't an obvious friendship. Crean was no larrikin. He was well educated and his purpose in Dublin was to study medicine at the Royal College of Surgeons. But his was an untamed soul and his *joie de vivre* could sometimes get out of hand. Johnston, on the other hand, with his boarding school education and military background, was a man reared on protocol and convention. The opposites attracted and they became firm friends, even if for the rest of their friendship Johnston suffered untold embarrassment because of the shenanigans of his sidekick.

Johnston's call-up to the Ireland XV in 1893 came on the back of several outstanding displays for the Wanderers. In 1893 the *Belfast Telegraph* carried a report on their match against Queen's College at Ballynaieigh, in which it described the Wanderers' winning try: 'Johnston, a minute later, got clean away at the twenty-five, and fell with Johns [the Queen's full-back] over the line, succeeding in scoring.'

Johnston and Crean were both loose forwards who played a similar game. They had a fair turn of speed and were also exceptionally big men for players of that era. On the eve of his Test debut against England, Johnston was listed in the team line-up as 6ft 2in and 13st 7lb, making him the heaviest player in the Irish side. Both men also used to take place-kicks which, though unusual for forwards in the modern game, was by no means out of the ordinary a century ago.

Johnston's Ireland debut against England on 4 February 1893 ended in failure, the visitors to Lansdowne Road winning by two tries to nil. He missed the Scotland match a fortnight later but returned for the game against Wales in Llanelli on 11 March.

The Irish were up against a formidable set of Welsh backs that included the vastly experienced Billy Bancroft and Arthur Gould, and a try from Gould's brother, Bert, was the only score of the match. Outclassed in the backs, the Irish forwards did what subsequent generations of their countrymen have made an art form and hustled the opposition to distraction. The *Athletic News* lavished praise on the bloody-minded Irishmen: 'They succeeded admirably in hampering the Welsh backs and in that way prevented a heavy defeat. Their tackling was sure, and the footwork of the forwards very clever and hard to stop. Possibly the anxiety of the forwards to rush out upon the Welsh backs was responsible for Wales' superiority in the tight scrummage. There was little to choose in the line-out; if anything, Ireland could claim the advantage.'

That was the end of Johnston's Ireland career. The following season in 1894 he had to be content with playing in a Wanderers side that won the Leinster Cup. Crean made his Test debut the same year and helped Ireland to their first Triple Crown.

While Crean was making hay on the international field – Ireland won the championship again in 1896 – Johnston continued to turn out for the Wanderers. He left the Royal Inniskilling Fusiliers in 1894 but nothing is known about the profession upon which he embarked. His heart clearly wasn't in it, whatever it was, because in 1896 he accepted an invitation to join an Anglo-Irish tour to South Africa, a trip that would mean three months away from home. The party, led by Johnny Hammond, contained twenty-one players of whom twelve were Englishmen and the rest Irish. Invitations had been issued to Scottish and Welsh players but for reasons unknown they declined to travel. The tour was the third such venture undertaken by a British rugby side – and the second to South Africa following an unbeaten tour in 1891 – but it was the first time that Irishmen had been present in the squad.

Where there was Johnston there was of course Crean and the two appeared side by side in the frontispiece of the tour's souvenir scrapbook. Johnston was resplendent in the uniform of the Inniskilling Fusiliers, head held high and a waxed moustache bestriding a lantern jaw. Crean too tried to convey an air of seriousness in bow tie and winged collar, but the twinkle in the eye undid his best efforts.

The squad embarked on 20 June 1896 with a reporter from the *Athletic News* present to report proceedings.

> 'To give the combination a hearty send off, a large number of well known footballers and supporters of the game assembled on Saturday morning on the No 1 platform of Waterloo Station. While waiting, telegrams came pouring in to various members of the party and then a hurried shake of the hand and "Goodbye, boys", "Good luck" and the Union Line Special steamed out at a quarter to twelve.'

The *Athletic News*, Britain's weekly sports newspaper, persuaded one of the players to send back regular reports from the tour and the first one appeared in a July edition under the pseudonym 'Tartar' (the name of the squad's ship). The hand of the team censor is clearly detectable in the first piece, which drew attention to the decorum of the tourists. 'About nine of the team adjourned to drink the usual toast of "Sweethearts and Wives". Lights were put out at 10.30 but most of us had retired to our bunks before that hour.'

The sea passage to Cape Town took eighteen days and 'Tartar', evidently a man with sea legs, took delight in reporting the discomfort of those team-mates less fortunate: 'Many were the tales of woe and distress we heard … the sacrifices to Neptune having been long and numerous.'

Activities available to the players on board the ship were limited but varied. They held a series of sports competitions as well as a tug of war contest and a concert for first-class passengers. The concert was held in the music saloon and Johnston was one of five players to perform a well-received solo. The tug of war contest consisted of teams of sailors, ship's firemen, first-class, second-class and third-class passengers. 'Tartar' described the event. 'The sailors beat the second- and third-class passengers and the firemen beat the first-class passengers [the tourists]. The firemen then beat the sailors.'

Furious with themselves for losing, the players challenged the firemen to another contest the next day and this time 'the team regained their laurels, Mackie, Lee, Clinch, Walker, Crean, Johnston, Hancock and Todd pulling the firemen over the line twice in succession'.

The tug of war embarrassment came on 6 July, just a couple of days before the ship reached Cape Town. It was the first sign of how far the players' fitness had declined after three weeks cooped up on a ship. That they had been shorn of their stamina became apparent in the opening match against Cape Town Clubs at Newlands. The tourists scraped home 14–9 but the *Cape Times*, which on first sight of the squad had gushed 'what lengthy specimens of manhood!', wasn't impressed by what it saw. 'The all round exhibition of the English team was very disappointing. The forwards are by no means fit yet and they have not settled into united work.'

The squad was treated royally off the field with the South Africans keen to show off their land to the men from the Mother Country. On 21 July the players paid a visit to the West End De Beers diamond compound where forty Zulus welcomed them with a tribal dance. 'The Englishmen,' commented one local paper, 'were objects of considerable interest to the natives.' The tourists reciprocated the curiosity, taking photographs until their plates ran out.

A week later there was a hunting trip to the veldt, which went down well with 'Tartar'. 'A capital day's sport was witnessed, the greyhounds killing several spring bucks. Some of the team were provided with mounts, and thoroughly enjoyed following the hounds whilst others ran on foot and so got themselves fit for the return match with Griqualand West. The day's outing did the team a world of good.'

It did Griqualand no good. They were beaten 16–0, a resounding defeat coming only a few days after they had been narrowly squeezed out 11–9 in their first encounter. The next match was against Port Elizabeth, who were beaten 26–6. The tourists had played themselves back to full fitness. Eastern Province were trounced 18–0 and Johnston had what the *Cape Times* described as his strongest game of the tour to date. His perseverance particularly caught the paper's eye: 'Johnston quickly getting possession again found his pathway disputed by Eaton … but not to be denied Johnston for a third time within one minute started off but Lyons grassed him now.'

The victory against Eastern Province was celebrated with dancing to the music of Signor Tasdugno's string band, which continued until the early hours of the morning. These post-match dances were a feature of the tour, growing ever more ostentatious as rival towns tried to outdo one another. After the British side had beaten Transvaal, the Wanderers Hall was the scene of what 'Tartar' described as 'a very delightful function, [although] the room was perhaps a trifle too crowded and on a future occasion it would be well to let comfort overrule sentiment to engage a more commodious room'.

Johnston's performances in the early tour matches earned him a slot in the starting line-up for the first Test against South Africa in Port Elizabeth on 29 July, which the British won 4–0.

The players now embarked on an itinerary that would have tested the stamina of David Livingstone. The day after the Test the squad left – by horse and cart – for Grahamstown where, on 1 August, they won 20–0. The next day, Sunday, they rose at crack of dawn and covered 36 miles along dirt tracks that were so bad the players frequently had to push the carts out of ruts. That evening they lodged at a place called Breakfast Vlei, although according to 'Tartar' beds were in short supply due to a breakdown in communications: 'Through some mis-understanding not a single hotel en route was prepared for us and we had to sleep where we could find a resting place, and eat what we could get.'

On Monday 3 August there was no improvement in travelling conditions and they didn't reach King William's Town until dusk. The entire population of this isolated town turned out next afternoon to see their boys put to the sword 25–0. The *Athletic News* carried an account of the game and picked out 'Johnston, Crean, Hancock and Mortimer as the best of the side'.

Just after eight o'clock the following morning, Wednesday, they left for East London for a Thursday match that was won 27–0. On Friday morning the boys were off again, 25 miles north to Queenstown, who were beaten 25–0 on the Saturday. Thus a twenty-one-man squad had played five matches in ten days, scoring 105 points and conceding not one.

The tourists' peregrinations took them next to Johannesburg, at the time a hotbed of political intrigue. Just a few months earlier there had been a disastrous attempt by several hundred pro-British mounted police to topple the Afrikaner Government that ruled Transvaal. The Jameson Raid, as it became known, was the brainchild of the avaricious and ambitious Cecil Rhodes who, as Prime Minister of Cape Colony, wanted to see Transvaal annexed to the Crown, thus ending a period of Afrikaner rule stretching back to 1881. Rhodes had hoped the sight of mounted soldiers galloping across the Transvaal would inspire the large number of foreign gold prospectors to rise up and rebel against the Afrikaners. The foreigners, 'Uitlanders' to the Afrikaners, sat tight and the raiders were rounded up and imprisoned.

Although pistols had been reholstered, the tension in the city was palpable. The British were looking for an excuse to invade the Transvaal as keenly as the prospectors were searching the Rand for gold. Into this climate of mistrust entered the Anglo-Irish party, not the last time that a touring party from the British Isles would court political controversy in South Africa.

The second Test was in Johannesburg and Johnston had his best game of the tour, perhaps inspired by the large number of women in the crowd who 'quite outnumbered the sterner sex ... and emulated the latter in their enthusiasm'. In the first few minutes Johnston and Larry Bulger, the Dublin University threequarter, broke out of defence after some sustained South African pressure and worked their way just short of the home team try-line. Later in the game Johnston had a hand in the decisive try, slipping a pass to Mackie, the Cambridge University centre, who sent Crean over to make it

10–0. South Africa fought back in the second half and Theo Samuels, a late replacement at full-back for Maxwell, had the honour of becoming the first player to score a try for his country.

Although now two Tests down, South Africa's steady progress continued in the third Test in Kimberley where they lead Britain 3–0 at half-time. The visitors stepped up the pressure in the second half, winning 9–3, but it was no great surprise when in the fourth and final Test South Africa won 5–0.

With the tour over Crean and Johnston decided to remain in South Africa. The pair were in their early twenties and had no ties in Ireland, so why not take advantage of the free passage? South Africa at that time was a land riven by distrust between the Afrikaners and the British. Maybe they sensed that an armed conflict was near and relished the prospect of adventure. More likely was the lure of gold. Their movements after the fourth Test in Cape Town would seem to indicate this was their motive for remaining in South Africa. Once Johnston had recovered from an attack of tonsillitis that sidelined him for the final Test, they retraced their steps to Johannesburg.

There is little evidence of what Johnston got up to in the years before the outbreak of war in 1899. He continued to play rugby, turning out for the Wanderers of Johannesburg, alongside Crean, who had a medical practice in the city. In 1897 he captained Transvaal in their defeat by Western Province in the final of the Currie Cup.

As the century drew to a close the political situation in South Africa deteriorated. Britain's Imperialist expansion policy was on a collision course with the Afrikaners' desire to remain a self-determining republic, free of outside interference. The same year that Johnston was appointed captain of the Transvaal side, the British Government appointed Sir Alfred Milner High Commissioner in South Africa. The Afrikaners looked askance at Milner, sensing that he was an agitator, sent to South Africa to exploit the resentment harboured by many Uitlanders towards the Transvaal government. The Uitlanders wanted a greater say in how Transvaal was run but President Kruger refused to grant them a role within the government. The decadence that had enveloped Johannesburg since the arrival of the Uitlanders appalled the stern, God-fearing Afrikaners. If the Uitlanders were given any form of power sharing the Afrikaners believed it would lead only to moral decay.

In the summer of 1899 the British Government was told by its representatives in South Africa that British citizens in the Transvaal were being treated as if they were no better than the blacks. This was intolerable to the Government and a week later 10,000 troops were dispatched to South Africa in the belief that this show of strength would serve as a shot across the Afrikaners' bow. It did nothing of the sort.

Kruger and his Government had been stockpiling a large arsenal for the past five years, most purchased from sympathetic contacts in Germany and France. Kruger didn't want a fight but he wasn't prepared to see his land swallowed up by the British Empire.

On 9 October he issued an ultimatum to the British Government saying it must withdraw its troops from the Transvaal border where they were massing. The following day the British cabled Kruger – his birthday – rejecting the ultimatum. The Boers moved quickly and on 11 October in a pre-emptive strike they invaded Natal with a force of some 15,000 men. On the face of it, the Boers stood no chance. They were up against reputedly the most powerful army in the world. They were a raggle-taggle bunch, aged from sixteen to sixty, with no uniform and no military training. But they had weapons – about 80,000 modern Mauser rifles supplied by Germany – and most Afrikaners were excellent riders and marksmen from the time spent hunting on the veldt, a terrain they knew how to use to their advantage. They also had in their ranks 2,000 foreign nationals, all motivated by a fear of British colonial expansion. They included Germans, Scandinavians, Americans, Italians and Russians. The largest contingent, however, were the 500 men from Ireland.

By the time the Boers crossed from Transvaal into Natal, Johnston and Crean were in uniform. The two had joined an irregular unit called the Imperial Light Horse. Most of the men who fought in this regiment were Uitlanders recruited from the gold mines of the Rand, further evidence that Johnston had dabbled in the trade. Johnston and Crean enlisted at the Pietermaritzburg Show Grounds in the first week of September when war was imminent. Johnston with his military background was given an immediate commission. Crean rejected the chance to become a medical officer and entered the ranks as a trooper. As the threat of war increased in early October the regiment received orders to prepare to strike camp and ride to Ladysmith. Crean, recently promoted to corporal, approached Captain Johnston with a request that became regimental folklore:

'Excuse me, Sir, may I have a few hours leave? – urgent private affairs.'

'Certainly not. You know all leave is stopped and I'm surprised that you, a non com [non-commissioned officer], should not set a better example.'

'Sorry, Sir, may I have a word with you personally, unofficially?'

'Yes, what is it?'

'Bob, you're a dirty –. You know well there's a bit of a spree on and it's spitefulness to keep me here. Bob, dear, just you wait until this war is over and I'll prove to you that you are no man by giving you the father and mother of a hiding – the Saints pity you!'

'Is that all, Corporal Crean?'

'Yes, Sir.'

'Break away.'

The Imperial Light Horse was safely in Ladysmith when the first salvos were fired in the war. The Battle of Talana Hill on 20 October was a victory of sorts for the British, although the high casualty rate presaged future disasters. The British learned from two prisoners that a Boer force under Commandant Kock had occupied the station at nearby Elandslaagte, capturing a supply train along the way. The Afrikaners had also cut telegraph lines and sabotaged the railway track.

General Sir George White, the cantankerous silver-haired commander of the British forces, was not pleased. This 'commando' style of warfare was alien to the 64-year-old who had been reared on orderly infantry charges. He ordered Major-General French to destroy the irritants. French descended upon Elandslaagte with five squadrons of the Imperial Light Horse, some infantrymen from the Manchester Regiment and the Natal Field Battery.

French would have had only a vague idea of the numbers of men ranged against him. He was aware, however, as were the men of the Imperial Light Horse, that the Boers occupying Elandslaagte station were commandos from Johannesburg. This was the fight the Light Horse wanted. Ever since the botched Jameson Raid in 1895 the Uitlanders had lived with the stigma of cowardice, a charge levelled at them by the Boers who ridiculed their passivity as the mounted insurgents tried to start an uprising. The Boers had even renamed the Uitlanders' city 'Judasberg'. As dawn broke on the morning of 21 October the unmistakable whiff of revenge hung in the air. The shriek of the two shells that rent the morning air was the last sound heard by several of the Boers caught napping in Elandslaagte. Before the Natal Field Battery had time to follow up their opening salvo, the thousand-strong force of Boers had beat a hasty retreat to a series of spurs 2,000 yards away on the opposite side of the valley.

From defensive positions dug several days earlier, the Boers retaliated with their two Maxim-Nordenfelt guns. One shell blew apart an ammunition wagon. The Boer guns outranged the British Seven Pounders and French decided to call up reinforcements. He sent a message to Colonel Hamilton in Ladysmith, asking for a squadron of 5th Lancers and 5th Dragoon Guards, a Royal Field Artillery Battery and a large infantry force consisting of one company from the Devonshire Regiment and five companies of Gordon Highlanders. By 3pm all the reinforcements were in place. The combined British force now outnumbered the Boers by about three to one.

There was one problem for the attackers, the topography of the battlefield. One British war correspondent present at the battle described it thus: 'When viewed from the flank they [the spurs] looked something like the teeth of a saw. To the front and on the flanks of this position stretched the rolling veldt, without any considerable cover, for at least 5,000 yards.'

At 4pm Johnston ordered his squadron to dismount. They would be going in on foot. The attack started half an hour later, with the artillery laying down a barrage under which the British advanced. The Devons launched a semi-frontal attack on the main spur, while the Light Horse, Gordons and Manchesters worked their way round the Boers' right flank. The affront of the combatants dismayed the gods, and the heavens opened to drench them in a torrential downpour. As the British advanced through rain and shrapnel, the sky behind the spur was illuminated by streaks of lightning.

The driving rain largely obscured the Boers' view of the British as they crossed the hideously exposed veldt. Once among the temporary safety of the boulders at the bottom of the spur, the soldiers had time to glance upwards, towards the top of the 800-foot spur that was their objective. The Boers had spent three days building fortifications on the spur and their diligence now wreaked havoc among the waves of British infantry clambering up the hillside. A thick fence of barbed wire blocked the path of the attackers. Those who were snagged were riddled with bullets from Boer marksmen hidden behind rocks or in trenches. In the few places where gaps appeared in the wire, the Boers concentrated their fire and the bodies of the British dead accumulated, effectively blocking the holes. As Johnston's squadron fought their way to the top they encountered a large number of German troops attempting a counter-flank, led by a Colonel Schiel. The Light Horse fell upon the mercenaries, slaughtering every one without mercy. The *Times* correspondent, climbing alongside the Light Horse, wrote the next day that it now 'ceased to be a general's battle; everything depended on company and even on section commanders, and gallantly the officers and non-commissioned officers did their work. If the men wavered and stuck under cover, the officers sacrificed themselves to furnish an example.'

The Boers would have been dismayed to hear such an assessment. The war was only a few days old but already they had realized that the British generals had little tactical appreciation of how to fight a guerrilla war. They were applying outdated strategies learned on the subcontinent against ill-disciplined and lightly-armed natives. Only when there was a change in military leadership in late 1900 did the British start waging a war more suited to the terrain and opposition.

But the Boers knew the British 'Tommy', if freed from the shackles of his bumbling generals, was a formidable foe. After the Battle of Spion Kop in January 1900, a humiliating defeat for the British caused by inept leadership, a Boer soldier said: 'We know the British soldier is the best in the world, and your regimental officer the bravest; it is your generals we rely on.'

At around 6pm these British Tommies, through a combination of superior numbers and unwavering courage, fought their way to the top of the spur and captured the Boer guns. The Imperial Light Horse had lost their CO, Colonel Scott-Chisholme, who had been shot in the ankle as he stopped to assist a wounded trooper. As he lay on the ground, he waved his men on with his red silk scarf, crying 'My boys are doing well.' Seconds later he was shot through the head.

The new occupants of the spur stood and surveyed their handiwork, justifiably proud of what they had done. But their jubilation was short-lived. The Boers launched a desperate final counter-attack, led personally by Kock, and the ferocity of the fresh onslaught temporarily demoralized the British troops. They turned and fled. Back they ran down the spur, past the body of Scott-Chisholme, red scarf still grasped in his hand, and the corpses of dozens of their comrades.

It was at this point that Johnston won his Victoria Cross. Along with Captain Charles Mullins and Lieutenant Brabant, both Imperial Light Horse, Johnston positioned himself in front of the fleeing soldiers and checked the retreat. Gathering up remnants from the Gordons, Manchesters and Light Horse, Mullins and Johnston led a fresh charge towards the ridge. Near the top they met the cock-a-hoop Boers, who thought the battle was theirs. Bloody hand-to-hand fighting ensued for several minutes as bayonets, rifle butts and bare hands were used in the final death struggle. The war correspondent of the *Morning Post,* who witnessed the frenzied climax of the battle, wrote: 'The ILH behaved with splendid recklessness. The final charge was magnificent. I was behind the Gordons and the Imperials and saw it all. I consider it the finest close fighting the world has ever known.'

Kock was killed in the mêlée, as were many of his commandos. The remainder either surrendered or fled. The *Times* correspondent reported that the battle was over at 6.30pm. 'I had just time to look round the laager below the hillside, strewn with dead and wounded, the Dutch and German gunners being distinguishable by their brown uniform. They had fought their guns splendidly.'

Johnston had been slightly wounded in the second charge up the spur. He joined a casualty list that graphically illustrated the ferocity of the battle; the British suffered 50 men killed and 213 wounded. The Boers had left behind 67 of their dead on the spur, with 100 wounded and over 200 in the hands of the enemy.

Captain Mullins, as senior officer of the Imperial Light Horse present during the Battle of Elandslaagte, wrote a report for the high command in which he paid tribute to the Gordon Highlanders in the face of terrible losses. As a result of the report the Victoria Cross was awarded to two of their number, Lt Meiklejohn and Sergeant-Major Robertson.

The lack of decorations bestowed upon the Light Horse, however, rankled with some of their officers. Was there a hint of prejudice in this oversight? As an irregular force composed of disparate nationalities the Light Horse were tolerated, respected even, but never loved by senior British officers. But even they had to concede that the Light Horse had played the decisive role in the battle and should be rewarded.

On 12 February 1901 the awards of the Victoria Cross to Mullins and Johnston were gazetted. The identical citation read:

'Charles Herbert Mullins, Captain, ILH, and Robert Johnston, Captain, ILH. On 21 October 1899, at Elandslaagte, at a most critical moment, the advance being momentarily checked by a very severe fire at point-blank range, these two officers very gallantly rushed forward under this heavy fire and rallied the men, thus enabling the flanking movement which decided the day to be carried out.'

While his family and friends raised a toast, Johnston remained unaware of the honour he'd received. Ever since 30 October he had been trapped inside the town of Ladysmith, along with 12,000 other British soldiers and 8,000 civilians.

General White was in command of the besieged town and he adopted a 'sit tight and wait' policy. Conditions worsened inside Ladysmith as food ran out and the Boers continued to shell the town with their two 'Long Tom' cannons. The greatest threat, however, was disease. Dysentery and enteric fever spread swiftly and on 26 December Johnston was admitted to the Intombi Hospital, which with the permission of the Boers had been established four miles outside Ladysmith to deal with the increasing number of sick and wounded.

There he lay until 19 January, racked by an undisclosed fever, dreaming, he said later, of suet dumplings and pears. He also had with him a 'siege brand of tobacco, a mixture of peach and wild geranium leaves', a little something to calm the nerves. And he needed it. As dysentery and enteric fever took a hold in the town, there was a greater demand for people with medical experience. Crean was given permission to leave the ranks of the Light Horse temporarily and work in the hospital. It must have been with a mixture of pleasure and trepidation that Johnston woke one morning to see his old friend standing over his bed. The siege was raised on 28 February 1900, when General Sir Redvers Buller finally succeeded in dispersing the Boers who had encircled the town. He marched triumphantly into Ladysmith the next day, ending 118 days of captivity for the starving soldiers and civilians.

Johnston continued to serve with the Imperial Light Horse for the rest of 1900. On 5 June he took command of 'C' squadron and was involved in the fruitless hunt for General Christiaan De Wet's commando. The following month he led his squadron in a skirmish against some Boers at Witklip, an engagement that rumbled on into the next morning when 600 commandos were seen coming towards them as they rode out on patrol. Johnston and his men, outnumbered by six to one, decided that discretion was the better part of valour and retired.

On 25 July 1901, he went to London to receive his VC from King Edward VII at St James's Palace, along with Mullins, who was now a cripple having been shot several times during a Boer ambush the previous year.

The next ten years of Johnston's life were spent back in South Africa. In 1902 he was appointed commandant of a concentration camp in Middelburg, 25 miles east of Pretoria. The decision by the British to establish a series of concentration camps in the latter half of the war, in which were housed over 150,000 Afrikaners – mainly women and children – left a bitter legacy among the Boers that remains to this day.

The idea of the concentration camp – first used by the Spanish in their campaign against the Cubans in the eighteenth century – as part of British strategy was Major-General Lord Kitchener's. He was of the opinion that the Afrikaner women were encouraging their menfolk to continue the resistance. By rounding them up and interning them, the men's resolve would weaken and the war would reach a speedy conclusion. Brutal as Kitchener's policy undoubtedly was, it worked, and on 31 May 1902 peace terms were signed.

Johnston's tenure therefore as commandant of the camp was brief. In 1903 he was appointed district commissioner of the Eastern Transvaal. He returned to Ireland at some stage during the decade, taking up a position with the Irish prison service in 1911.

After fifteen years Johnston was back home, but Ireland was about to undergo a period of unrest not dissimilar to that which had torn apart South Africa. Johnston's loyalty, however, remained with the Crown and, although his war wounds prevented him joining up in 1914 at the outbreak of the First World War, he was made Commandant of the prisoner of war camp at Oldcastle in 1914. For a brief spell in 1915 he took up a post as Governor of Portlaoighise Prison, but the following year he was back in charge at Oldcastle.

Years in the company of Tom Crean had not dulled in any way Johnston's sense of propriety. He was still very much an establishment man at heart. In 1918 he was appointed Registered Magistrate for County Roscommon, and two years later transferred to County Clare. That was a short appointment, however, for he stepped down when the Irish Free State government came to power in 1920.

The rest of Johnston's life was spent among the rolling hills of Kilkenny where he raised thoroughbred cattle and indulged his love of golf and fishing. The tranquil surroundings he enjoyed had been well earned by his deeds on the veldt, with both ball and rifle. He died in a Kilkenny nursing home aged seventy-seven on 24 March 1950.

CHAPTER TWO

Tom Crean

Tom Crean, the greatest rugby forward of his day, was like his friend Robert Johnston only in his love of rugby and his fearlessness. A handsome charmer, he travelled the world seeking adventure, women, drink and fighting.

Tom Crean would have been a rich man if he'd been born a hundred years later. A talent such as his would have been rewarded handsomely by professional rugby union. In the 1890s he was the greatest forward in the world. In the 1990s he would have been the world-class flanker Ireland never had. His physique was perfect for today's back-row forward, 6ft 2in and 16 stone. He could cover 100 yards in 10.5 seconds and his power was legendary. He was memorably described by one Irish writer, Jacques MacCarthy, as crossing the English try-line 'festooned with Saxons'.

Crean was also spectacularly good-looking. He had a strong face, with firm yet kind features, but it was the green eyes that people found most appealing. They trusted those eyes but when Crean smiled there was a mischievous twinkle about them. The few ladies that could resist his physical charms soon found themselves overpowered by his wit and charisma.

Crean, however, would have hated professional rugby. Life for him was an escapade, an adventure, to be enjoyed without restrictions. The routine and monotony imposed by professional sport would have suffocated Crean. He would also have been ideal tabloid fodder. For he was a quixotic character who gallivanted across the world, seeking excitement wherever and whenever he could find it. Women, drink and fighting, he loved them all.

Crean came from a respectable and loving middle-class Catholic family from Dublin. His father, Michael, left Ireland in 1860 to fight in the Papal Brigade against Garibaldi and his Redshirts at the Battle of Spoleto. He was decorated by Pope Pius XI and when his sixth child, Thomas Joseph, was born thirteen years later, he passed down to his son his courage and his roving, or what another Irishman born a year later, Ernest Shackleton, came to call his 'wanderlust'.

Tom Crean was born in Morrison's Hotel, owned at the time by his maternal grandparents. Charles Parnell, the forefather of Irish Home Rule and leader of the Nationalist Party from 1877, was arrested by the British in Morrison's in 1881. It was the only link between Crean and politics. Politics to Crean wasn't much fun and if there wasn't entertainment to be had out of something he wasn't interested.

Crean was sent to Clongowes College and his outstanding physical prowess was already apparent, as the *Clongownian* noted in his obituary:

> 'He won many events in the sports, his best distances being the quarter and half mile ... he was also a very fine swimmer and figured prominently in athletics and [rugby] football.'

From Clongowes Crean enrolled at the Royal College of Surgeons in the autumn of 1891. He made an instant impression on his classmates. Handsome, athletic and intelligent, Crean was also something of a celebrity thanks to an incident a few weeks earlier at Blackrock. A young art student called William Ahern had gone swimming at Blackrock and found himself out of his depth a quarter of a mile from shore. Crean went to his assistance and, with the help of a Mr Leachman, was able to bring Ahern back to the shore. The rescue made the newspapers and Crean and Leachman were awarded the Royal Humane Society's Testimonial for saving life at sea.

Crean's diversion from his medical lectures was rugby and in 1891 he joined the Wanderers. The rather earnest Robert Johnston was another new face at the club and the two young men struck up a friendship that endured until it was severed by death.

Crean leapt the chasm of self-doubt from schoolboy to senior rugby effortlessly and soon established himself in a Wanderers pack that contained Ireland internationals Jimmy Roche and E G Forrest. Crean was awarded the first of his nine caps in 1894, a few weeks before his twenty-first birthday. His international career began in auspicious circumstances. Ireland beat England 7–5 at Blackheath to record their first victory on English soil. Scotland and then Wales were also dispatched and Crean's first season had coincided with Ireland's first Triple Crown triumph. There were further celebrations in Dublin a short while later when Wanderers, with nine capped players in their XV, beat Trinity 5–0 to win the Leinster Cup for the first time since 1888.

In the 1895 International Championship Ireland finished with the wooden spoon. One or two writers ascribed the fall from grace to a complacency that had tiptoed its way into the Irish dressing room, but the majority pinned the blame on the pack. The correspondent for the *Athletic News* tore into the Irish forwards with a ferocity that was in his opinion missing from their own play. 'It was palpable there were several shirkers in our scrummage … the pushing mainly devolved upon O'Connor, Crean and Clinch, and if they could not carry the mauls against eight opponents all three played up in sterling fashion.'

Ireland did at least have an excuse of sorts against England. A sharp frost that had gripped the country in the days leading up the match was broken by a thaw on the Friday night. The pitch quickly turned into a slushy mess on top, but with a layer of frost underneath. It all made for trying conditions, as the *Athletic News* described: 'The once spotless white jerseys [of England] were besmeared with mud and the green clothing of the Irishmen assumed a darker shade, and from head to foot the players were moving masses of Hibernian real estate … the players slipped and splashed, and staggered and fell about like drunken men.'

Ireland finished their 1895 campaign in much the same way as they had started, said the *Athletic News*, defeated up front, this time against Wales: 'Asked to explain the defeat I should first of all mention the poor scrummaging of the Irish forwards … although Forrest, Crean and Clinch worked hard.'

Crean's life changed forever in 1896. He went international with his talent and charisma, and discovered a world outside the British Isles. He graduated from the Royal College of Surgeons and helped Ireland erase the humiliation of the previous season with another championship title. It wasn't a Triple Crown, a 0–0 draw against Scotland scuppered that dream, but wins against England and Wales gave them the title. Crean was the outstanding player in an Irish pack that was unrecognizable from the shambles of 1895. Against England, the *Athletic News* wrote: 'Crean was perhaps the best of a fine lot. He shoved like a demon and was nearly always first away from the mauls.' One of his contemporaries in the Irish scrum wrote in after years that Crean was 'the foremost figure and pride of the pack – a raging, tearing, rampaging, terrible opponent. His six feet of brawn, handsomely proportioned, his fair curly hair and his always laughing face gave him the semblance of a Greek god – or an outsize in naughty cherubims.'

Shortly after the end of the 1895–6 season Crean was invited to tour South Africa with an Anglo-Irish squad. If he had possessed a conventional bone in his body, Crean might have politely declined, opting instead to pursue his medical career. Instead, he leapt at the chance. What could his father say? When he had been the same age he had left Ireland to fight Garibaldi. Now Crean was off to fight the South Africans. The poor South Africans never quite knew what hit them. Crean hurtled round the country, leaving a trail of bruised opponents, awed admirers and broken hearts. When it was time to return home, Crean thought better of it and decided there was more fun to be discovered in South Africa. The boat back to England was a quieter place than on the outward journey.

Crean was lucky to tour with a group of men who, by and large, shared his philosophy of life. It was, remembered Walter Carey, one of Crean's team-mates, 'a very happy tour'. Even the Englishmen in the party, hitherto manacled by conservatism, managed to loosen their shackles and enter into the spirit of things.

The squad sailed from England on 20 June 1896 with one of them filing reports for the *Athletic News*. His first column described the sports day held on deck: 'The Irish contingent were well to the fore in everything. Indeed, it was a case of "Crean first, the rest nowhere …" Crean won the high jump. The half mile was a time race and won by Crean in 2 min 46 sec …. The quarter mile was also a time race and [Louis] Magee and Crean were each clocked to do 1 min 13 sec.'

Once on dry land, Crean's dichotomous nature quickly became apparent. He was one of three Catholics in the squad and when an excursion to Hout Bay was arranged for the first Sunday the trio asked to be excused. It would mean missing their fourth Mass in a row and such impiety worried them. The tour manager accommodated their wishes and the trip was rescheduled.

Such reverence wasn't in evidence before the third tour match against Western Province. Crean was captain for the day, standing in for Johnny Hammond, and the tourists passed an agreeable pre-match lunch as guests of Prime Minister Sir Gordon Sprigg. Sir Gordon produced his finest champagne and asked Crean if he would allow the players to have a glass. Crean, no doubt having wrestled with his conscience, thought it decorous to accept the offer, though he insisted the players be restricted to 'only four tumblers of champagne each'. The subsequent scoreless draw was the only one of the seventeen provincial matches they failed to win. When the tourists played Western Province a few weeks later, presumably having told Sir Gordon they had a prior engagement, they won 32–0.

The Anglo-Irish XV won the series three Tests to one and the verve of Crean caught the eyes of a claque of South African correspondents:

> 'Crean came through the next scrum and dribbled away half the length of the field. Lawton took the ball from him, but could not escape the dashing Irishman's clutches ... Crean broke away from the scrum which ensued on the 25 line and with a dribble that was perfection itself carried the ball to the Cape Town line ... Individually Crean was the most brilliant forward on the field, doing grand work and never slacking for a minute ... Crean stood head and shoulders above everyone; he played a superb game from start to finish.'

Crean was as captivating off the field as he was on it. His loquaciousness led him to be cast as the squad's after-dinner speaker. One suspects he didn't put up much resistance. The *Athletic News* described the tourists' visit to the De Beers diamond compound on 21 July: 'Loud cries of "Crean" resulted in that gentleman making a capital little speech, in the course of which he expressed the opinion that if football continued to improve as it appeared to have done recently, South Africa would be able to teach England, Scotland

and Ireland how to play the game. He then proposed the health of every Colonial-born man in the room.'

After the tourists had thrashed Port Elizabeth 26–3, Crean tried to salve any damaged egos among his adversaries: 'We have played six matches in South Africa but today's match was the nicest we have yet played. We played against men who played for the love of the game and were worthy of the game of rugby football.'

The last match of the tour ended in defeat for the tourists. They lost 5–0 to South Africa in Cape Town. That evening an Irish banquet was held in the Masonic Hall. Crean said a few words and was his usual eloquent self. But it was also a sentient speech. Perhaps he had spent enough time in South Africa to see that the distrust that existed between the Afrikaners and the British would soon erupt into open warfare. His speech, paraphrased in the *Athletic News,* was unequivocal about his allegiance: 'He said he had heard Irishmen were always "agin the Gout [*sic*]" but he had been playing for England and would do so again with a heart and a half. He was an Irishman who would go hand in hand with England as long as he lived (to loud cheers).'

Crean and Johnston bade farewell to their team-mates a short while later. They had decided to remain in South Africa along with a third Irishman, Walter Carey. His reasons, however, for staying behind were more pious. He later became the Bishop of Bloemfontein, but always retained enormous affection for Crean, even if he occasionally blushed at some of his high jinks. 'He was the most Irish, the most inconsequent, the most gallant, the most lovable personality one could ever imagine and he made the centre of the whole tour.'

Crean worked for a while at the Johannesburg Hospital, but in 1897 he opened a practice in Boxberg in the Transvaal. He proved a popular doctor, so popular, in fact, that a new patient once forced his way into the consulting room after hours. It wasn't clear who was more surprised, Crean by the intruder, or the trespasser who found himself confronted by a giant Irishman wearing nothing but a vest. 'Is it no manners that you have intruding upon the privacy of a gentleman?' roared Crean, who had been enjoying a wash and a shave. The quaking man mumbled an apology but Crean's blood was up. 'Your face is a cruel one, it needs hitting. Will you fight me?'

The intruder bolted and Crean, despite his deshabille, gave chase, shaking his fist and telling the man where he was going to stick his shaving brush.

George Fleming Gibson, in his book *The History of The Imperial Light Horse*, took up the story: 'The quarry gained shelter in his house and locked, bolted and barred the door. Tommy stood on the mat and pleaded with him to "Come out and fight". A crowd collected, and on the arrival of a policeman Tommy suddenly realized the extreme innocence of his vesture and, always a man of prompt decision, offered to fight the policeman for his trousers. Eventually he made good his sartorial deficiencies by borrowing a jacket from a bystander, which he rigged about him kilt-wise, and thus attired made his stately way back home.'

Far from damaging his reputation, Crean's standing was only enhanced by such tomfoolery. His mix of Irish bluff and blarney proved irresistible. When he joined the Imperial Light Horse as a trooper in September 1899, the regiment's campfires crackled with tales of Crean's carousing. One of the soldiers' favourites was of the time he played cupid.

A friend of Crean's had fallen in love, but was diffident in front of women. He asked Crean to represent him and present his suit to the object of his affections. This he did and reported back to his friend that he thought the young woman might requite his love. Overjoyed, the wooer purchased a diamond ring to be bestowed upon his beloved. Crean set off to present the gift but returned, a few hours later, with a cabload of alcohol.

'What the devil does this mean?' cried the suitor.

'My boy,' declared Crean, 'I've saved you. She's a withered crone, of no intelligence, and I've decided she's unworthy of you.'

His ashen-faced friend tried to stammer a reply.

'Ah, now,' soothed the doctor. 'I knew your heart would be breaking with sadness, so I sold the ring and I've come to help you drown your sorrows.'

Crean fought at the Battle of Elandslaagte in October 1899, where Robert Johnston won his Victoria Cross, and was one of the 213 British wounded. His wounds weren't serious, however, and when the Imperial Light Horse regiment were among the 12,000 soldiers besieged in Ladysmith from November to February 1900, Crean took an active part, playing soldier and saviour.

On 6 January 1900, there was heavy fighting on Wagon Hill, a position of strategic importance to the captives a few hundred yards to the south-west of Ladysmith, when the Boers tried to capture some British artillery pieces. One hundred men of the Light Horse, Crean among them, had formed a picket to protect the artillery. The skirmishing began just after midnight when sentries heard the Boers moving up the hill. The Light Horse repelled the first attack and the three remaining squadrons of Light Horse arrived to reinforce their comrades. When the sun rose the combatants had gone to ground among the brush and rocks of the hill. In some places they were separated by no more than the length of a decent dropped goal. Sergeant Rumbold, Rifle Brigade, found himself among the Light Horse on Wagon Hill: 'To move was certain death … others were plucky enough to crawl back for assistance, but out of the four that went, three were shot through the head, dead. Thus we had to lie all day in the scorching sun, not daring to move, and ever on the alert for the slightest sign from the front …The rain came down in torrents about 4pm and soaked us all to the skin, but we had to lay in it like ducks, for the Boers had their eyes upon us. Then at 6.30, just as it was getting dark we fixed swords [bayonets] and rushed the position, driving the Boers down the hill and knocking them over like rabbits.'

Wagon Hill remained in British hands but the cost had been high. Seventeen officers and 152 soldiers had been killed and 250 wounded. The hospital couldn't cope with such an influx of casualties, there wasn't the staff. Crean responded to a request for people with medical experience. Along with a trooper Nixon, formerly a doctor from Heidelberg, Crean was temporarily transferred from the Light Horse to work in Intombi Hospital.

The siege was finally broken on 28 February. A fortnight earlier the town of Kimberley had also been wrested from the Boers, who had surrounded it for nearly three months. Mafeking, under the command of Colonel Robert Baden-Powell, was now the only British garrison still under siege. Crean turned from besieged to siege-breaker. He was part of a 1,100-strong force under Colonel Bryan Mahon that rode from Kimberley at the beginning of May to relieve Mafeking, 250 miles north.

Riding alongside Crean was his good friend, David Maxwell. In a letter to his sister he described the march to Mafeking. On 13 May they were ambushed by a group of Boers in a 'miserable short little fight of an hour … [but] found that our loss had been very heavy – 6 killed and 27 wounded … Stood to without offsaddling all night and marched to water at sunrise (14th) about five miles and which we had to dig for in the sandy bed of a river. Marched again at 3pm till 1am.' The next afternoon the Light Horse ran into another Boer force. This time Maxwell considered it to have been a 'good fight ... mostly artillery and then advanced on foot till dark. When a patrol was sent in to see if the road was clear they reported all right.'

He then turned to more mundane matters. 'The days are hot but the nights are bitter. Tommy Crean, a huge Irish giant, and I always share our blankets and as he is a restless person I usually wake up to find his enormous mass of flesh weighing about 18 stone lying over me – uncomfortable but warm.'

On the evening of 17 May the relief was effected as the last of the Boer besiegers vanished across the veldt. The inhabitants were overcome with joy. They had been immured since 13 October, 217 days. The news was also welcomed in London, an early birthday present for Queen Victoria a week before she turned eighty-one. She sent a telegram to Baden-Powell, saying:

> 'I and my whole Empire greatly rejoice at the relief of Mafeking ... I heartily congratulate you, and all under you, military and civil, British and Native, for the heroism and devotion you have shown.'

By the end of 1900 Crean had been commissioned and given charge of his own squadron (at full strength around ninety men). His commanding officer, recognizing that Tom Crean's ebullient personality would overpower any malcontents, ordered his squadron to garrison a Boer village for a short while.

Crean quickly became a favourite among the children. His sense of fun and beaming smile were a pleasant change from other stony-faced British soldiers. Their mothers, when they discovered he was a doctor, put aside their distrust and dislike of the British army and came to him with their sick children. Crean was winning the 'Hearts and Minds' of hostile civilians years before it became accepted as an important military strategy of any invading army. It wasn't that he set out to win over the townsfolk. It was just his natural compassion and his innate ability to meet people on any level, whatever their background and persuasion.

Unlike a lot of the Light Horse Regiment, Crean bore the Boers no grudge. While he certainly didn't identify with their cause – rising up against perceived British oppression – like a great many Irishmen (they made up the preponderance of mercenaries fighting alongside the Boers), he respected the Boer soldier for his courage and fighting qualities. A deputation of Boers came to see Crean one day in his role as garrison commander to ask him if they could have some of the Light Horse's forage. Drawing himself up to his full 6ft 2in, he addressed the Boers in regal fashion:

> 'Her Majesty, God bless her, has personally deputed to me the care of this noble city and I labour night and day in your interests. Go to your homes and be assured that I have no more sacred duty than to promote your welfare, both here and hereafter. I have spoken. God Save the Queen.'

Determined to finish with a flourish, Crean ordered his trumpeter to sound 'Killarney'. The Boers returned to their homes, not entirely sure what the big Irishman had been talking about, but confident he would see them right.

In June 1901 Crean relinquished command of his squadron on the orders of his commanding officer. His complete disregard for his own safety in battle alarmed the CO, who could not afford to lose such a capable officer. Crean was persuaded to become the regiment's medical officer. For the next few months surgeon-captain Crean's energies were centred on the operating table. The war had swung the way of the British but pockets of Boers continued to prove intractable. In the Orange Free State, Christiaan De Wet, the originator of the commando tactics that had for so long infuriated the British, was continuing to strike at enemy targets. At 8am on 18 December, De Wet and some 800 mounted burghers swooped on what he thought was a munitions convoy as it travelled through Tygerskloof on its way to Harrismith. But the convoy was a column of fighting troops, the Light Horse among their number.

The initial attack was fought off but the burghers dismounted and went to ground in the long grass and for twenty minutes engaged the British in a terrifying firefight. Several Light Horsemen had been wounded in the Boer assault and one of the casualties, Corporal Peter Malan, was unable to move because of a bullet in his leg. Trooper Arthur Peckitt went to his aid but was himself wounded as he tried to drag Malan to cover.

This was Crean's chance for some action. Seeing the plight of the two men, he sprinted forward and dressed the wounds of both soldiers. The Boers tried to pick him off but with no success. Crean then heard the cries of Lieutenant J O'Hara. As he moved to give succour to the wounded officer, one of the Boers drew a bead on Crean and shot him through the arm.

Crean reached O'Hara and was dressing his wounds when he was shot in the stomach. Legend has it – in some quarters – that in the moments after Crean was hit he cried 'By Christ, I'm kilt entoirely'* and tried to get to his feet only to collapse. Such swagger would have been improbable.

Crean was almost certainly struck by a bullet from a Mauser, the rifle supplied in great quantity to the Boers by Germany. It was the latest in weapon technology and its smokeless cartridges meant the Boers could shoot at the British from a safe distance without giving away their position. Its one drawback, in the eyes of its owner, was that the bullets weren't as destructive as those of the Martini-Henry, the standard issue among British troops. The 11.4mm bullets of the Martini-Henry caused fearful wounds to the Boers because they were soft-leaded and expanded on impact. The Mauser bullets, by way of contrast, were made of harder lead. To counterbalance this discrepancy, it became common practice among the Boers to alter Mauser bullets to 'dum-dums', by filing down or flattening the tip, so that they too, like the British bullets, expanded when they hit their target. The bullet that hit Crean was probably a dum-dum, judging by the gloomy assessment of the doctor who examined him later that day. He gave Crean little chance of survival and for several days his life hung in the balance. That he eventually pulled through was attributed to his strength, vitality and willpower.

Crean was helped in his recuperation by the news that he had been awarded the Victoria Cross for his courage at Tygerskloof. The Cross was gazetted on 11 February 1902:

> 'During the action with De Wet at Tygerskloof on 18 December 1901, this officer continued to attend to the wounded in the firing line, under a heavy fire at only 150 yards of range, after he had himself been wounded, and only desisted when he was hit a second time, and, as it was first thought, mortally wounded.'

Crean was invalided back to England and the speed of his recovery surprised medical staff. He was fit enough to receive his Victoria Cross from

---

* Surviving family members dismiss this as apocryphal, saying that Crean spoke with a gentle brogue and not with the thick Irish accent that has been attributed to him in some accounts of his life.

King Edward VII at Buckingham Palace on 13 March, but he was still recovering from his wounds when peace was declared at the end of May 1902.

To be confined to a hospital bed was purgatory for Crean. He grew restless and frustrated, but put the time to good use, applying for, and winning in September 1902, a commission in the Royal Army Medical Corps. Once he was passed fit for service, he asked for a posting overseas. Possibly he requested Africa. He had fallen in love with southern Africa in 1896 and perhaps now wanted to explore more of the continent. He was sent to the west coast of Africa and remained there from May 1903 to September the following year. Unfortunately, there is little clue as to what exactly his duties were during these sixteen months. Crean married in 1905, thus proving wrong those among his friends who had claimed there wasn't a woman capable of taming Tommy Crean. His wife was a beautiful Spanish lady called Victoria, only daughter of Don Thomas Heredia of Malaga. In 1906 he resigned his commission and left the army. He opened his own practice and settled down to a much quieter life with Victoria.

They lived comfortably in London and were a popular couple on the social circuit. The war hero and the exotic Latin beauty were usually top of most invitation lists. Crean's war record brought its own cachet and opened doors for him that might otherwise have remained closed. In 1910 a new hospital was opened at the royal enclosure at Ascot to much public acclaim. In an edition of the *Daily Mirror* in June, the paper described it as a 'miniature hospital to be used in case of accidents'. Accompanying the story was a picture of the hospital with its Chief Medical Officer posing outside, replete with straw boater and twinkling eyes. Tommy Crean was making headlines again.

The hospital had only been open a short while when its worth became apparent. A jockey was thrown from his horse during a meeting but Crean was by his side in minutes. The jockey had serious head injuries and Crean decided to use a trepan to remove a circular section of bone from the man's skull in order to relieve the pressure on his brain. The jockey survived and Crean was required to pose for more photos. It would be trite to say Crean had put his wild days behind him. Certainly, he enjoyed a happy and productive marriage to Victoria, who bore him two children, Patrick and Carmelita. But when Britain declared war on Germany on 4 August 1914, he was back in uniform eight days later. He was now in his early forties but his lust for adventure remained as strong as ever.

The army shipped Crean to France on 15 August. They clearly recognized his worth. By the end of the month he was retiring from Mons with the rest of the British Expeditionary Force. The Battle of Mons on 23 August had been the first engagement in the war between German and British land forces. The British, reputedly dismissed by the Kaiser a week earlier as a 'contemptible little army', checked the German advance although outnumbered two to one.

Then the order came to fall back and Crean, medical officer attached to the 1st Cavalry Brigade, found himself trying to manoeuvre his ambulances past munitions trucks advancing towards the front. At one point the congestion became so bad that the officer in charge of the munitions trucks ordered Crean to move his ambulances to the side of the road. 'By whose orders?' he demanded to know. The munitions officer, a chap called Brierly, stormed over to the ambulance and confronted Crean. For a fleeting second it seemed the two would come to blows, but then they roared with laughter and embraced. The last time they had seen each other had been thirteen years earlier at Tygerskloof when Crean won his VC.

Crean had pulled a few strings in order to get to France with such swiftness. General Briggs, commander of the 1st Cavalry Brigade, had been one of Crean's officers in the Imperial Light Horse. When he heard Crean wanted to come out to France he insisted he serve with him. Crean was promoted to Major and boarded the first available troopship. Briggs later described Crean as 'the most fearless man I have ever seen'.

An American, Frederic Coleman, who served under Crean as a stretcher-bearer in 1914–15, was of the same opinion. In his book *From Mons to Ypres with French*,* Coleman wrote: 'Crean ... one of the bravest men who ever won the Cross, was doing the work of a dozen. Thinking Wulverghem would soon become unhealthy, he started moving the wounded from a temporary hospital in an estaminet which faced the end of Wulverghem's main street. Inspired by some intuition, he hurried the ambulances up and filled them in unusual haste. The last wounded man was out of the house and the last ambulance 50 yards down the road toward Neuve Eglise when a howitzer

* Field Marshal Sir John French, the British cavalry officer chosen to lead the BEF to France in 1914. He was replaced by Field Marshal Sir Douglas Haig in December 1915.

shell fell, crushing the estaminet like an eggshell.'

Crean received the Distinguished Service Order in June 1915, a month after he was mentioned in despatches. At the beginning of 1916 he was handed command of the 44th Field Ambulance in France. As in South Africa in 1901, his courage in the trenches was construed as recklessness by some of his superiors. In one indiscriminate bombardment during the Battle of the Somme his General, sheltering in a dugout with his staff officers, saw Crean striding along the trench puffing on a cigarette and unconcerned about the shelling. The General tore him off a strip for being a bloody fool by needlessly exposing himself.

> 'Needlessly, is it?' said Crean, with the confidence of a Victoria Cross winner. 'Are not all my bearers killed or wounded? Is there a soul to help the boys? I must go myself.'
> 'I forbid it,' spluttered the General.
> 'But, sir...'
> 'Don't "But, sir" me. You'll most certainly be killed if you attempt to reach the forward line and you'll be of no earthly use to us if you are killed. I order you to stay here.'

Crean looked at the General, then pushed aside the barrier of rank and spoke to him man to man: 'It's written that I'm to die in my bed,' he smiled.'My boys need me. Go I must.'

Crean was right, he did die in his bed. The last years of his life were unkind to him. The spark had begun to go out of his eyes in the trenches. The Boer War had been fun for Crean. The virtues he cherished such as courage and boldness could more often than not see a man through. But the First World War, that was different. It was slaughter on a scale Crean couldn't comprehend. Machine-guns, gas and high explosive. His type of warfare had been overtaken by weapons that took no account of a man's pluck and resolve.

Crean was invalided home from the trenches at the tail end of 1916 suffering from diabetes. He was humiliated by his illness and the deterioration in his health embarrassed and frustrated him. When he caught sight of himself in the mirror he couldn't believe that this was the man who had charged down the Lansdowne field 'festooned with Saxons'. He tried to recreate his youth by other means, spending money freely and living beyond his means. This just got him deeper into debt. Before the outbreak of the First World War his medical practice had been worth around £3,000 per annum (£150,000 in today's terms). In 1922 he was in the Bankruptcy Court, answering charges that he owed two money-lenders over £50,000. The case was reported in the newspapers, inflicting upon Crean more pain than any bullet had ever managed. He assured his creditors he would pay off his debts and explained that his ill-health had forced him into a nursing home and he was at present unable to work. That would soon change, Crean promised, once he returned to his practice.

He never did return to work. He died at his Mayfair home on 25 March 1923, surrounded by his family. He was just forty-nine. Although Crean was denied the joy of seeing his children grow up, he would have been proud of them. Patrick, having inherited his father's swashbuckling nature, trained as a Shakespearean actor, and became an expert swordsman, who was employed by film studios to choreograph sword fights. Carmelita is remembered by the Crean family as a woman whose looks were as stunning as her mother's. She died in 1970 having never married. Few men could compare to her father.

CHAPTER THREE

Donald Bell

*D*onald Bell was a schoolteacher who became a professional foot-baller with Bradford in 1913. He enlisted when war broke out a year later and the Victoria Cross he won in 1916 is the only one awarded to a professional footballer.*

'It is evident these men are without any feeling for their brothers of the field, and do not care a farthing about anybody but themselves.' The editorial of the *Athletic News* on Monday 19 October 1914 caused quite a shock to the constitution of many an Englishman. For others, the vitriol that spewed forth from the pen of Britain's weekly sports paper was deserved and long overdue. It depended on one's allegiance. Supporters of Manchester United were dismayed to read such disparaging remarks about their team. Fans of other clubs, who had tired of the arrogant posturing of United players, were delighted to see them get their comeuppance.

The editor of the *Athletic News* continued his diatribe: 'They have not, at a time of stress without precedent, at the first real crisis since football became an institution, any idea of hanging together like jackdaws in a steeple. They are birds of prey. The people of Manchester now realize the type of creature they have been cheering.'

The attack on United by the *Athletic News* illustrated the depth of feeling stirred up by football in the months following the outbreak of war. Within a month of Britain having declared war on Germany on 4 August the game was being castigated by many for the players' perceived reluctance to 'do their bit' for the war effort. While other sports had closed down football continued on its merry way, seemingly indifferent to the fighting on the other side of the English Channel.

Attendances at matches fell precipitously, a result not just of fans enlisting but also because men of non-military age refused to pay money that would line the pockets of men they thought should be fighting for their country, not chasing a ball around a field. By the end of September several of the smaller clubs were on the verge of bankruptcy and the Football League decided to act. It issued a directive that asked all forty League clubs to donate a percentage of their gate money into a pool that would support the most stricken clubs. The League, however, having done its sums, realized they needed more money. It asked the bigger clubs to put a proportion of their players' wages into the relief fund. Some of the players, when informed of the proposal, blew their top.

The first to refuse were Manchester United, something, said the *Athletic News,* that 'will not cause any surprise when we announce that [they] have refused to permit reductions on the plea that they do not approve of the scheme … We can understand their objection, which arises from intense selfishness and an everlasting tradition in the club to be "against the government" … we have every sympathy with the directorate [of the club] who have always been afflicted with a body of men who have given more trouble than any set of players in the whole of the kingdom of football.'

The *Athletic News* took delight in noting that Manchester City and Liverpool, United's two fiercest rivals, had accepted the League's proposal without a murmur. The following week the *News* gleefully recorded that Manchester United had fallen into line after several days of prolonged abuse from all quarters. But the paper named and shamed a further five clubs whose players had refused to fall into line: Tottenham Hostpur, Sheffield Wednesday, Sheffield United, Aston Villa and Bradford City. 'It is amazing to us that the players of the five clubs should refuse to help in a movement for the benefit of their mates,' the paper wrote.

A fortnight later, however, on 16 November 1914 – the day on which the

Battle of Flanders ground to a halt and the Allied and German armies embarked upon four years of trench warfare – the *Athletic News* rode into battle in support of football. Its censure of a number of clubs had led to a barrage of national condemnation with the more strident accusing players of rank cowardice in not enlisting. The *News* could not tolerate what it considered a calumny: 'We strenuously protest against the attack made upon professionals who are mostly married and who have contracts for employment ... if a professional chooses to volunteer like Arthur Grimsdell of Tottenham ... we respect him for his loyalty ... but we fail to see any reason in the assertion that the professional footballer should enlist any more than other professionals ... we wish there were more Grimsdells but he does not stand alone as suggested.'

The *Athletic News* then listed several professionals who had joined up, including Alfred Stevenson of Plymouth Argyle and Coventry's Jack Jarvis, both of whom had been wounded during the fighting in Flanders. Then there were the three Newcastle players who had enlisted only last week. It could have also mentioned Donald Bell of Bradford Park Avenue.* But it didn't.

If Bell had spotted the oversight at his army training camp, he would have shrugged his shoulders and sighed. Being overlooked was nothing new to the twenty-three-year-old. It had happened during much of his professional football career with Bradford.

Bell was one of those irritatingly gifted sportsmen who could turn their hand to any sport and make it appear easy. Although it was football at which he excelled, Bell won his colours for rugby, hockey, swimming, cricket and football while at Westminster College in London. Archie White, who knew Bell as a schoolboy, and also won a VC in the same war, recalled many years later that his friend was a 'deviation from the ordinary ... [he was] six feet high and over fourteen stone, he had the build of a hammer-thrower; he could never have been a runner. Yet he had a unique gift of acceleration; he could start from zero on the centre line, be in top gear in two strides, and cover thirty, forty or fifty yards at the speed of a sprinter on a running track. That is what made him so valuable as a footballer.'

Bell fell into professional football by accident. Born in Harrogate in 1890,

* Bradford Park Avenue were commonly referred to as Bradford, while there was also a Bradford City in the League.

he had six siblings, only one of whom was a brother. His five sisters ignored the exhortations of Donny – as Bell was known to his family and friends – to come and kick a ball around in the garden. Deprived of such athletic pastimes, Bell immersed himself in books and set his heart on becoming a teacher.

He played amateur football in his teens for Starbeck, Mirfield United and Bishop Auckland but when he left school in the summer of 1909 he moved to London and enrolled at Westminster College training to be a teacher. Bell enjoyed the lectures and teaching theory but he needed an outlet for his energies. He joined Crystal Palace as an amateur and played at right-back during the 1909–10 season. The following season, cajoled by a fellow trainee, Bell combined football with rugby, making use of his powerful physique in the back row for Westminster. After a handful of matches he was selected for the Hertfordshire County XV, to the chagrin of his friend, who had been trying for such an honour for years. Bell's dalliance with rugby was short-lived. He qualified as a teacher and moved back to Yorkshire as soon as possible. London was pleasant enough, but it was too dirty and the people weren't that friendly. He was appointed assistant master at the Starbeck Council School, not far from Harrogate, and joined Newcastle as an amateur at the start of the 1911–12 season.

Few children misbehaved in Bell's classroom. His performances for Newcastle made him the hero of his pupils and occasionally, if they were very good, he would show them a few tricks with the ball. It wasn't just the children who admired him. One local paper described Bell as a 'tall man of fine physique, and for a person of his build he was wonderfully fast'. It also suggested that perhaps his ideal position was centre-forward. A while later his manager decided to try out the idea and moved Bell up front for a game. It was not a stroke of tactical genius. Bell missed several sitters and after the match admitted to a journalist that 'until I went back into the defence we never looked like getting a goal. Then we got several.'

His displays in defence, however, were altogether more composed and authoritative. They caught the eye of a watching scout from Bradford Park Avenue and at the start of the 1912–13 season he joined the second division side as an amateur. Bell got few chances to prove himself in his first season, as Bradford pushed for promotion. He found it a struggle to teach algebra while in the back of his mind he was trying to work out ways to stop

Saturday's centre-forward from scoring. But the 'boot money' he received came in handy, a welcome supplement to his weekly teaching salary of £2.10s (£2.50).

Bell decided to turn professional at the start of the 1913–14 season. He was twenty-two and in his physical prime. Now was the ideal opportunity to give it his all, particularly as Bradford had won promotion. The prospect of playing against forwards of the calibre of Sunderland's Charlie Buchan and Billy Meredith of Manchester United was altogether exciting, if a little daunting.

Bell warmed up for the coming season with a tour to Denmark as a member of the Yorkshire XI. When he reported to Bradford in August he felt he had a good chance of dislodging Watson, the incumbent right-back, from the first team.

For the first couple of months Bell didn't get a sniff of first-team action. If he hadn't been such a cheerful character he might have begun to get downhearted. He waited patiently and was rewarded with his first appearance on 3 November, against Leicester. Bradford won 3–2 and Bell's performance impressed the correspondent of the *Athletic News,* who wrote that 'Bell is coming on at the back'.

Bell wore the number two shirt again the following week in an away match against Wolves after Ewart was ruled out through injury. The Yorkshire side were expected to be turned over by a Wolves team containing several internationals and flying high at the top of the table. But it took a Sam Brooks goal in the eighty-first minute to settle the match and give Wolves an undeserved victory. The *Athletic News* described the goal in its report: 'Brooks slipped round Garry and ran a step or two across the left front of the goal, and before Bell could intervene, whipped the ball into the net.'

Bell's narrow failure to block the goal didn't detract from another confident display. The *Athletic News* wrote that: 'Mason was very safe in the visitors' goal, but his work was not of a most difficult character for he had in front of him two sterling backs in Bell and Watson, who kept their rivals so well at bay that most of the shots which came in were from a fairly lengthy range.'

The next week, when Hull came to Bradford for a local derby, Bell was back in the reserves, dropped to accommodate the return to fitness of Ewart. He played a couple more matches for the first team but at the beginning of

1914 he picked up a bad injury late in the game against Notts County. It was a cruel blow, said one local paper, when it reviewed Bradford's prospects for the season. It described Bell as 'one of the best type of the professional footballer … broadminded in outlook and scrupulously fair in his play. Had it not been for an accident he would probably have secured a regular place in the side. Indeed, some of his displays, particularly those in the matches with Notts County at Trent Bridge and Wolverhampton Wanderers at Molineux, were good enough for any team in the country.'

The summer of 1914 was gloriously warm and sunny, for thousands of young men one final opportunity to make hay before the world called time on their lives. Bell was happier than most. Not only was he looking forward to the start of the new season with Bradford, but he was also hopelessly in love with a local girl, Rhoda Bonson. Occasionally they took picnics in the Yorkshire dales; at other times they simply sat and talked about their future together. Neither paid much attention when they heard that some obscure archduke had been assassinated in Sarajevo on 28 June.

Bell was already training with Bradford when Europe tumbled into a war precipitated by the murder of Archduke Franz Ferdinand, heir presumptive to the throne of Austria-Hungary. Bell maybe used his teaching skills to explain to his team-mates the sequence of events that had led to war. Most were ambivalent, but Bell had already begun to think about enlisting. He considered it his duty but would the club hold him to his contract?

He wrote to the club's directors, saying:

'I have given the subject very serious consideration and have now come to the conclusion I am in duty bound to join the ranks. Will you therefore kindly ask the directors of the Bradford Football Club to release me from my engagement?'

A few days later the response came from T E Maley, the club secretary:

'With the utmost pleasure the directors accede to your desire, and in wishing you a safe return and an honourable career they feel sure that your estimable character and strong personality will obtain for you all that a soldier deserves.'

It was a generous gesture by Bradford, and they must have rued Bell's decision, as he doubtless did. His departure added to the shortage of defenders within the club, following transfers and retirement. Shortly after Bell was released from his contract – and with Bradford having conceded 16 goals in four matches – Maley went in search of replacements, recruiting J Crozier from Middlesbrough, and W G McConnell, an Irish international.

Bell entered his local recruitment office determined to join the cavalry. He departed an infantryman, a private in the West Yorkshire Regiment. There was no way such an athletic individual was going to be wasted astride a horse. The recruiting sergeant had been an astute fellow. Bell was a natural soldier. Within a couple of months he had been promoted to NCO and was being marked down as officer material.

Early in 1915 Bell was still in camp in England, disgruntled and keen to get over to France and have a go at the Germans. He was also becoming a bit fed up with the life in the ranks. Then one day in camp he had a chance encounter with Archie White, an old friend from Harrogate, who was an officer in the Green Howards. The two got talking and White expressed his astonishment that Bell wasn't an officer. He rolled his eyes and said 'If only'. White took Bell by the arm and introduced him to his commanding officer, Lt-Col E H Chapman. According to White, his CO 'had one look at him and recommended him for a commission on the spot'.

In June Bell left the ranks and became Second Lieutenant Bell, 9th Battalion, The Yorkshire Regiment, better known as the Green Howards. He skipped home and told Rhoda his news. Perhaps it was at this point Bell asked her to marry him. If not, it might have been in November 1915, shortly before he left for France with his regiment. Whenever he proposed, his girlfriend accepted and they agreed they would discuss possible dates in the letters they promised to write to one another.

Bell was a prolific letter-writer, though his fiancée, mother and sister all demanded constant correspondence. On 5 January, he sent his mother details of a bombing raid involving his regiment, though he reassured her that he hadn't participated: 'All our men came back with several slightly wounded. The Germans retaliated by shelling our line and our company had a hot time. Two of our officers were wounded, one slightly but the other very severely.' The Yorkshires saw sporadic action during the next six months, but little in the way of actual fighting against the Germans. The nearest they got to the enemy – except the odd trench raid – was when they had to shelter from a barrage of shells. When Bell left his regiment for two weeks' leave he would have had little to tell his family back in Yorkshire. Even if he had, though, they probably wouldn't have listened; his sisters certainly wouldn't have been interested. They had more pressing matters to attend to – their brother's imminent marriage to Rhoda Bonson. They had finally settled on a date that coincided with Bell's leave and on 5 June they walked down the aisle, while the organist valiantly struggled to drown out the sobs of happiness from Bell's five sisters.

Two days later Bell returned to the front. As he kissed his wife goodbye he reminded her that she was to regard his sisters as her own, and if she ever felt down she was to go and see them. Rhoda squeezed her husband's arm and told him not to do anything silly. 'Don't feel you always have to lead by example,' she whispered through her tears.

The Battle of the Somme is synonymous with unutterable destruction. It was the offensive that, so the British supreme command promised, would be the beginning of the end for the Germans. By Christmas it would all be over and the war would be won. 'Now where have we heard that before?', the more cynical British soldier muttered under his breath. But cynics were in the minority in 'Kitchener's Army' of June 1916. These were, after all, the men who had volunteered two years earlier, swept along on a tide of patriotic fervour that engulfed the whole of the British Isles. They were factory workers, shop assistants, bank clerks, stockbrokers, all of whom had seen the poster of Earl Kitchener, Secretary of State for War, with his penetrating stare above the finger that seemed to be pointing at each of them individually. By the beginning of September 1914, 33,000 men were volunteering each day.

The Somme offensive had been planned originally as an Anglo-French effort; its aim to kill so many Germans that their army would crumble. But the scale of French losses at Verdun in early 1916 switched the emphasis from a joint attack to one dominated by the British, who would supply sixteen divisions to France's five.

The battle began at 0728 hours on 1 July. By the end of the day 20,000 British soldiers were dead, and another 40,000 had been wounded. It was, and remains, the most catastrophic day in the history of the British Army. In those few hours a generation was destroyed; husbands, fathers, sons, brothers obliterated by shellfire; Englishmen, Welshmen, Scots and Irish mown down by the German machine-guns they had been promised would be destroyed by the week-long British artillery bombardment that preceded the battle. And for what? 'Whatever was gained,' one Welsh corporal reflected years later, 'it wasn't worth the price that the men had paid to gain that advantage. It was no advantage to anybody. It was just sheer bloody murder. They are the only words you can use for it.'

Sadly, very little had been gained in exchange for the cream of a nation's manhood. There had been a few small gains with villages such as Montauban and Mametz being taken but along most of the 30km front the German guns had savagely resisted all British attempts to advance. Bell and the Yorkshires had spent 1 July held in reserve at a place called St Sauveur. If any of the men spoke French they would have appreciated the irony of the name. Perhaps the British High Command did have a sense of humour, after all, billeting them in a village whose English translation was St 'Saviour'. The sound of battle a few miles to their north convinced them they had been saved from an unpleasant ordeal. But for how long?

On 3 July the battalion received orders to march up the Bapaume Road towards the German-held village of Contalmaison. When they reached the Tara-Usna Ridge they rested and awaited further orders, although the Germans dug in on high ground along a 1,500-yard stretch of frontline called Horseshoe Trench suggested themselves as the obvious target. Sure enough, when the order came through it was to capture Horseshoe Trench.

Several other battalions had tried to wrest the trench from the Germans on 4 July and the following morning, but had failed. Bell and the Green Howards moved into position on the afternoon of 5 July. They were more successful and, despite heavy casualties, Bell and his men were in possession of Horseshoe Trench shortly after 6pm. They began to clear the trench of German dead, tossing their bodies up and over the parapet, or using the corpses to shore up a section of the trench that had been demolished by shellfire. Suddenly a German machine-gun began firing into their left flank. Several men were killed in the mad rush to take cover. Bullets thudded into the sandbags and the bodies of the Germans, as the British took cover.

Bell scrambled along the trench, his head bowed so low that his knees nearly touched his chin as he ran. He crouched down beside Corporal Colwill and Private Batey, two of the fittest and hardest men in the regiment. Stuffing a couple of grenades into his tunic pocket, Bell told the pair he was going to try and silence the machine-gun. The two soldiers volunteered to come with him. Grabbing a grenade each, they followed Bell along the trench, keeping out of sight until it petered out at its extreme flank. The machine-gun team hadn't spotted them. But between them and Bell's men lay thirty metres of exposed no man's land. Bell looked at Colwill and Batey, the latter only nineteen years of age. The sweat dripped from under their helmets and zigzagged down their faces, streaking the grime that seemed to permanently encrust them all. He calmly told them what they had to do, and emphasized the need for speed. They would have just a few seconds before the German turned the gun on them. 'Once I give the order you run like hell and throw your grenades. OK, boys?' Colwill and Batey nodded. They shook hands and edged towards the end of the trench.

The German gunner saw the three out of the corner of his eye as he swept the main trench with machine-gun fire. But by then three or four seconds had elapsed and Bell had already covered half the distance. A couple of years earlier he had been fractionally slow in closing down Sam Brooks before he scored for Wolves. This time, however, it was Bell sprinting to get into a good shooting position. As the German swung the gun round, Bell, now about fifteen metres away, threw a grenade. It exploded a metre in front of the gunner, killing him and destroying the gun. They jumped into the trench and advanced along it until they heard guttural voices drifting up from the depths of a dug-out. Taking their remaining grenades, they removed the pins and hurled them down into the darkness.

Two days later Bell sat down and wrote several letters home. This time it wasn't such a struggle to think of things to say. To his mother he wrote:

> 'When the battalion went over, I with my team, crawled up a communication trench and attacked the gun. I hit the gun first shot from about twenty yards and knocked it over. We then bombed the dugouts and did in about fifty Bosches ... I must confess that it was the biggest fluke alive and I did nothing. I only chucked one bomb, but it did the trick. The CO says I saved the situation for this gun was doing all the damage.'

He couldn't resist having a playful dig at his father who, much as he loved him, had bored him to tears at times during his adolescence, with his continual lectures on why sport was an irrelevance: 'I am glad to have been so fortunate, for Pa's sake, for I know he likes his lads to be top of the tree. He used to be always on about too much play and too little work, but my athletics came in handy this trip.' Archie White maintained years later that only a soldier of Bell's speed and athleticism could have taken out the German machine-gun. 'Laden by steel helmet, haversack, revolver, ammunition and Mills bomb in their pouches, he was yet able to hurl himself at the German trench at such speed that the enemy would hardly believe what their eyes saw.'

Bell also wrote a letter home to a former teaching colleague. It was a strange letter, one of those that soldiers at the front must have found difficult to pull off convincingly: a juxtaposition of the banal with the brutal. He touched briefly on his part in killing the German machine-gunner, describing it jauntily in a style acceptable to those back home, a depiction that only added to the illusion held by most civilians that the war was a noble crusade and not a dehumanizing slaughter. 'There is a chance of me getting a Military Cross or something of the sort,' Bell wrote. 'Talk about luck! Fancy just chucking one's bomb, even if it was a bull's eye.' The next paragraph concerned an outing to the seaside. 'As regards Blackpool, I know Rhoda [his wife] would be very keen to go. I will write straight away to give her your address and here is hers, so that you can write to her and make arrangements.'

By the time Bell's letter reached his wife, with the address of the friend, he was dead. He was killed on 10 July, displaying similar courage to that which he had shown five days earlier.

Once again he had attacked a machine-gun position that threatened to inflict heavy casualties on his men. Dusk was descending as Bell spotted the gun being brought up into position. A fellow officer described what happened: 'Bell dashed forward with an armful of bombs, and started to clear out a hornet's nest of Huns who were ready to take toll of our advancing troops. He advanced with great courage right up to where the enemy were posted. He took careful aim, and bowled out several of the Germans. Unfortunately he was hit.' A bullet pierced the front of Bell's helmet,* grazing his forehead and leaving him momentarily stunned. As he lay on the ground

* The helmet Bell was wearing when he was killed is displayed in the Green Howards regimental museum and bears vivid testament to his bravery.

he was probably confused for a few seconds, unsure if he was badly wounded or not. He scrambled around on the ground and put his steel helmet back on. Most men would have beat a hasty retreat after such a near miss. Bell charged towards the machine-gun. The British officer wrote that: 'For a while he fought on, but was hit again. He got weaker, and had to relax his efforts. He collapsed suddenly and when we reached him he was dead.'

Bell was buried close to where he fell. His men, several of whom wept openly, hammered a piece of wood into the ground and placed his helmet on top. That allowed them time to carve a proper cross. A few days later they erected it, with the words 'He gave his life for others' etched into the wood.

Bell died without knowing he had been awarded the Victoria Cross for destroying the German machine-gun on 5 July. However, the conclusion of the citation implied that it was an award for his conduct during the whole week leading up to his death:

> 'This very brave act saved many lives and ensured the success of the attack. Five days later this gallant officer lost his life performing a very similar act of bravery.'

Bell's VC was presented to his wife by King George V at Buckingham Palace. His Majesty presented many posthumous VCs during the war but perhaps none was given in such pitiful circumstances as Rhoda Bell's. What words of comfort can you offer a woman whose marriage had lasted thirty-five days?

She received dozens of letter of condolence following her husband's death. T E Maley, secretary of Bradford football club and the man who had given Bell permission to be released from his contract, wrote:

> 'He has triumphed, and if a blameless and unselfish and willing sacrifice have the virtue attached with which they are credited, Donald is in the possession of eternal happiness, and in his glorious record and great reward there is much to be envied.'

Bell's commanding officer wrote that 'everyone in the 9th Yorkshires will I know be delighted to see the announcement in the Gazette [concerning

Bell's VC] and will be proud to know that your husband belonged to our battalion'.

But amid all the jarringly exultant letters one moved Mrs Bell through its simplicity and sincerity. It was written by John Byers, Bell's batman at the front. She had written to him some time after his death asking for details, even if it was just a snippet, of her husband's final days, so she could at least have something to cling to in her grief.

Byers wrote:

> 'I sit down and write these few lines in deepest regret. Believe me I am most sorry that it should be so. I would to God that my late master and friend had still been here with us, or better still, been at home with you … [The Company] worshipped him in their simple, whole-hearted way and so they ought, he saved the lot of us from being completely wiped out, by his heroic act … We have lost the best officer and gentleman that ever was with this battalion and we have lost some good ones. He was called to go to the 8th battalion of this regiment, that was just on our right, so that we heard nothing of his death until the next day … The last time we were on the Somme, some of our lads came across Mr Bell's grave and they told me it was being well cared for, and that there is a cross erected over it … I am pleased his valise arrived to you and you think it was alright. You would find in the souvenirs that we got on the 5th of July in the first great attack, a Prussian helmet, bayonet and pair of boots. I packed them all in it but I cannot quite remember whether his little toilet bag was packed, or he carried it with him at the time of his death … You ask me if I smoke, yes, but not cigarettes, only a pipe and tobacco so if you will send some, I will be very grateful to you. Believe me, wishing you the best of health and wishes.'

Rhoda Bell never remarried. She probably never found anyone to match Donny, and, anyway, there wasn't exactly an abundance of men from which to choose. At least she didn't belong to the massed ranks of the 'Superfluous Women' of the 1920s; the cruel name given to the single women in Britain who never married because there weren't enough men to go round. Mrs Bell was married for five weeks, yet in that time she spent just two days with her husband. As she sat alone in her house, with only a Victoria Cross to keep her company, did she wish, maybe, that the man she had loved so deeply had not been so brave?

CHAPTER FOUR

Gerald Patterson

O n demob, in 1919, Gerald Patterson entered Wimbledon, and won the men's singles at his first attempt. The public liked the war-hero sportsman, and he led a fine life, winning many titles and Davis Cup matches before becoming a tennis administrator and a successful businessman.

'Big Bill' Tilden and Gerald Patterson were the two stars of men's tennis in the years immediately after the First World War. Tilden, an American, was as flamboyant and camp as the Australian Patterson was rugged and muscular. Those who liked their tennis stars to play with panache, verve and gracefulness adored Tilden. Fans who admired power, determination and an utter refusal to admit defeat pinned their colours to Patterson. Tilden was the more gifted tennis player – he won ten Grand Slam tournaments to Patterson's three – but he was never as respected as the Aussie.

The reason was their war records. While Tilden had served in some obscure backwater with the Service Corps, Patterson had been in the front line for three years, winning the Military Cross and coming through some of the most brutal campaigns of the war. The public never forgot this distinction and British fans in particular worshipped the man who had sailed to England to enlist in the artillery and fight for Britain.

Patterson was commissioned as a Second Lieutenant shortly before his twenty-first birthday. He was posted to 102 Brigade, Royal Field Artillery, with whom he remained for the duration of the war. When he joined the brigade in August they were firmly ensconced in the Somme Valley, taking part in the biggest offensive of the war so far. Patterson remained in the Somme until the end of the battle in mid-November, passing through villages whose names, Thiepval, Martinpuch and Becourt, came to symbolize the horror of the murderous battle.

By the turn of the new year Patterson and 102 Brigade were in the Ypres Salient preparing for the offensive on the Messines-Wytschaete Ridge that was planned for early summer 1917. There had been stalemate in the Salient since May 1915, when the British had dug in after considerable German advances the previous month, a success gained against French colonial troops who had become the first soldiers in warfare to experience the terror of gas as a military weapon.

Fortunately for the Allies the Germans in the front line were just as scared of the gas and they failed to exploit fully the chaos caused in French ranks. The British Second Army consolidated their defensive positions in a tiny area that enclosed the Belgium town of Ypres in a loop and in the north ran along the western side of the Yser Canal. General Sir Herbert Plumer, commander of the Second Army, and one of the few generals in the war who was innovative and not tied to outdated warfare strategies, sat down and devised a plan to launch a new British offensive.

The problem facing him was that the Germans sitting in their trenches on the Messines-Wytschaete Ridge occupied virtually the only high ground on the Salient. From their positions they had a perfect field of fire down on to the British soldiers dug in on the flats of the boggy Flanders plain. If the Germans weren't removed from the ridge any attempt to advance would end in appalling casualties.

So early in 1916 Plumer instructed work to begin on a series of tunnels underneath the ridge. Once these tunnels stretched as far as the ridge, huge mines would be laid directly under the Germans. Miners from the pit towns of England, Scotland and Wales were brought in for the task of tunnelling and they were joined by Cockneys who had worked on the London Underground. They dug away grimly while all the time the Germans, who knew something was going on, dug their own tunnels to try and discover what the British were up to.

At times the Germans came so close to discovering the tunnels, the British soldiers digging could hear them talking to one another. But the British luck held and one by one all nineteen mines were laid in place ready for 0310 hours on 7 June when they would be simultaneously detonated. As the final touches to the mines were being added a massive artillery bombardment involving 2,266 guns began on 31 May. For the past month the men, guns and ammunition needed for such an enormous and sustained bombardment had been discreetly moved up into position. By 6 June the British had fired 3,561,530 rounds at the enemy in a devastating display of firepower.

Despite the constant pounding the British were giving the Germans Plumer knew that all his well-laid plans could go awry if the communication lines between the infantry and the artillery were not perfect.

The Messines-Wytschaete Ridge hid from the British Observation Posts the German second line and thus their artillery positions. The concern was that once the British troops approached the second line the artillery would be unable to see the German guns if they launched any local counter-attacks. It was imperative therefore that there was a communication link between the infantry and the artillery. To solve this concern a number of artillery officers were attached to infantry regiments as liaison officers; their role to go over the top with the soldiers and report back to their brigades on the positions of the German guns.

Patterson had the dubious honour of liaising with the 8th Yorkshire Regiment, just one regiment in an attack that would consist of 80,000 infantrymen, including a large number of ANZAC troops.

At 0310 hours the nineteen mines were detonated at the same time that 756 heavy guns/howitzers opened up with two specific aims: to neutralize the German artillery and provide a creeping barrage under which the infantry, and Patterson, could advance. The British Prime Minister, David Lloyd George, at work in his office at Downing Street, felt the tremor when the guns opened up. William Beech Thomas, war correspondent of the *Daily Express*, told his readers two days later about what he had witnessed: 'I have seen several of the heaviest bombardments ever conceived by scientific imagination; none of them approached this in volume or variety or terror, and one moment in it will live for ever in the mind of all who were within range as a spectacular miracle of the world. An hour before dawn, as we stood over the dim valley, where the black treetops looked like rocks in a calm sea, we saw what might have been doors thrown open in front of a number of colossal blast furnaces. They appeared in pairs, in threes, and in successive singles. With each blast the earth shook and shivered beneath our feet.'

The infantry attack was a resounding success and by 0900 hours the British and ANZAC troops occupied the ridge from where they could see the German rear positions. All around them Germans surrendered in droves, dishevelled, shell-shocked and broken, but glad to be alive after such a terrifying few hours.

Once there, artillerymen moved their guns up on to their new ground and prepared to resist the inevitable German counter-attack. It came at 1400 hours but by then the artillery were in position and they opened up in a defensive barrage that destroyed the inferior German artillery. The 102 Brigade's war diary noted that: 'A defensive barrage was maintained in front of the infantry during the remainder of the day and night. Excepting for a heavy defensive barrage the enemy artillery during the attack was extraordinarily quiet, the Field Artillery batteries being left pretty well alone.' The whole offensive had been a resounding success. The infantry had captured 144 German officers and 7,210 soldiers, as well as 48 artillery pieces and 218 machine-guns, but of far more significance the Messines-Wytschaete Ridge was now in their possession. On 9 June King George V cabled Field-Marshal Sir Douglas Haig, Commander-in-Chief of the British Forces on the Western Front, with his congratulations.

> 'I rejoice that, thanks to thorough preparation and splendid cooperation, the important Messines Ridge, which has been the scene of so many memorable struggles, is again in our hands. Tell General Plumer and the Second Army how proud we are of this achievement, by which in a few hours the enemy was driven out of a strongly entrenched position held by him for two and a half years.'

Shortly after Patterson and two other officers of the 102nd Brigade were awarded the Military Cross for their conduct on 7 June. The citation for Patterson's MC ran:

'For conspicuous gallantry and devotion to duty. He went forward under very heavy fire and sent back most valuable information. He set a splendid example of courage and initiative throughout the operations.'

A dozen officers from 102nd Brigade acted as liaison officers during the Messines Ridge offensive and three were killed. Patterson emerged unscathed and he lived a charmed life throughout the rest of the war. So many of his fellow officers weren't so lucky, their fates wearily recorded in 102nd Brigade's war diary. On 11 June 1917 a gas shell scored a direct hit on a dug-out, leaving two officers in hospital with severe gas poisoning. The following day a Second Lieutenant was badly injured by a shell. On 13 and 14 June three Lieutenants were victims of gas shells. In July Captain W R Pasteur, one of the two other officers awarded an MC on 7 June, died of wounds after being hit by shell shrapnel.

The killing continued. On 4 August a German shell landed on Patterson's 'B' Battery and left four dead and six wounded. In a particularly ferocious week in early October 1917 eight officers from 102nd Brigade were evacuated with gas poisoning. A high-explosive shell claimed the lives of two officers a week later. Patterson's luck, however, held and when the brigade was relieved from the Battle of Passchendaele at the end of October, he was one of the few surviving officers of the original brigade.

From Belgium Patterson's brigade moved to Italy to bolster their defences against a mighty Austro-German offensive at Caporetto that had been launched on 24 October. Nine Austrian and six German divisions broke through Italian defences and by the end of the day had advanced twenty-five kilometres in the greatest push in one day since the Battle of the Marne in 1914. The Italian army fled in disarray with 400,000 discarding their rifles and deserting. What saved them from total collapse was the scale of the breakthrough. The Germans hadn't the transport to move supplies up to the infantry and, after falling back 70 miles, the remnants of the Italian army dug in and called for Allied help.

By the beginning of December six French army divisions and five British were in frontline positions. There wasn't much to do but that didn't bother Patterson. For him and the rest of the brigade December was a chance to relax after the horrors of Ypres. Christmas was celebrated with, as the war diary gleefully recorded, 'turkey, bacon, vegetables, plum pudding, fruit, nuts, beer, wine, sweets and cigarettes'. On New Year's Eve the war diary reflected on the past month: '[December] has been uneventful. It was spent, chiefly, in camouflaging and fortifying battery positions, establishing and fortifying Ops [Observation Posts] on the Montello Hill, and selecting and making alternative, second line and reinforcing positions.'

The rest of 1918 passed in much the same desultory fashion. Towards the end of March the brigade moved on to the Asiago Plateau, part of a mountainous area to the north-east of Verona in northern Italy. For the men this proved no easy task, as the war diary noted on 24 March: 'The Guns went up mountain to the nearest point on roads to Battery Positions, drag ropes then being used to pull the guns up paths to position. In some cases pulleys and ropes had to be employed.'

Although Patterson was involved in the war up to the very last he was not called upon to take part in any of the desperate final battles that were being waged on the Western Front. The war diary entry for 11 November 1918 was a masterpiece of understatement: 'Brigade marched to Favaro Veneto – North of Mestre.' Lieutenant Gerald Leighton Patterson's war was over.

He was demobbed in early 1919, a twenty-three-year-old Australian in London with an accountancy qualification and a hangover. One of the few people he knew in England was Norman Brookes, an Australian Wimbledon champion in 1907 and 1914, and a good friend of Patterson's father. Brookes had figured large in Patterson's early tennis education. As a young boy in Melbourne he used to act as ballboy to Brookes and his dad when they played their weekly foursome on the family court in the affluent suburb of Kew. Patterson shared Brookes' grim demeanour on court, as well as the belief that there was no such thing as a lost cause. But Patterson, for all his strength and athleticism, could never match the artistry of his mentor.

Brookes wangled Patterson an invitation to join the other 127 competitors in the Wimbledon men's singles, a record number of entrants, on the strength of his achievements in Australia in 1914 and his triumph in a pre-Championship tournament in Surbiton, where he didn't drop a set in any of his four matches.

In his first round match Patterson demolished Gilbert of Britain 6/0, 6/4, 6/0. The host country provided him with his victims in rounds two and three, before compatriot Stanley Doust was thrashed 6/2, 6/0, 6/2 in the fourth round. In the semi-final Patterson dropped a set – the only one in the entire championships – against Britain's Major Ritchie. That win took him through to the final where he disposed of another Englishman, Algernon Kingscote, 6/2, 6/1, 6/3.

Patterson had won the All-Comers' Singles title but the format of Wimbledon at the time required him to meet the defending champion in the Challenge Round to determine the outright winner; thus the defending champion was not required to play in any matches other than the Challenge Round.* As the defending champion was Norman Brookes it meant that for the first time in Wimbledon's history the men's singles title would be contested by two Australians.

Unfortunately the match failed to live up to the expectations of the crowd, who had been anticipating a duel of contrasting styles: the finesse and touch of Brookes against the power and pace of Patterson. What transpired was a one-sided, three-set affair in which Patterson dropped only ten games on his way to victory. After a nervous start Patterson grew more masterly as the match progressed. *The Times* reported that: 'He was confidence itself in the third set. In one game he made Mr Brookes a canvas for a masterpiece. He passed the first of that redoubtable man's services across him forehanded; did the same by the next backhanded; took the third point when at the base line by a drive straight at him and too fast to be volleyed, and the fourth with a low sudden push that entangled him in his own foot.'

Nevertheless, the manner of Patterson's 6/3, 7/5, 6/2 victory left many spectators feeling that they had witnessed not the arrival of a new star but the demise of a former great champion. In particular, they wondered, would anyone be able to cope with the strength of his serve. Wallis Myers, writing in the *Daily Telegraph*, painted a colourful description of Patterson's strength. 'This tall, vigorous Australian, emerging mysteriously from No Man's Land, brought into the firing line a weapon of attack so destructive that only [Major] Ritchie could check its career for a set. With lion-like strength Patterson beat all-comers, almost conferring on Brookes himself the docility of a lamb.'

Patterson headed next to the USA where there were more lambs waiting to be blasted off court. Or so he thought. But lying in wait for Patterson was

* This antiquated format was ended after the 1921 Championships following fierce lobbying by the players.

American Bill Johnston, known universally as 'Little Bill', and he had in his quiver an arrow that would fell the Australian Achilles. Patterson met Johnson in the last sixteen of the US Open. Johnson, although dwarfed by Patterson physically, had a whipping forehand and a volley nonpareil, but above all, he possessed a tennis brain, and he had soon figured out that Patterson's Achilles' heel was his backhand. Time and again he returned Patterson's booming serves to his backhand and each time the Australian's response became more ragged. Several shots ended up on the clubhouse roof and one particularly stinging backhand caught the umpire a hefty blow that nearly knocked him out of his chair. It was soon christened the 'Windy-Woofer'.

Johnston was leading two sets to one and 4/1 in the fourth when Patterson's weakness was reined in by his great strength, his indomitable spirit. Suddenly he reeled off five successive games to level the match two sets apiece. Johnston pulled himself together in the final set to take a 5/3 lead but back came Patterson, his service more fearsome than ever and his backhands ... well, somehow they were landing in court. He levelled the set at five games each, but Johnston's class showed in the end and he took the match with a 7/5 victory in the final set.

Patterson was evidently unconcerned by the manner of his defeat against Johnston and the next year returned to Wimbledon to defend his title. In the Challenge Round he faced a rejuvenated Bill Tilden. The previous year he had lost to Johnston in the final of the US Open and so disgusted had he been that he had locked himself away for six months working on his weaknesses.

Against Patterson Tilden turned his practice into perfection, winning in four sets after handing his opponent the first set 6/2. The American, who had sought the advice of Johnston on how to play Patterson, spent the first set adjusting to the pace at which the Australian hit the ball before unleashing his full repertoire of shots in the second set. The magazine *Lawn Tennis and Badminton* wrote that Tilden's performance led to 'the complete exposure of the cyclonic Gerald Patterson's limitations ... The Australian had betrayed certain weaknesses last summer which were bound to be exploited sooner or later by a player with as many deadly weapons of attack and the necessary tactical ability. The American had evidently made up his mind to ignore Patterson's destructive service by adopting the bold policy of slogging the return at the incoming volleyer's body. What was the result? Patterson found himself faced with the stern proposition of making his own angles, and he failed lamentably. He found his king covered by an ace every time.'

Patterson's 1920 Wimbledon singles campaign had ended in disaster but he hadn't helped himself by declining to play in any warm-up tournaments. His woes continued that year in America when the USA thrashed Australia 5–0 in a Davis Cup tie and along the way Johnston slaughtered him 6/3, 6/1, 6/1. He sailed back to Australia determined to do something about his backhand.

When Patterson returned to Wimbledon in 1922 it was to the new venue at Church Road (it had previously been Worple Road) and to the new format that involved no Challenge Round. Patterson's backhand had been reconstructed – although Bill Tilden still remembered it in later years as the 'Tennis Tragedy of the 1920s' – and he reached the final where he faced Randolph Lycett.

The 1922 Championships were beset by torrential rain. The final was switched to a Monday as a result and Patterson defeated Lycett 6/3, 6/4, 6/2 in a match that was as one-sided as the victory over Brookes in 1919. In fact, Patterson's hardest match had been the semi-final win against compatriot Jo Anderson when, once again, he showed his resilience in winning a five-setter, despite trailing two sets to one.

Despite the rather dour nature of the final, no one quibbled with the result and Patterson was richly acclaimed in the papers. The *Daily Herald* commented that: 'He is a fighter of the first degree, and his great physique is made full use of by his Australian grit ... [his honour] was richly deserved, for he had all the great players in his portion of the draw. For sheer determination the champion is unequalled. He concentrates his whole mind on the business at hand, and, above all, he is an excellent sportsman.'

The improvement in his backhand had not gone unnoticed, as *Lawn Tennis Magazine* pointed out in its review of the Championships. 'Patterson may be acclaimed a better champion than in 1919, for his first service seems to be faster than ever, his second to break more, and his volleying to be at least as good. His backhand is also decidedly improved. Nevertheless it remains a vulnerable point, although it requires a master to exploit this weakness.'

Business commitments and the journey time prevented Patterson from defending his Wimbledon title in 1923 and it wasn't until 1928 that he reappeared at the Championships in what turned out to be his last hurrah.

The previous year he had won the Australian singles title for the first time, beating Jack Hawkes in a classic encounter that went the full five sets and lasted just under four hours. Patterson once again came from two sets to one down to snatch victory in a game still considered one of the finest to grace the Australian Open.

Patterson arrived at Wimbledon in 1928 having captained Australia in a Davis Cup tie against Italy in Genoa and, although he was now aged thirty-two, his stamina and determination showed no signs of taking early retirement. He contested an epic third round encounter with Britain's Charles Kingsley that was finally won by Patterson 10/8, 9/11, 10/8, 5/7, 6/2. The Lawn Tennis Association had to pay £100 in overtime payments to its staff as they waited for a winner.

In the fourth round Patterson clearly showed signs of tiredness against Jacques Brugnon of France and he slipped to a four-set defeat that marked the end of his association with Wimbledon. Over the course of nine years Patterson had played nineteen matches, winning seventeen of them and dropping only thirteen sets. More significantly he had been the champion the tennis world craved in the years after the First World War.

So many gallant young men had died in the trenches that the public wanted a champion who had the same qualities as those who had perished. Patterson's determination, courage and fighting spirit struck a chord not only with other survivors but also with fathers, mothers, sons and daughters who had lost loved ones in the war. Patterson represented all that was best about the young men who had died fighting and, by supporting him, the public felt they were keeping alive the memory of relatives who had fallen. That's also why Tilden, for all his class, was never as popular as Patterson.

Patterson remained heavily involved with Australian tennis after he had retired. He rose to become a respected administrator within the sport and in 1946 returned to Wimbledon as the non-playing captain of the Australian Davis Cup team. He was also a successful businessman and, in the early 1930s, was bequeathed a small fortune by an aunt who had always doted on her favourite nephew.

Patterson married and had two children, one of whom, Bill, was Australian motor-racing champion in 1961. Six years later, on 13 June 1967, Patterson died in Melbourne after a long illness aged seventy-one. Tributes flooded in from around the world, although the most poignant was written in Patterson's local newspaper, Melbourne's *The Age*, by Ian Mair.

'Who ever thought I would be going to Gerald Patterson's funeral today? Because if anybody seemed immortal to a young fellow just after the First World War, it was G L Patterson. He gave me – and, if me, then thousands of other countless strangers to him – so many uncounted hours of pleasure.'

Georges Carpentier

Georges Carpentier's philosophy on life was simple; it was to be enjoyed, and enjoy it he did. The French boxer won the European Heavyweight title in 1913 when he was still in his teens. Carpentier's film-star looks and charisma won him an array of fans. Women loved him, men admired him, but fame didn't change him. When war broke out in 1914 he joined the air force and insisted on a front line posting.

'I would stroll along the Avenue des Acacias wearing a black bowler, light yellow gloves, a fancy waistcoat and patent leather boots with dove-grey uppers ... and, of course, I always carried my ivory-headed cane.'

Georges Carpentier was a dandy, a self-confessed fop, from the top of his bowler down to his dove-grey uppers. He was also a ladies man, a teetotaller and he fancied himself as a movie star. Then, of course, there was his nationality. French. All in all, he didn't appear to have many qualities that would make him the darling of British boxing fans in the first quarter of the twentieth century. They preferred their boxers to be less swanky and more, well, savage. Men like 'Bombardier' Billy Wells, Ted Smith, the former sailor with a tattoo for every girl in every port, and Joe Beckett, the heavyweight with the battered face and baleful scowl. The problem they had was that

Carpentier beat the lot; whipped their hides, sent them sprawling across the canvas seconds after the sound of the bell. Beckett lasted sixty seconds, much to the displeasure of the Prince of Wales, sitting in the front row. 'My cigar had gone out,' he later explained. 'I had just time to light it again and look up – and the fight was over.'

So why did the British public adopt Georges Carpentier as one of their own? What persuaded hundreds of Englishmen to cross the Channel to cheer him on against an American in Dieppe? And how did he come to mix with royalty? He was hugely charismatic, undoubtedly, with a Gallic streak that appealed to a country whose own sporting heroes were more austere and conservative by comparison. Carpentier was the first in a line of French sports stars who have mesmerized the British public with their élan. Where Carpentier led, Suzanne Lenglen, Jean Borotra, Henri Leconte, Serge Blanco and Eric Cantona followed.

A cheeky smile and a music-hall broken English accent, however, wouldn't have been enough to win over the sort of men who crammed into the Holborn Stadium and Olympia to watch Carpentier fight. These were hard men leading hard lives. They came often from the slums of London, saving up for weeks to afford the three guineas to stand and see him box. They liked what they saw. This French bloke, they said to one another, might dress like a beau, but he knows how to scrap and he's got guts aplenty. They also saw him as one of them. Not just because of Carpentier's humble origins in a drab mining town in northern France, but because when the First World War broke out, he, like they, volunteered and went off to fight at the front. He didn't wangle himself a cushy little number in some quiet backwater, like a lot of sportsmen who were keen to be photographed in uniform but a little less keen to rough it on the front line with the ordinary working man. Carpentier refused to accept a sinecure, badgering his superiors until he saw some action and subsequently distinguishing himself in combat. Yes, Carpentier was one of them, from the top of that daft bowler right down to those dreadful dove-grey uppers.

Carpentier was born in 1894, in a small village just outside Lens in the Pas-de-Calais region of France. He was the youngest of five children and money was always a struggle for his mother and father, a collier at the local pit. This was the route followed by his older brother, Gustave, who began working in the mines aged twelve. He worked ten hours each day and had three francs to show for it. 'That was the settled order of things for people like us,' recalled Carpentier.

Georges might have taken the path of his father and brother had it not been for his boxing skills. They were first spotted by a local man. One afternoon he broke up a brawl between a group of teenagers and a ten-year-old. The youngster was outnumbered four to one but he landed several good punches in the mêlée. After he had shown the back of his hand to the teenagers the man turned to the ten-year-old Carpentier. 'I run the gymnasium in town,' he said. 'Why don't you come along? I'll teach you something better than fighting in the street.' The man's name was François Deschamps. If the truth be told he was a bit of a chancer, a dreamer, someone who was always telling his friends how he was going to hit the big time. But his heart was in the right place. When he saw Carpentier he thought he was just another lad who would enjoy boxing at his gym with the other boys. Within ten years he would be the manager of one of the most famous boxers in the world, negotiating six-figure purses and accepting invitations to fight in America.

Carpentier's first serious bout was in December 1906, shortly before his thirteenth birthday. He fought an infantry corporal called Legrand, a man twice his age and twice his size, and won. There was much hilarity in the barracks that night. Two years later Carpentier turned professional and beat an Englishman called Ed Salmon in his first fight. He took home 150 francs, a tidy sum for a boy whose brother wouldn't earn that in a month. His rapid progress as a boxer during 1909 and 1910 outstripped his physical development. In two years he lost just three of his 34 fights, and those were to opponents whose physical maturity had been reached.

When he turned seventeen in January 1911, Carpentier tipped the scaled a fraction under ten stone but his speed and agility in the ring caught the eye of Jack Johnson, the American heavyweight champion who was touring Europe. He sparred some rounds with him in exhibition bouts, cutting Johnson's lip with a wayward right. 'That little fellow of yours will go far,' he told Deschamps afterwards as he nursed his swollen mouth. Word of Carpentier's exploits drifted across the English Channel and reached the ears of 'Bombardier' Billy Wells, the British heavyweight champion, who was training for his fight against Johnson that autumn. Wells' camp invited Carpentier to England to spar with their man and pass on a few trade secrets. In return, they promised a lucrative contest would be arranged for him against Sid Burns.

Carpentier was nervous about accepting the offer. Not so much because he feared Burns, or Wells, but because he had heard strange tales about the inhabitants of this peculiar little island: 'In French cartoons ... all Englishmen had long teeth, wore caps and went around in bright checks,' he said later. However, the 5,000 franc purse on offer for fighting Burns overcame Carpentier's reluctance.

He sparred with Wells, beat Burns and enjoyed England. The English liked him too, especially after his forceful defeat of Burns. They offered him another fight, against Young Joseph, the European welterweight champion. Carpentier conceded a couple of pounds in weight to his opponent but he was far too quick for Joseph. The fight ended in the tenth round when, as *La Boxe et les Boxeurs* reported: 'Suddenly [Carpentier] let fly. He used his right in a series of swift upper cuts and hooks, so fast as to be almost invisible.'

Carpentier was acclaimed upon his return to France. Hundreds gathered at the Gare du Nord to welcome him home and promoters clamoured for his attention. At the start of 1912, having just turned eighteen, Carpentier fought Jim Sullivan for the European middleweight championship in Monte Carlo. At the weigh-in the Frenchman noticed that his opponent's features were 'unmarked and he looked like a man not used to taking punches – more a boxer than a fighter'. Sullivan, in fact, lasted a few seconds of round two before Carpentier delivered a left upper-cut to his chin that, in the words of one Parisian newspaper, left the Englishman 'on his back, his arms outspread and [he] lay there motionless. It was a knock-out, complete and absolute.'

Carpentier had now built himself quite a reputation as a decent boxer with fast hands and a powerful punch. But the sceptics' doubts remained. They looked askance at his good looks. Wait until someone goes to work on his pretty little face, they muttered, then we'll see how tough he really is. That someone appeared in June 1912 in the hulking shape of an American middleweight called Frank Klaus. His nickname was the 'Pittsburgh Bear', and it was apt. He had the build of a grizzly and he fought in the same wild and remorseless style. Carpentier watched him box a compatriot shortly before they met in the ring and wrote later: 'He was on the attack all the time, seemingly irresistible to the blows his opponent dealt him.'

The fight was fixed for Dieppe, a relatively convenient venue for the French fans and the many British supporters who had taken Carpentier to their hearts. When the two boxers met at the pre-fight press conference, Klaus gave a derisory snort when he saw Carpentier. 'He looked at me,' remembered the Frenchman, 'laughed rather unpleasantly and said something in English I didn't understand, but the journalists obligingly translated, "He says your jib's too pretty for a boxer's".'

When Deschamps intervened to save his man from further punishment in the nineteenth round there was little prettiness to be found in Carpentier's face. Harry Pearson, an English boxing promoter, was at ringside and by the end of the bout his dinner jacket was speckled with Carpentier's blood. 'His condition was terrible,' he wrote later. 'Battered, bruised, only his indomitable spirit kept him on his legs, fighting ... a minute of the 19th had gone when Klaus drove in a blow to the pit of his stomach ... Georges staggered. Blood gushed from his mouth.' Deschamps leapt into the ring but Carpentier pushed him away: 'Go away, François! Let go! What are you doing, madman?' Deschamps, tears streaming down his face, took his boxer's head in his hands, 'I will not have you killed.'

Carpentier was disqualified, his face a congealed mess of blood and sweat, but only one of the two boxers went out on the town that night. Klaus retired to his bed, triumphant but shattered. Carpentier was similarly exhausted, but even so, 'I made it a point of honour to show myself at the Casino that evening. I liked to appear in public after a fight.'

The next morning Carpentier had more to reflect upon than just his gambling losses. Klaus had been outboxed for much of the fight but his greater strength had won him the fight. For the first time Carpentier realized that his skill, speed and accuracy were weapons that could take him only so far. If he wanted to reach his holy grail, and become the heavyweight champion of the world, he would need to sharpen their edges on an anvil of destruction. 'The problem,' he reflected later, 'was how to render profitable the muscles Nature had endowed me with, rather lavishly perhaps, in the thighs and calves ... consequently for months and months I practised how to bring the weight of my thighs into play for the use of my punch.'

By the start of 1913 Carpentier had a formidable arsenal. It was too much for Marcel Moreau, Bandsman Rice and George Gunther, who were all beaten by an increasingly ambitious Carpentier. His aspirations were guided by Deschamps, who arranged a contest in June for the European heavyweight crown against Billy Wells, the British champion. It was a 'big risk' to accept the fight, Carpentier remembered, since he would be surrendering three stone to his opponent, but 'it would have been silly to turn down such an opportunity'.

The fight in Ghent began badly for Carpentier. Twice in the first round he was knocked to the floor, and as he rose for the second time he could hear the boos echo around ringside. The fans who had made their way from Paris and London felt cheated. This was a farce and a waste of money. But it was a different Carpentier who emerged at the start of round three. He began attacking Wells' midriff, pummelling his stomach with a series of punches as though he were a lumberjack trying to fell an English oak. Carpentier continued his work in the fourth round, landing blow after blow until the oak swayed and then, with a punch above the heart, toppled and crashed to the ground.

Wells was nothing if not game. He asked for a rematch at the end of the year, and got it. Carpentier was paid 77,000 francs for the fight and laughed all the way to the bank. Wells had lasted sixty-three seconds, much to the fury of the 1,500 spectators at the National Sporting Club in London who roared their disapproval. As Wells tried to leave the arena, and was confronted by the former British featherweight champion, Jim Driscoll, screaming 'Coward! Coward! Coward!' inches from his face, the correspondent from L'Echo des Sports filed his copy: 'One, two, three; left, right, left to the stomach. And then slowly and limply as though all the strength had gone out of his great body the English champion staggered along the ropes. His legs gave way under him and he collapsed, an inert mass which did not even twitch as the chronometer ticked off the fatal ten seconds.'

Carpentier had earned more money in a minute than his brother could earn in a lifetime working in the mines. And his skill as a boxer brought with it other rewards, too, as Carpentier was delectably discovering. A few hours after dispatching Wells, the Frenchman was pursuing more captivating adversaries in the nightclubs of London. They put up sterner resistance than Wells but while the night was still young enough for romance Carpentier had departed with a woman who 'wasn't a tart, but I don't think she was altogether a lady either. However, she was very pretty and she pleased me. It was clear, too, that I did not displease her. In short – as my friends did not fail to observe with a twinkle in their eyes – the affair was well away.'

Carpentier's conquests out of the ring were as legendary as those inside the ropes. He was the first boxer to trade on his film-star looks. Women who were normally poised and refined threw themselves at his feet, kissing his dove-grey uppers and offering themselves up for his gratification. He had lost his virginity at the age of thirteen, an experience he remembered with clarity many years later, 'but not for the usual reasons ... It happened one night in a garden in which there was also a savage dog chained up, and the whole time it barked furiously ... I have always been fond of dogs but I deplored that one's lack of consideration.'

His first encounter with a groupie was in Monte Carlo after Ed Sullivan had impeded his progress to his favourite nightclub by a little over three minutes. He was eighteen at the time, precocious with it, and the twenty-four-year-old woman got straight to the point when they met after the fight. 'I noticed you were looking at me [in the ring],' she cooed. Carpentier looked her up and down, and smiled, 'I don't remember.' It was the line to her heart. They embarked upon an affair and Carpentier later wrote that 'she came into my life just at the right moment to teach me a good many things it was high time I learned.'

Carpentier's appeal was universal and, in one or two cases, intoxicating. Long before the word 'stalker' had been coined, he was unnerved by a high-society English woman who seemed to crop up all over the world whenever he fought. 'The thing had become an obsession,' he said. 'On more than one occasion on leaving my hotel in a town in which I had only just arrived I would catch myself instinctively casting a furtive and harassed look each way along the street, in the fear that I would see the well-known figure of the lady ... bearing down on me.'

The boxing promoters soon realized they could exploit Carpentier's allure. They suddenly became ardent supporters of the Suffragette movement and demanded equality for the fairer sex. Why should women not be allowed to attend boxing contests in Britain, they demanded to know. The promoters got their way and when Carpentier fought Gunboat Smith in London in July 1914, women were in the audience for the first time. Maybe Emmeline Pankhurst wasn't there, but dozens of other young ladies were, swooning as Carpentier danced to victory.

At the beginning of August 1914 Carpentier was still in London, negotiating the contract for a fight against an American boxer called Young Aherne. His knowledge of English was limited but just a quick scan of the newspapers told him all he needed to know about the seriousness of the situation in Europe following the assassination of Archduke Ferdinand of Austria. On 2 August France declared war on Germany and, when Britain followed suit two days later, Carpentier and Deschamps were already steaming across the Channel.

On 6 August, Carpentier enlisted in the air force and was posted to Saint-Cyr, a clearing camp where airmen awaited a further posting. His first mission was to the Quartermaster's Stores and it was a distressing experience for Carpentier, like being struck below the belt. He came out, he said, looking 'like a scarecrow'. The cut of his military uniform appalled him – this was no way to go to war – so when the opportunity presented itself he fled to Paris and 'had myself a uniform made to measure'. While back in town he also picked up one of his favourite cars, a Bellenger. His commanding officer watched with eyebrow raised as Carpentier returned to camp that evening; the following night in the mess he took delight in telling his fellow officers that he was being chauffeured by the European heavyweight champion in the finest automobile in the French army.

The first months of the war passed slowly for Carpentier, too slowly for a man who was used to moving quickly in life, be it in the ring, pursuing women or making money. He led a dissolute life for most of 1914, 'painting the town red almost every night … there were parties at the place of this one or the other … [and] there were other temptations – women, pretty women, of deplorably easy virtue.' He later looked back on those months with disgust, ashamed of his gallivanting while a few miles north on the Marne 300,000 Frenchmen were shedding their blood as they stemmed the German advance and then slowly pushed it back.

The death of his friend and fellow sportsman, Jean Bouin, compelled Carpentier to confront his commanding officer. Bouin, who had won a silver medal in the 5,000 metres at the 1912 Olympics, had been killed on the Argonne front. His self-sacrifice deeply disturbed Carpentier who found himself 'a quiet corner where I could howl unobserved'. The next day he demanded to be posted to the air base at Avord where he could learn to become a pilot.

His persistence brought its reward. He qualified as a pilot after six weeks and was posted to a fighter squadron at Belfort. His first missions were escorting bombers across German lines but within two months he had been transferred to Squadron F14: 'I was put on reconnaissance operations together with an observer and we directed artillery fire, noted enemy positions and took aerial photographs.' It was while on one of these patrols that Carpentier ran into trouble. The motor of his plane spluttered and died, forcing him to crash-land in a field over French lines. The plane was wrecked and both he and his observer were badly bruised but the mishap allowed him a week's convalescence. 'I soon felt all right again, and Paris was quite close. The temptation was impossible to resist.' Carpentier had no compunction about going on a splurge in Paris now that he was doing his share of the fighting.

Shortly before he was due to return to base Carpentier made whoopee one final time. He dined on the rue Duphot and on leaving tried to hail a cab. As he waited a car drove by containing four men, one of whom leaned out and told him to take an aeroplane home, or words to that effect. 'Naturally, I replied to the rudeness in kind,' Carpentier recalled. The car stopped. 'A hefty type got out and rushed at me, aiming a heavy blow at my face. It was unexpected but at least he had come to the right address.' Carpentier dropped him with a right to the chin. 'In a moment his three friends were on me, but one after the other I sent them down to join their pal in the gutter, each with a well-placed right.'

Carpentier's next posting was to Squadron MF55 in Le Cheppe. Within a couple of days of his arrival he learned of the death in battle of another sporting contemporary. He was an Englishman called George Mitchell,* a good sort with bags of pluck and an impenetrable sense of humour. Shortly after Carpentier had knocked out Billy Wells in sixty-three seconds he received a challenge from Mitchell to fight him in Paris. Carpentier tapped his ivory-headed cane against his boots as he considered the proposal. He stared at Deschamps and repeated what he had just been told by his manager: 'So let me get this straight: this Mitchell chap will pay me 5,000 francs to fight him just so that he can win a £1,000 bet with some friends that he can last longer in the ring than Wells?' Deschamps nodded enthusiastically. 'And is Mitchell a boxer?'

Deschamps' brow furrowed: 'I think he has done a bit; they tell me he is a

---

* Second Lieutenant George Mitchell, Black Watch, was killed on 22 July 1915 aged twenty-six.

reasonable amateur boxer in a place called Yorkshire.' Carpentier pondered the challenge and then accepted. 'I found the proposal amusing.'

A date was agreed in April 1914 and the Doerr School of Boxing in Paris was chosen as the venue. As the two men waited to enter the ring, Carpentier was approached by an anxious Mitchell: 'Monsieur Carpentier, I beg you not to spare me in the slightest degree. Clearly, that wouldn't be fair to the people with whom I have made this bet, and apart from that it would disappoint me too.' Carpentier gazed at Mitchell. 'I quite understand. You can count on me to make it the real thing.'

Mitchell was knocked down by Carpentier's first punch, but he rose after a count of nine. He was felled twice more and before a minute had passed he was bleeding heavily from cuts above his eyes. The referee allowed the fight to continue for fifteen seconds after the agreed time of sixty-four seconds before he stopped the contest. Mitchell, unsteady on his feet and wiping the blood from around his eyes, beamed broadly: 'Thank you from the bottom of my heart, Monsieur Carpentier, the thing went off absolutely correctly.'

Mitchell's death, like those of all his friends, grieved Carpentier, but the mask of bonhomie rarely slipped from his face. He continued to exude an air of sang-froid, a devil-may-care attitude to war and living. When the French launched the Second Champagne Offensive on 29 September 1915 – to coincide with the British attack at Loos – he was heavily involved in reconnaissance work. 'There was plenty of action,' he recalled, as the Allies attempted unsuccessfully to push the Germans back towards Belgium. 'On more than one occasion we ran into enemy ack-ack or were pursued by enemy fighters.' Carpentier's brevity in describing his role in the offensive concealed his courage. The squadron was mentioned in despatches for their work and Carpentier was awarded the Croix de Guerre. The medal was welcome but the additional forty-eight hours' leave was even more appreciated. He spent the two nights at the Théâtre des Capucines, 'for which preference there was a very special reason'. He never revealed her name. She must have captured the heart of Carpentier, for the next time he returned to Paris to see her was on an unauthorised trip that resulted in him facing charges of 'desertion in the face of the enemy'. He was placed under arrest and thrown in the cells. When his commander discovered his own staff car had been used for the tryst his whiskers twitched with indignation. Within two days Carpentier was transferred to Squadron F8 at Vadelaincourt.

The commander would have been pleased to know that Carpentier had a thoroughly miserable time at his new home. His quarters in May 1916 were a series of decrepit wooden huts, infested with rats, vermin that had always frightened Carpentier. He had also arrived in the midst of the battle for Verdun, which had been at the centre of a monstrous battle between the French and German armies since February. That summer 'things were very hot' as far as the aerial war was concerned. Carpentier remembered that 'there were far more planes engaged on both sides than ever before, particularly fighters, and the air fighting was at its fiercest.'

Carpentier was assigned to a role that suited his personality; it required courage, enterprise and gall.

> 'My job was to keep our forward command posts, which were hidden well underground, supplied with information by morse code or by dropping weighted messages concerning the dispositions of the enemy and of our own advanced troops.'

To carry out his orders Carpentier had to fly very low, in all weathers, running the gauntlet of fire from the battlefield below. The risks were obvious and he was nearly brought down by one shell that exploded directly below his plane, spewing up a violent concoction of shrapnel and mud: 'When I got back to base I even found stones embedded in the fuselage.'

On 24 October the French troops retook Fort Douaumont, which had been captured by the Germans eight months earlier provoking scenes of wild triumphalism back in Germany. Church bells had been rung across the country, children had been given a special holiday and newspapers had predicted the imminent collapse of France. The French had staved off such a calamity, thanks in part to the obduracy of the new commander appointed in the immediate aftermath of the Douaumont debacle, General Philippe Pétain, whose first Order of the Day upon taking charge read simply: 'France has her eyes on you.'

Over the following months France prised the fort from German hands finger by bloody finger. When they finally took possession in October, France celebrated as manically as the German civilians had done all those months earlier. Among the men who had fought at Verdun and floundered through the fiendish mud amid the shrieks of the dying, there was just insensibility. Carpentier flew over the fort on the day of its recapture. Years later he wrote:

> 'That day made an impression on me I was never to forget. I could see the bodies of the defenders strewn around the fort where they had been blasted by our shells, while our *poilus* climbed up what was left of the ramparts. When I got back to base I climbed on my bed and lay there for about three hours, mentally and physically k.o'd.'

Carpentier was awarded the French Military Medal for his distinguished conduct at Verdun. This time there was no whoop of delight when he was informed of the decoration. The war had lost its sheen for Carpentier. When he had rushed back from England to enlist in August 1914 the steamer had been full of men eager to join up because 'the war would not last more than a few weeks'. In the weeks after Verdun he spent much of the time lying on his bed, staring numbly into space, too drained even to go on a spree in Paris.

The French Supreme Command was as traumatized as Carpentier. During the ten months of fighting at Verdun France had suffered 377,000 casualties. The morale of the French public could not afford to be eroded further. In particular the sporting patrimony of the country must be preserved and so the French military ordered all well-known personalities to be removed from the firing line. In January 1917 Carpentier found himself sent on a course at Joinville. It became a course of indefinable length. He was still at Joinville on 11 November 1918 when the Armistice was announced.

The two years Carpentier spent on the Western Front had, as with millions of other young men, left their imprint on his soul. He had sparred during his time at Joinville and in his first few fights in 1919 he defeated Dick Smith, middleweight champion of Britain, and a French heavyweight called Croiselles. But when he stepped in the ring after the war it wasn't with the unbridled *joie de vivre* that had characterized his fights before 1914. Life wasn't such a wild gallop through a meadow of pleasures: 'The five-year gap brought about by the war had undoubtedly blunted the fine edge of my enthusiasm … when I did return to boxing after the war … it was without quite the same ardour and freshness.'

His first real test was in December 1919 when he fought Joe Beckett, the new heavyweight champion of Britain, at the Holborn Stadium. Carpentier now weighed twelve stone but he still gave away over a stone in weight to the Englishman. Fred Dartnell, writing in the *Daily News*, suggested that 'the probability is of something sensational in the way of an early finish', although he leaned towards Beckett and his superior weight and strength.

Among the 4,000 fans at ringside were a plethora of notables from the worlds of politics, society, literature and the theatre. George Bernard Shaw was one of them, a lapsed boxing fan who had been commissioned to write an article for *The Nation*. He had heard all about Carpentier but this was his first chance to see him in the flesh. Beckett was first to enter the ring. Carpentier, like all born showmen, kept his audience waiting. Shaw stroked his beard impatiently as he waited for the entrance of the Frenchman. On hearing a commotion he turned round and was startled by what he saw emerge from the shadows: 'Nothing less than Charles XII, "the madman of the North", striding along the gangway in a Japanese dressing gown as gallantly as if he had not been killed almost exactly 201 years before.' Shaw stifled a chuckle at the effrontery of Carpentier, writing that 'he was at home with it; he dominated it; he picked out his friends and kissed hands to them in his debonair way quite naturally, without swank or mock modesty, as one born to move assemblies.'

Beckett, watching from his corner, dissolved into a bundle of nerves as he observed the swaggering entrance of his opponent. He had lost the fight in his mind before the sound of the first bell. He lasted 74 seconds, eleven more than his predecessor, Billy Wells. Carpentier, ever the gentleman, helped him back to his corner and bowed before the Prince of Wales. Then, wrote Shaw, '[he was] hoisted up to be chaired, dragged down to be kissed, hung out by the heels from the scaffold to be fondled by a lady'. All in all, it had been a satisfactory night for Carpentier, who the next day gave an exhibition of his skills before a lunch party including King George V and Queen Mary.

In 1920 the unthinkable occurred – Carpentier married. It was a blow to millions of women the world over, but a blessing to Deschamps. He had ambitious plans for his man and he was confident the love of a good woman would focus his mind on the prize they had eyed for the past fifteen years, the world heavyweight crown.

The three of them had sailed to America in the spring of 1920, ostensibly to dispose of Battling Levinsky, the world light heavyweight champion, who was nonchalantly mastered in four rounds. Levinsky's head hit the canvas seconds before a red rose, gracefully thrown from the hand of Alice Delysia, a French actress in Broadway, who had come to watch her compatriot. Bob Edgreen, an American boxing journalist, liked the look of the dashing Frenchman: 'Carpentier is the great champion we were told he was. It wasn't an inferior Levinsky he met and yet he beat him even more decisively than Dempsey succeeded in doing.'

Carpentier and Deschamps smiled when they read Edgreen's words. Dempsey was, after all, the real reason they were in America. He was heavyweight champion of the world and the man they had to dethrone. Negotiations began shortly after the victory over Levinsky and on 5 November the relevant parties agreed terms. What they announced in the ballroom of the Claridge Hotel stunned the sporting world.

Dempsey would earn $300,000 and twenty-five per cent of the motion picture rights and Carpentier would receive a similar share of the film rights and $200,000. The *New York Times* warned in an editorial that the continued commercialism of boxing would one day kill the sport, while *The Times* said: 'From the financial point of view of Carpentier and Dempsey, the enormous purses which are being offered may be satisfactory, but a bubble, when it is blown sufficiently large, is certain to burst.'

To justify these enormous fees, promoter Tex Rickard needed strong publicity to attract a huge gate. He shamelessly used Carpentier's war record in comparison to Dempsey's. Dempsey, in fact, had been deferred for service because he was supporting a large family. But near the end of the war, his otherwise astute manager, Doc Kearns, made a mistake, arranging for Dempsey to pose for recruitment purposes in the Sun Shipyard, Philadelphia, wearing striped overalls and pretending to use a riveter's machine. Unfortunately, the pictures published in the press showed Dempsey wearing his street clothes underneath, with expensive suede shoes sticking out beneath the overalls. His riveting was clearly a fake, and the public, assuming that Dempsey was trying to disguise the fact that he had dodged the draft, labelled him a 'slacker', and it took years for Dempsey to overcome the ensuing unpopularity. This suited Rickard, whose publicity posed the swarthy 'slacker' against the debonair, handsome war hero. Possibly uniquely in a big American boxing match, more of the crowd wanted the foreigner to win than the American.

Carpentier, however, probably knew he had taken on a fight he could never win. Dempsey was two stone heavier and a born fighter. Unlike the British heavyweights who had capitulated to the speed and power of Carpentier's punches, the American seemed to enjoy taking blows as much as he delighted in throwing them. So why did Carpentier accept the fight? Money was obviously a factor. To say otherwise would be disingenuous, but he was pushed into the ring by more than a love of the filthy lucre.

He had long dreamed of becoming world heavyweight champion of the world. It had sustained him during the tough early years, when he had fought for purses of 150 francs in deserted village halls, and it probably spurred him on through Verdun, giving him a purpose as he tried desperately not to be dragged down into the dark abyss that seemed to threaten him. This was his one chance of fulfilling his dream and, even though it was a long shot, Carpentier was a risk-taker by nature and he was now prepared to gamble his reputation.

The fight was staged on the outskirts of Jersey City on 2 July 1921. The crowd numbered somewhere in the region of 90,000, paying nearly two million dollars, twice as much as any previous fight. Tex Rickard, the promoter, should have been a happy man but he was troubled by a nagging thought. It wouldn't do much for his reputation if Carpentier died in the 18-foot ring. Shortly before the fight got under way at 3pm he sought out Dempsey. 'Listen Jack,' he said, slipping an arm round the American's massive shoulders, 'this Carpentier is a nice feller [sic], but he can't fight. So I want you to be careful and not kill him.'

Carpentier entered the ring first escorted by two policemen. He was wearing a dove-grey dressing gown but also, according to a correspondent from the New York Tribune, the look of a 'clever, elusive, but guilty young gentleman, who knew at last that the jig was up and was going along to headquarters to face the music'. Dempsey's appearance brought forth a gasp from the women in the crowd. He looked so big and so powerful in comparison to the man they had come to cheer. It seemed to them that Dempsey could snap Carpentier's neck between his thumb and forefinger.

In the first round Carpentier shed ruby tears from a punch that cut him above his right eye. When he unleashed a couple of blows to Dempsey's thick torso they failed to make any impression. Carpentier's axe was blunt. Or was the bark too tough?

In round two Dempsey closed in to finish the fight but in his eagerness he exposed his chin and Carpentier sent in a straight right that landed just below his left cheekbone. 'Dempsey wavered,' recalled Carpentier, 'his eyes flickered and he went back into the ropes. But he didn't go down.' Dempsey had been hurt by the punch and some journalists watching from the front row thought he was there for the taking. One, Heywood Broun, wrote that Carpentier 'was within a punch of the championship ... the tragedy of life is not that a man loses but that he almost wins'. The punch from Carpentier had been intended for Dempsey's chin but at the most crucial moment in his career his accuracy had deserted him. If it hadn't Dempsey might have gone down for a long count. Instead, he was dazed but vertical and Carpentier had broken his thumb in two places and sprained his wrist from the misdirected blow.

It didn't take Dempsey long to realize Carpentier had injured his hand. The grimace on his face told its own story. Carpentier remembered that by the start of round four his hand was just a 'useless lump of flesh and bone that hurt agonizingly'. It was now just a matter of time before Dempsey finished him off. The big American was kind. He knocked him down halfway through the fourth and then as the bell approached he sounded the death knell for Carpentier's dreams: 'With one knee on the canvas,' Carpentier said, 'I sought to regain my breath. I could see Dempsey's face screwed up and dripping with sweat that might have been mistaken for tears ... the referee steadily counted me out and then Dempsey came forward to help me up. "No," I thought, "not that!" With my last remaining strength I managed to get to my feet before he was able to make the gesture.' Carpentier had evaded the *coup de grâce* but his boxing ambitions had ceased to be.

The power of Dempsey had been matched only by the courage of Carpentier. Women sobbed quietly into their handkerchiefs while the men in the audience shook their heads in admiration. Some would never be able to warm to the Frenchman's ostentatious displays but his bravery demanded respect. The *Times* correspondent was as affected as the rest by what he had seen: 'My own imagination is haunted by the spectacle of Carpentier, springing on to the raised ring, a blithe and smiling model for any sculptor, and of his appearance less than twenty minutes later as he lay dazed and disfigured by the terrific punishment he had received.'

Carpentier continued to fight for another four years but he was going through the motions. After the Dempsey fight he knew he didn't have the weight to win the heavyweight championship. 'The feeling of fulfilling a mission which had sustained me for so long had deserted me ... I therefore went on as before, but now only as a man pursuing a lucrative profession.'

He retired in 1926, scared of becoming a washed-out old pro boxing in front of the size of crowds he had last seen as a thirteen-year-old in Lens. Many boxers are notoriously inept at forging a new life for themselves outside the ring, but Carpentier had no such problems. When he announced his retirement he already had another career lined up. With his looks, his charm and his natural showmanship, the cinema beckoned. He had made his first film appearance in 1920 in *The Wonderman*, the first of twelve movies in which he starred. Some of them, he breezily admitted, were eminently forgettable. He appeared in *The Gypsy Cavalier* in 1922 but when he tried to recall its plot years later he was unable to 'remember what *The Gypsy Cavalier* was about any more ... in fact, I don't think I ever knew.'

He spent much of the summer of 1929 at the holiday home of Arthur Loew, vice-president of Metro-Goldwyn-Mayer. He rubbed shoulders with Douglas Fairbanks and his son, Douglas Fairbanks Jr, and their respective wives, Mary Pickford and Joan Crawford. There were drinks parties with Al Jolson, George Gershwin and Gloria Swanson, while with Charlie Chaplin he chased women. On one occasion the pair competed for the charms of a showgirl they were watching. 'We'll make a bet,' laughed Chaplin, 'we'll invite the girl over to our table and then see which of us she prefers.' The young lady, they discovered, was English and called Kathleen. 'Chaplin and I competed for her favour,' remembered Carpentier. 'Result: "No decision." After having talked to us for a while she made her excuses and went to another table where an unknown rival was sitting alone.'

One woman not quite so resistant to Carpentier's charms was the Hollywood siren Greta Garbo. The two met when he was filming *Hold Everything*. She invited him for a swim at her house. 'I kept the appointment,' said Carpentier, 'but swam alone. The great Garbo had certainly put on a swimming costume ... but she contented herself with watching me, asking from time to time whether the water was cold.'

Carpentier's fortunes nose-dived in 1929. He lost 'enough money to sink a battleship' in the Wall Street Crash and began to tire of the decadence of Hollywood. He was at heart a Frenchman who felt happiest in the bosom of his country. He returned to Paris and in 1935 opened an upmarket bar.

Business was good and within a few years he was running two more cafés. It was a blissful existence for Carpentier who would chat to boxing aficionados from around the world while examining 'the many pretty women who daily ornament the place'.

In 1965, aged seventy-one, Carpentier stepped down from his work as a congenial proprietor. The following year he accepted an invitation from the *Sunday Telegraph* in Britain to report on the impending fight at Highbury Stadium between Cassius Clay and Henry Cooper. Carpentier, who had always retained an affection for the eccentric race across the Channel, met both boxers in the build-up to the fight. When Clay challenged him to a knockabout spar, Carpentier sprung to his feet and shadow-boxed with the American champion. 'I boxed with my arms low and loose,' he told Clay. 'You know,' said Clay, turning to his manager, Angelo Dundee, 'this guy talks sense, he's a good fighter'.

Carpentier died on the evening of Monday 27 October 1975. He suffered a heart attack and passed away in the arms of his only child, Jacqueline. 'My father had the death he wanted,' she told reporters, 'because he had always had good health and he had a horror of sickness.'

His passing brought France to a standstill. Every newspaper carried his picture on its front page and the main television channel cleared its evening schedule to transmit a tribute to his remarkable life. The headline in *France Soir* caught the mood of the nation: 'The Death of Carpentier – with him goes the era when boxing was a noble art.'

Thousands of words were written in the eulogies that followed as journalists struggled to capture the essence of Carpentier. None truly succeeded. After all, who exactly was Georges Carpentier? Was he the preening fop who flitted from one woman to the next? Or was he the magnificent warrior who proved his courage in the ring and who in war served his country with uncommon bravery? He is best remembered as a boxer, one who in 1991 was inducted into the International Boxing Hall of Fame. That would have tickled Carpentier, but more agreeable to him would have been the two words included in a tribute written by *Le Monde*. Remembering his appearances at Les Palais des Sports to watch the latest French hopefuls, the paper recalled that with each passing year he looked more fragile. However, there remained one constant. He was without fail, declared the newspaper, whatever the occasion, always *'chic inimitable'*.

CHAPTER SIX

Charlie Buchan

Charlie Buchan was Sunderland's star striker in those golden days just before the outbreak of the First World War. His talent as an inside-forward earned him an England call-up but within a few years he was representing his country on the battlefield as a guardsman. He fought in some of the most brutal battles of the war on the Somme, at Passchendaele and Cambrai but survived to continue his remarkable football career for Arsenal and England. Buchan had left his mark in war and peace.

Charlie Buchan knew all about hard men. He spent all of his sporting life trying to avoid their wild lunges and high elbows. In the early years of his football career with Sunderland he was intimidated by their aggressive posturing. He discovered they came in all shapes and sizes, and occasionally as part of a double-act, as was the case once during a match in Lancashire. 'If you try any of your tricks today,' the left-back hissed in Buchan's ear, 'I'll kick you over the grandstand.' The right-back sidled up behind him, 'Aye, and I'll go round the other side and kick you back on the field again.'

Then came the First World War. Buchan spent three years with the Grenadier Guards and soon realized that the gap between what constituted 'hard' on the football field and 'hard' on the battlefield was as wide as a drill sergeant's shoulders. Raymond Asquith, son of the then Prime Minister, Herbert, would have been kicked off the football pitch if he had dared take on one of the game's hard men. He had led a privileged life – Winchester and Oxford – and preferred more cerebral pastimes. Yet in 1916, Asquith, one of Buchan's officers in the Guards, was shot in the chest during an attack on the Somme. Anxious to show his men that he was not badly wounded, Asquith lit a cigarette and shouted encouragement to his Company as they continued to press the attack. He died on the way to the dressing station.

Having lived and fought alongside such men, Buchan came to despise the football hard men who tried to throw their weight around, particularly when they were also shirkers. After two years on the Western Front Buchan found it depressing to return to England and find fit, young men unashamedly gallivanting around the football pitch when, in his opinion, they should have been doing their bit at the front. He came across one such man playing in a wartime match for Huddersfield against Birmingham in 1918. The Blues' defender, who had just finished a shift at the local munitions factory, took delight in kicking Buchan black and blue. Eventually, his patience snapped: 'I've had as much fighting as I want,' he smiled matter-of-factly. 'If you fancy a scrap, join the army.' With one well-placed verbal hand grenade the man's bravado had been blown to smithereens.

Probably no other professional footballer saw as much action in the First World War as Charlie Buchan. Certainly none was as lucky. He fought his way through the Somme, Passchendaele and Cambrai, three of the most abhorrent battles of the war. Shellfire scattered hundreds of his mates to the four winds. Others were caught in murderous machine-gun fire. But Buchan's number never came up. He didn't claim to be a particularly religious man, but someone was watching out for him during his two years on the Western Front. Or perhaps he just had a lucky face.

If he did, there wasn't much evidence of it during his football career. Twice he appeared in an FA Cup Final, and both times he finished a loser. Then there were the England appearances, or lack of them. Six caps in eleven years, yet he had been considered the most gifted forward of his generation. But none of this much bothered Buchan. In fact, nothing bothered Buchan, save the odd FA official. Buchan's phlegm was inherited from his father, a former colour-sergeant in the Highland Light Infantry. He moved from Aberdeen to

London when he left the army and found a job as a blacksmith at the Royal Arsenal in Woolwich. All of his sons were instilled with the qualities he considered important: courage, perseverance and stoicism. Buchan was born in 1891, a year before Rudyard Kipling published his *Barrack-Room Ballads*. They would have appealed to his dad. 'Tommy' and 'The Road to Mandalay' probably featured regularly in his boys' bedtime stories.

Just up the road from the family home was Plumstead Common, the manoeuvring ground for the Royal Horse Artillery. The hooves of a thousand horses had scuffed away all the grass, which was supplanted by gravel, dirt and horse manure. It was here that Charlie and his brothers learned their football. The conditions underfoot were far from salubrious but the boys learned how to stay upright in the face of the most determined challenge. Three of the brothers became professional footballers. Few ever remembered seeing them take a fall.

Buchan grew up a committed Arsenal fan and he signed for them as an amateur on 26 December 1909. He played only a handful of matches for the reserves before he left after a row over expenses. It was a bold gesture on the part of Buchan, a risky one, too, for an ambitious teenage footballer. Most would have held their tongue and their grievances in check. But Buchan had a keen sense of probity. Perhaps it was innate, or it might have been another of life's lessons drilled into him by his father. Either way, Buchan believed throughout his football career that there was a correct way to behave. In this case Arsenal had served him an injustice and he walked out on the club. Such virtue soon earned Buchan a reputation as a gentleman player. Those in football authority, however, came to view him as a truculent rebel.

From Arsenal he moved to Northfleet in the Kent Senior League and then to Leyton, a professional club in the Southern League, in the summer of 1910. He did enough in one season at Leyton to attract the attention of First Division clubs. Two goals in a win against Southampton impressed Bob Kyle, manager of Sunderland. He approached Leyton and in March 1911 Buchan was transferred north for £1,250. His contract would earn him the maximum wage of £4 a week. He also received a £10 signing-on fee, which Kyle suggested he put to good use by buying a new overcoat. 'It can get pretty cold where you're going,' he warned Buchan. Charlie took his advice. He cut a fine figure of a man when he turned up at Sunderland for his first day, decked out in a new tweed suit and a fur-lined overcoat.

The Roker Park fans weren't quite sure what to make of this lanky nineteen-year-old inside-right. His first home game was against Middlesbrough. He played well in a 3–1 win. 'If you keep playing like that you'll be king of Sunderland,' team-mate Jimmy Gemmell told him as they walked off the field.

Buchan had played too well, however. Opposition teams got wind of this wonderkid and decided to rough him up. It wasn't too hard. Standing just under 6ft, he was unusually tall for his age, but he weighed less than ten stone. The shoulder barge had yet to be outlawed and Buchan spent less time in play than the ball.

In the next fourteen games, he scored just once. The fans began giving him what he remembered later as 'the bird'. But Buchan never let his head drop, even though he was just nineteen, and hundreds of miles from his family and friends. A lesser man might have packed his bags and caught the train back to London. But Buchan couldn't do that. It would be an admission of defeat. What would his father say? He persevered and his luck began to change. He also began to fill out. He soon put on more weight and sprouted a couple of inches. It wasn't long before he looked ridiculous in the tweed suit and fur coat.

Sunderland started the 1912–13 season in atrocious form, winless after the first seven league matches. No one gave them much of a chance against FA Cup holders Bradford in November, but they thrashed them 5–1. A month later Liverpool suffered a humiliating 7–0 defeat. Buchan banged in five. 'Four of them,' he said, 'I just touched into the net.' The Sunderland fans saw things differently. Buchan was the new idol of Roker Park.

Their form carried over into the new year and in April they reached their first FA Cup Final and what seemed like the entire population of the city flocked down to Crystal Palace. Sunderland's opponents, Aston Villa, were one of the best supported teams in the land and the two sets of fans produced a record crowd for a Cup Final of 121,919.

It wasn't a memorable one, however, with Villa's Tom Barber scoring the only goal. The game was dominated by two defences that seemed more intent on kicking lumps out of forwards than trying to play football. Two of the players, Sunderland's Scottish centre-half, Charlie Thompson, and Villa and England centre-forward, Harry Hampton, waged their own private war. The FA later banned the pair for the first month of the new season. The *Times* correspondent, however, while calling the match a dull affair, didn't see much wrong in the physical confrontation. In fact, he took the opposite view to the FA and denounced the modern player as soft: 'These expensive professionals seem to be very fragile creatures; the smallest hack, which no public school boy would think of noticing, is enough to send them to earth in a well-acted but supremely ridiculous agony of pain ... the FA ought to appoint an official matron to mother these tender creatures, to kiss the place to make it well.'

Four days later the two teams met again in the League. This time it finished one apiece. The point meant Sunderland needed two more from their remaining three games for their fifth championship title. The following Saturday they got them in a 3–1 win over Bolton. On the last day of the season they defeated Bradford to set a new league record of 54 points from 38 matches.

In the same season Buchan had won international recognition, but it wasn't an auspicious occasion. He was picked for the match against Ireland at the Queen's Club. It was the start of a relationship with the FA selectors that was as warm as the North Sea wind that blew across Roker Park. Before Buchan had even put on the England shirt he became embroiled in an argument over expenses. He put in an advance claim for £12 19s 10d. The FA was outraged. Buchan politely pointed out that he lived in the far north of the country. The FA queried a taxi fare, asking why he couldn't take a tram. The trams, explained Buchan, didn't run on a Sunday before midday. That was no good to him when he would arrive back in Sunderland at 9am. Grudgingly, the FA paid up.

Buchan enjoyed a satisfactory individual debut, even though the match was a disaster for England. He scored the opening goal but Ireland fought back to win 2–1. The *Times* correspondent once again ran his mordant eye over proceedings: 'Except for some very clever work between the Sunderland right wing pair of Mordue and Buchan, there was a singular lack of combination among the forwards.'

Buchan sat 'despondent' in the dressing room. Next to him, with his head in his hands, was George Elliott, the Middlesbrough forward. On the other side of Elliott was one of the linesman. Buchan was mulling over his performance when the linesman began talking to Elliott:

'He passed some remarks about the right wing – Mordue and myself – that I could not help overhearing and did not like. So with the hot-headedness of youth, I told him just what I thought about him. He turned out to be a member of the FA Selection Committee.'

He didn't win another England cap for seven years.

The 1913–14 season was one of mediocrity for Sunderland. They finished seventh in the league and were knocked out of the Cup by Burnley in the fourth round. The following season, however, was even worse. 'Scarcely had the next season started,' Buchan recalled, 'then the First World War broke out. It was my unhappiest season. I wanted to join up but, when the League decided that the competition should run until the following April, I was reminded that I had a contract to carry out.'

The fires of Buchan's angst were stoked by a bitter debate that raged in the national press about football's response to the war. Many prominent people – most of whom were unable to distinguish a goal line from a firing line – rushed to condemn professional footballers for what they perceived to be reluctance to join up. In November 1914, Lord Durham referred to the Sunderland team in a recruiting appeal that was paraphrased by the *Athletic News*: 'He did know there were eleven men wearing Sunderland colours who, he thought, ought to have preferred wearing khaki. He did not know whether it was ignorance or – he was almost ashamed to say the word – cowardice on their part. If it was the latter, could Sunderland people go to look at a football match?'

Buchan enlisted as soon as the league finished in April 1915. The British Army didn't have many strapping six-footers in its ranks; it had even fewer international footballers. He was a good catch. The recruitment officer knew just where to send him – the Guards.

Buchan strolled into Caterham Barracks the following Thursday evening. He knocked on the guardroom door and strolled in, pipe in hand, coat slung over shoulder. He later remembered: 'The sergeant looked me up and down and greeted me with, "We don't tame lions here, we eat them."'

Charlie Buchan found himself at the bottom of the rung once more. His England cap meant nothing to the drill sergeants of the Guards. Their job was to winnow the wheat from the chaff. John Bouch, who suffered the same ordeal as Buchan in 1914, remembered it well: 'We were subjected to a volume of abuse and scorn which is difficult to imagine. I found out swear words I'd never heard before.' When the aspiring Guardsmen weren't being sworn at, they were being drilled. 'You're in the Guards, remember!' they would scream at the trembling recruits. 'This is *not* a regiment of the line. You are supposed to be the people to guard the Sovereign, God help him!'

To Buchan, Bouch and thousands of other disconsolate souls who suffered on the Caterham parade ground, there must have been times when they sat on their beds, with blistered feet, aching knees and ringing heads, wondering what was the point of so much drill. The point, said the Guards, was to instil discipline. Lord Gort commanded the 4th Battalion, Grenadier Guards in 1917: 'The great thing is drill. No doubt you want something to help you over your fears and if you get control of the nerves, as you do in drill, it helps largely, and it helps to drive the man forward in war ... the feeling of unionism – of moving together – is a great help, and this is brought out by the soldiers' training – drill.'

Buchan spent a year at the Guards depot. He had clearly inherited from his father the qualities that made a good soldier and at the start of 1916 he was promoted to acting lance-corporal. In May that year his draft was notified they would be sailing shortly to France. There was a routine medical inspection to ensure all the Guardsmen were in tip-top condition. Buchan failed because of his teeth. He listened incredulously as the doctor told him he would have to remain in England to have them repaired. Buchan was unable to tolerate the idea that his mates would go to France without him, and all on account of a couple of bad teeth. Somehow he persuaded the doctor to turn a blind eye. 'We were so keen at the time,' Buchan wrote wistfully many years later. 'A short spell in the trenches quickly changed my opinion.'

Buchan arrived in France two weeks after the Battle of the Somme had begun. As he stood on the Calais dockside he was confronted by the reality of war. The broken bodies of hundreds of troops lay on stretchers as far as the eye could see. The walking wounded pushed their way past the Guardsmen, their eyes bearing witness to everything they had experienced at the front.

Buchan joined the 3rd Battalion, Grenadier Guards at their camp in Mericourt, a small village a few miles behind the front line. Now a lance-sergeant, he had a comparatively easy time of it for the first few weeks. The Guards continued to be held in reserve, and so Buchan was given the responsibility of managing the Grenadiers' XI. During one match their activities were reported to a German artillery battery and half a dozen shells came their way. Unperturbed, and adamant the game must continue, Buchan and the other players simply 'packed up and restarted on another pitch'.

By the end of August Field-Marshal Haig was ready for another push on the Somme. Since the cataclysmic events of 1 July, when 60,000 British soldiers had been killed or wounded in one day, there had been a series of small assaults along the front, but nothing as big as the offensive planned for 15 September. Haig had also decided this would the ideal time to blood the Guards.

The Battle of Flers-Courcelette was an attack over a ten-mile front. For the first time on the Somme, the Canadians were going to be used. There was also a leading role for the New Zealanders. The Guards, however, were allotted the hardest task of the battle, to capture the village of Lesboeufs.

The British had also decided to alter their battle tactics. There would be no preliminary bombardment. The Germans, safely ensconced in cavernous dug-outs, had been subjected to a week-long barrage before the attack on 1 July but all that had done was to warn them that an attack was on its way. Instead, this time the artillery would lay down a creeping barrage under which the infantry would advance fifty yards behind.

The Guards spent the weeks preceding the attack practising the advance. The beat of drums represented the artillery. Everything went swimmingly. On 10 September the Grenadiers moved up into the front line, replacing the 47th Brigade whose trenches were not of a standard suitable for Guardsmen. They spent the next twenty-four hours carrying out repair work. On 13 September the commander of the 4th Army issued a communiqué from within the walls of his chateau at Querrieu, calling for 'bold and vigorous action' during the attack.

On the following evening, an officer in the Scots Guards, Captain Sir Iain Colquhoun, wrote in his diary that it had been 'rather a horrible day as everyone is a little on edge'. That evening, Buchan and the Grenadiers moved into position, ready for zero hour at 0620 hours. The battalion war diary noted that they were at the jumping-off positions by 0300 hours. The next few hours must have played on the nerves of every man, particularly those whose experience of battle was restricted to the training camp. A few men managed to get their heads down and sleep for a couple of hours. Others sat around in silent groups or by themselves, lost in thought. As dawn broke and the rum ration was issued, some soldiers scribbled short letters home. Perhaps Buchan wrote a line to his wife, or to Alderman Taylor, the Sunderland coal exporter who had supplied Buchan with a reference when he enlisted.

The Grenadiers knew their order of battle. They were to attack in waves, four platoons forward and four in support, each on a forty-yard front. They were to be supported in their assault by ten tanks (the first time they had been used on the Western Front).

The war diarist recorded the first moments of the battle: 'At 6.19am the whole Brigade rose to its feet and advanced. Our left front company was met by machine-gun fire as soon as they got up.'

The right flank of the Grenadiers had fared better in those opening minutes of the attack, but they too were soon hosed with machine-gun fire. The discipline of the Guards, however, drilled into them at Caterham, held firm and the advance continued unabated. The fire came from several machine-gun positions located in an irregular line of shell-holes in front of the German front line. These were brave Germans. But when the Guards overran their positions the war diarist noted that the Grenadiers were in no mood to take prisoners: 'Every German in this trench was either shot or bayoneted.' But the German fire had broken up the wave formation so assiduously practised by the Guards in training. The battlefield was now a chaotic jumble of dead and living. Scots Guards, Irish Guards and Grenadier Guards forgot their traditional rivalry and shouted encouragement to one another above the din of battle.

There were hardly any officers left standing. Asquith savoured his final cigarette, while a couple of hours later, a man who would follow in the footsteps of Asquith's father and become Prime Minister was lying badly wounded in a shell-hole. Captain Harold Macmillan of the 2nd Battalion, Grenadier Guards, was only saved thanks to the courage of a Grenadier sergeant. He relived the memory over sixty years later:

> 'I can see him now ... bottom of shell-hole, sloped rifle: "Thank you, sir,
> for leave to carry you away," as if he'd been on parade ground!'

One of the few Guards officers still on his feet was Colquhoun. 'Within 30 yards I found myself in front of the Grenadiers with a few of my men. Our barrage was about 50 yards in front of us, and the whole landscape was obscured by smoke, and it was impossible to see anything or keep direction.'

Colquhoun, together with two Irish Guards officers and one from the Grenadiers, Captain Oliver Lyttelton, who later called the battle 'the most wonderful day of my life', led a mixed bag of about 120 guardsmen – mostly Grenadiers from the 3rd battalion – 800 yards into the German trench. They had reached the first objective. It was an empty trench running along the bottom of a small gully. In front of the trench were standing crops. Behind the foliage lay the village of Lesboeufs. Their target was within sight, but to push on with so few men would have been madness.

Colquhoun placed Lewis gunners on the flanks of their position and then 'went down along the trench to try and get reinforcements and take Lesboeufs'. It was now just after midday.

Colquhoun returned on his own. The only men he came across were dead. All they could do was sit and wait for reinforcements to be sent up from reserve. The Germans, however, had begun to sense the enemy had played themselves out. By mid-afternoon, the braver among them were edging cautiously forward, trying to determine the strength of the British. All the time the Guards glanced anxiously to the rear, hoping to see fresh troops coming to their rescue.

Buchan made a passing reference to the battle in his autobiography, although it was merely to confirm he had fought in it and survived intact. But one can speculate with confidence that he was one of the men in the trench. Colquhoun had gathered together just about every Grenadier from the 3rd battalion still standing and Buchan's lucky face had brought him through the initial charge unscathed. But would his luck hold?

At 5pm a battalion of Germans was seen advancing towards the battlefield. An hour later and the Guardsmen were fighting for their lives. Colquhoun marshalled his dwindling number of men magnificently, but gradually the Germans worked their way nearer using the crops as cover. Suddenly 250 of them sprung from the crops and charged the trench at a distance of forty yards. The British met them with fixed bayonets and the Germans were momentarily stunned by their discipline and defiance. Before the Germans came again Colquhoun gave the order to retire. The Guards disengaged themselves from the enemy and withdrew in orderly fashion. The casualty list for the attack made for grim reading. The 3rd Battalion Grenadier Guards had lost 380 men, and eighteen of their twenty-one officers had been killed or wounded. Buchan would need to introduce some new faces into the battalion football XI.

For the rest of 1916 the Grenadiers remained on the Somme, licking their wounds and settling into a routine of three to five days in the line, three to five days in billets and a longer time in musketry camp. They suffered sporadic shelling from the Germans but there were lighter-hearted moments too; a rat-catching competition was won by the 2nd Battalion, who snared 386 rodents and earned the approbation of all and sundry.

At the start of 1917 the battalion moved north-east to Ypres. Their fighting strength was twenty-six officers and 834 men. Fighting, however, there was little of for the first six months of the year. Much of April and May was spent on improving the conditions of the rail and road networks around Le Mesnil. Such a mundane task might have been appreciated by other regiments, but the Guards spent most of the time grumbling at the end of their spades. This wasn't why they were in France.

By July they were back in the trenches near Poperinghe, taking casualties from shellfire on a daily basis. It was a useful way of allowing the new Guardsmen, drafted in to replace those who had died at Lesboeufs, to become inured to the sounds and sights of the front line. Although the new additions to the Grenadiers lacked experience, they had undergone the same rigorous training as every man in the regiment. It was another unique feature of the Guards. Unlike other regiments, the Guards didn't fill their depleted ranks with half-trained men rushed out from Caterham. The drill sergeant would rather break bread with the Kaiser than let a Guardsman he didn't think was ready pass off the parade ground.

This would have been music to the ears of Field-Marshal Haig, for he had another task for the Guards Division. Enjoying the warmth of his Headquarters chateau near St Omer, the commander of the British forces had it in his mind that the German army was on the brink of collapse. Hadn't they been routed at Messines a few weeks earlier? Wouldn't one final push in Flanders achieve the breakthrough that would win the war? Haig was convinced this was the case. A massive new offensive, involving twelve divisions attacking an 18km front east of the Belgian town of Ypres was planned for 31 July.

Charlie Buchan, busy ducking the shells and trying to find a dry place to sleep, might not have shared the opinions of Haig. The Guards, on the extreme left of the front, began their advance at 0424 hours and the war diary recorded events as they happened. At 0540 the first reports of casualties began to arrive; at 0600 the battalion captured one of their objectives, 'The Black Line'. At 0714 they advanced towards the next objective, 'The Green Line' and met 'considerable opposition from concrete blockhouses along the railway'. Nonetheless by 0755 the Green Line was in the hands of the Grenadiers and the Vulcan Crossing, the most troublesome blockhouse, had been captured intact with three officers and fifty other ranks. It was one of the few British successes of the opening day. The Guards had advanced nearly two miles across a 2,000-yard front. Other divisions to their right weren't having such an easy time of it. The 51st Highland Division had launched their assault half an hour before the Grenadiers and about a mile further south. They walked into a maelstrom of shellfire. A lieutenant in the Royal Scots remembered seeing one of his boys hit with a huge shell fragment: 'It sliced him straight in two. He dropped his rifle and bayonet and threw up his arms in the air, and the top part of his torso fell back on to the ground … the legs and kilt went on running, just like a chicken with its head chopped off.' Amid such scenes of horror, the Grenadiers had got off lightly. Just under 150 officers and men killed or wounded, a third of the casualties they had taken on the Somme.

Buchan's name wasn't on the casualty list. Once again he had survived. He dogged it out for the next few months as the Ypres offensive ground to a halt amid rains of almost biblical proportions. Locals couldn't remember such a wet August. The mud became the arbiter of destiny for British and Germans alike. One soldier likened it to walking through caramel, and distances came to be measured not in yards but in mud.

Buchan was now an old hand. He had fought in two major battles and hadn't picked up a scratch. New recruits would have stuck close to him, hoping some of his luck might rub off on them. His conduct and leadership qualities had been noticed by the battalion's officers, who discussed nominating him for a commission. Then they were overtaken by more pressing matters.

Haig had continued sacrificing men in Flanders until the village of Passchendaele, reduced to little more than a few bricks, had been captured on 7 November. It brought the Third Battle of Ypres to an end. Haig said the battle had served its purpose. No one was really quite sure what he meant.

Why exactly had over 300,000 Allied soldiers died?

Haig was unperturbed. Pausing only momentarily to allow fresh cannon fodder to be brought to the front, he launched a new offensive forty-five miles south of Ypres, at Cambrai. For the first time in modern warfare tanks were used in large numbers. Haig had wanted to introduce them at Ypres, but the Tank Corps politely pointed out that tanks hadn't been designed to float. On 20 November, 381 tanks advanced five miles and tore a massive hole in the ranks of the Germans, incoherent with terror. The British infantry, mopping up, took 10,000 prisoners and suffered only 1,500 casualties, a triumph when compared to the mindless slaughter of the Somme and Passchendaele. Then things went wrong. The infantry couldn't keep pace with the tanks. The Germans, initially stupefied by these iron monsters, regathered their senses and counter-attacked. A week after the initial attack the British were bogged down, again.

Up went the cry, 'Send in the Guards', much to the displeasure of their commander, Major-General Fielding. The GHQ wanted the Guards Division to attack across a front that included the 100-acre Bourlon Wood and the village of Fontaine. Fielding attended a meeting to discuss the proposed attack. He pointed out that his men were being asked to 'advance across a stretch of country in full view of the enemy's gunners ... to capture an undemolished village which would be stoutly defended'. He looked around at the faces of the British top brass. None held his gaze. He left the meeting barely able to contain his fury.

It was the Grenadiers who were asked to attack the village of Fontaine. Fielding returned to the Guards Division and outlined the objectives with as much sang-froid as he could muster. The company commanders only learned of their objectives at midnight on 26 November. They quickly briefed their junior officers and word soon spread. The Guardsmen took it as one would expect. No fuss, no cursing, just a quiet determination. In the early hours of the following day, as the snow started to fall, the 3rd Grenadiers began moving up into position. Somewhere among them was Buchan, hoping that his luck would last and wishing he was back at Roker Park.

The Germans had anticipated the attack and at 0600 hours their artillery struck up the overture to battle. Shells rained down on the assembly point. Even before the Grenadiers had begun the assault, dozens were ripped apart by lethal splinters of shells. A shiver of apprehension passed through the men

TOP LEFT: The victorious Wanderers XV that won the Leinster Cup in 1894. Robert Johnston stands seventh from the left at the back, while Tom Crean is perched on the far right of the middle row.

TERRY LONG/WANDERERS FOOTBALL CLUB

ABOVE: The Boer Commandos in 1900 had little respect for the British Generals, but they called the regimental officers, men like Johnston and Crean, 'the bravest in the world'.

HULTON ARCHIVE

TOP RIGHT: Tom Crean won the VC in the Boer War and the DSO in World War One. He died in 1923, aged 49, a man broken by his experiences on the battlefield.

COURTESY OF PATRICIA MOORHEAD

ABOVE: Donald Bell towers above his family in a 1913 photograph. Dorothy, sitting at her father's feet, lived until the 1980s and retained strong and proud memories of her brother.

GREEN HOWARDS REGIMENTAL MUSEUM

RIGHT: Second Lieutenant Donald Bell of the Green Howards, the only professional footballer to have been awarded the Victoria Cross.

GREEN HOWARDS REGIMENTAL MUSEUM

TOP: Australian troops atop the Messines-Wytschaete ridge on June 7 1917, just a few hours after the Germans had been blasted off the ridge – an attack in which Gerald Patterson was awarded an MC.

ABOVE: Australians Gerald Patterson (left) and James Anderson with mascots at the start of their 1922 Wimbledon semi-final. Patterson went on to win the title.

ABOVE LEFT: The charismatic
Carpentier was a world champion,
war hero and film star, who chased
women with Charlie Chaplin and
partied with Douglas Fairbanks.
POPPERFOTO

ABOVE RIGHT: Georges Carpentier
in 1915, in the military uniform he
had had made to measure, unable as
he was to face going to war looking
'like a scarecrow'.
HULTON ARCHIVE

RIGHT: Not even Carpentier's
extraordinary courage was able to
resist the superior punching power
of Jack Dempsey when the two met
in their 1921 world heavyweight
title fight.
HULTON ARCHIVE

LEFT: 'We don't tame lions here,' a sergeant told England striker Charlie Buchan when he strolled insouciantly into the Guards' depot in 1915, 'we eat them.'

NORMAN BARRETT

ABOVE: Stretcher bearers move up towards the front line on the eve of the Battle of Flers-Courcelette in September 1916. Buchan, 3rd Battalion Grenadier Guards, was in the thick of the fighting, but he made it back to his own lines without the assistance of the medical corps.

IWM PHOTOGRAPH

ABOVE RIGHT: Buchan of Arsenal shakes hands with Southampton captain Harkus before their 1927 FA Cup semi-final. The Gunners made it through to their first Cup final but lost 1-0 to Cardiff thanks to a bizarre own goal.

HULTON ARCHIVE

ABOVE: Mobbs recuperating from wounds in June 1917, just a few weeks before he was mortally wounded. His body was never recovered; he is one of 42,000 British soldiers who fought in the Third Battle of Ypres and who has no known grave.

COURTESY OF JENNY EDWARDS

TOP: Edgar Mobbs (middle row, second from the right), wins his second cap for England against Wales in Cardiff in 1909.

RUGBY FOOTBALL UNION ARCHIVE

ABOVE RIGHT: Of the 264 men who enlisted in Mobbs' Sportsmen's Battalion in 1914, only 85 returned home. They marched for the last time in 1921 when they placed a wreath at the foot of Edgar Mobbs' statue in Northampton.

COURTESY OF JENNY EDWARDS

BELOW: This photo, taken the day after the Zeebrugge raid, shows the *Intrepid* and *Iphigenia* lying in the mouth of the Belgian port. The photo was a morale boost for the British public, though the Germans suffered little inconvenience as a result of the daring raid.

IWM PHOTOGRAPH

TOP LEFT: Lt-Commander Arthur Harrison is the only British rugby international to have been awarded the Victoria Cross.

RUGBY FOOTBALL UNION ARCHIVE

ABOVE LEFT: A group of officers aboard the *Vindictive* a few hours before she sailed. (From left to right): Hawkings, Harrison, Osbourne, Adams, Walker and Dickenson. A few hours later Harrison and Hawkings would be dead.

COURTESY OF ROSEMARY FITCH

ABOVE RIGHT: This detailed map shows clearly where Harrison and the raiding parties landed on the Mole, while the final resting places of the blockships in the canal mouth are also marked.

HULTON ARCHIVE

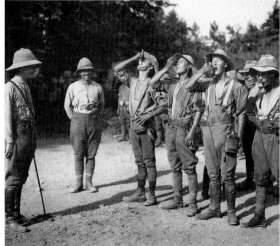

TOP LEFT: 'What a pity we can't stay young,' Aubrey Faulkner told Jack Hobbs in 1930. The following week he committed suicide, a victim of depression brought on by his war service and increasing ill-health.

TOP RIGHT: British troops gulp down their daily 5 grams of quinine in Salonika in a vain attempt to combat malaria. Half a million British soldiers reported sick during service in Salonika, the majority the victims of malaria.

ABOVE: A casualty clearing station during the Battle of Arras in April 1917. Herby Taylor had the good misfortune to miss the battle, but Arnold Jackson was wounded during the fighting.

at 0620 hours as they heard the familiar command: 'Fix Bayonets. Deploy. Extended Order. Advance.'

Just over an hour later the commanding officer received reports that the two left companies had managed to fight their way into the village. His boys hadn't let him down. He waited anxiously for news of the two right companies. It was they that Fielding had in mind when he expressed his fears. At 0840 the first reports filtered through: 'The two right companies of 3GG on the south side of the main Cambrai road have been practically obliterated by machine-guns from La Folie which our artillery failed to silence.'

The Guardsmen, their khaki uniforms silhouetted against the snow, presented an inviting target to the machine-gunners in La Folie wood, 1,500 yards to the right of the Grenadiers. The layer of snow that covered the ground was soon a dark red.

Meanwhile, those guardsmen already in Fontaine, of whom Buchan was probably one, now found themselves fighting for their lives in a series of frenzied clashes amid the ruins of the village. A sergeant led six men as far as the church in the middle of the village before they were driven back, while on the outskirts a maniacal battle was fought over a chalk pit. The Grenadiers lost all but one of its officers in the struggle but, as the war diarist noted with pride, the Guards 'killed forty of the enemy with the bayonet'.

Back at regimental headquarters Fielding shook his head in wonderment at the magnificence of the Grenadiers' feat. They had established a foothold in the village and taken over 600 prisoners. But the Germans had developed a curious attachment to the little that remained of Fontaine. Hundreds of reinforcements were brought up and the war diary recorded that 'little by little we were forced to withdraw before the enemy who were in great strength'.

The Grenadiers, along with the Coldstreams on their left, fell back scrambling over the grim detritus of battle. They were so few in number that they had to release their prisoners. The Guards Division had lost fourteen officers, while another twenty-four were wounded. Nearly 600 other ranks were killed or missing and a further 471 wounded. The roll call that afternoon was a quiet affair. But Buchan was present to answer his name.

Fifteen months later he was back at Roker Park. He still couldn't believe it; this was what he had dreamed of for three long years. A lot had happened to

Buchan since he'd survived Fontaine. That had been his last major action of the war. He had been nominated for a commission in December 1917 and at the start of 1918 he'd returned to England to attend the Officer Cadet Battalion in Catterick. Buchan had a certain cachet at his new residence, one that came with having won the Military Medal.

The medal was gazetted on 12 December, although like the majority of such decorations there was no citation. With a modesty typical of his generation, Buchan in his autobiography neglected to mention how he came to win the medal. Similarly, the battalion war diary, as was standard procedure among the Grenadier Guards, didn't comment on the award. Coming as it did, two weeks after the fighting at Fontaine, it would be reasonable to suppose Buchan earned it for an act of conspicuous gallantry during the battle.

If Buchan had any trouble adapting to civilian life, it didn't show. By early 1919 he was combining his football with a teaching job at the Cowan Terrace school. Indeed, the only change in Buchan in the opinion of his wife and friends concerned his waistline. He now weighed fifteen stone. He had clearly found the life of an officer an agreeable one.

League football resumed on 30 August 1919, and Sunderland beat Aston Villa 2–1. Buchan scored one of the goals and was the best player on the park. War? What war? It was as if Buchan had never been away.

For six consecutive seasons either side of the war Buchan was Sunderland's leading scorer. In 1922–3 he finished with thirty, the top striker in the first division. His reputation was such that defenders adopted bizarre methods in an attempt to curtail his scoring power. Against Newcastle United, Buchan stepped off the pitch to tie his shoelace. All the while Peter Mooney, the opposition half-back, stood over him. 'Sorry, Charlie, but I've been told not to leave you for a second.'

The England selectors couldn't ignore Buchan any longer. His war record had gone some way towards expiating his earlier conduct, so he was given another chance. He shone out in a dire England performance against Wales at Highbury. The pitch, reported the *Daily Mirror*, was a quagmire. This didn't worry Buchan. At least there wasn't a German machine-gun at the other end of the field.

Buchan opened the scoring for his country, as he had done in 1913 against Ireland. But the rest of the match unfolded as it had done seven years earlier.

Two goals from the visitors sunk the English. 'The Welsh forwards won the game for their side,' wrote the *Mirror*, 'and as a line were incomparably better than the Englishmen, although there was perhaps no one so good individually as Charles Buchan ... The England forwards could never get going as a line, and it must have been heartbreaking to Buchan to see all his best efforts go asking because of the ineptitude of the other forwards.'

The next season Buchan was again considered for international selection. He was invited to play for the North against an England XI at Turf Moor. The trial match was on the Monday so Buchan booked himself into a Burnley hotel on the Sunday. The hotel manager, honoured to have a man of Buchan's repute as a guest, loaned him the use of his own armchair. Buchan was snugly encased in it on Sunday afternoon when a member of the FA walked into the lounge.'You will have to get out of that chair, Buchan, when Mr Lewis [one of the FA heavyweights] arrives.' Buchan seethed silently. A few minutes later Mr Lewis strolled into the lounge, accompanied by his flunky. 'Buchan, here's Mr Lewis.' Buchan looked up from his book, gazed upon the corpulent figure of Mr Lewis, and turned the page.

Buchan's desultory England career finally petered out in 1924. He won a further cap in 1921, a couple in 1923 and made the last of his six appearances against Scotland in the first international to be staged at Wembley. He was given the captaincy against France in 1923 but it was somehow inevitable that Buchan would clash with the FA along the way. Sure enough Buchan was hauled in front of the FA after he had been seen shaking the hand of one of England's goalscorers in the 4–1 win. He received a 'severe reprimand' from his *bête noire* because 'it seemed hand-shaking was one of those things that wasn't done'.

Buchan began to wind down his football career in 1925. He had bought a sports' outfitters in Sunderland in partnership with a friend in 1920, and five years later took over sole ownership of the shop. He was serving behind the counter one day in May when Herbert Chapman walked in. The manner in which he strolled up to the desk made it plain he wasn't after a new kit for the Arsenal team that he had just started to manage. 'I've come to sign you,' Chapman peremptorily declared. Buchan at first thought he was joking. An England discard, he was nearly thirty-four and past his best. The astute Chapman, however, was adamant that Buchan was his man.

Buchan accepted Chapman's offer. That left only the transfer fee to decide.

Sunderland wanted £4,000. Sir Henry Norris, Arsenal's director, laughed. There was no way he was prepared to stump up that sort of cash for someone who would be thirty-four in a few weeks. They settled on an arrangement whereby Arsenal paid Sunderland £2,000 and an additional £100 for every goal Buchan scored in his first season. A smiling Norris handed Kyle a cheque for £2,000. Twelve months later he was writing out one for £2,100. It hadn't been the best bit of business he'd ever done.

Buchan's twenty-one goals were just a small part of his contribution to the club in the three seasons he was at Highbury. In tandem with Herbert Chapman, he devised the 'third back' game to counter the relaxation of the offside rule in 1924–5. This converted the centre-half, previously an attacking half-back, into a stopper, and pulled back an inside-forward into midfield. Arsenal dominated English football throughout the 1930s and their strategy had a lasting effect on the game. Football formations all over the world were revolutionized, and the 'back-four' and '3–5–2' of today are developments of the thinking of Chapman and Buchan in the 1920s. Also with Chapman he instilled within the club an attitude that accounts for much of Arsenal's strength in the 1930s. 'The club comes first,' he would say. 'Teamwork is not allowed to suffer from petty squabbling.'

Arsenal had finished 20th in the first division the season before Buchan arrived. They were runners-up in 1925–6, the club's highest position in its history. The following season he led Arsenal to Wembley for their first FA Cup Final. It ended ignominiously, however, with Cardiff winning 1–0 thanks to what remains the most farcical goal ever to stain a Cup Final. Cardiff's Hughie Ferguson sent a tame shot the way of Dan Lewis, the Arsenal goalkeeper, in the 73rd minute. Lewis gathered the ball on one knee and Buchan called for it downfield. Lewis rose to his feet but his knee hit the ball out of grasp and sent it bouncing towards the goal. 'In trying to retrieve it,' remembered Buchan, 'Lewis only knocked it further towards the goal. The ball trickled slowly but inexorably over the line with hardly enough strength to reach the net.'

At the end of the following season Buchan retired a few months short of his thirty-seventh birthday. Aside from his leadership skills, he had also scored 56 goals in 120 league and cup appearances. Before his last game against Everton, Buchan was presented with a briefcase and writing set of fountain pen and pencil. It was in recognition that where one door had shut, another now opened. Buchan was to become the football correspondent of the *Daily News* (later the *News Chronicle*).

Buchan had contributed articles to the *Daily News* – and to papers in the north-east – since before the war. Now, however, he was a full-time journalist with deadlines to meet and copy to file. The transition wasn't as seamless as he would have liked. For the first game of the 1928–9 season, Buchan turned up an hour early and absent-mindedly tried to get in the players' entrance. He also discovered that his eye for the goal hadn't deserted him: 'The number of goals I scored from my seat was phenomenal. Chances look so easy from a position high up in the stand. They aren't so simple on the actual field.'

Buchan had never given that impression during his career. His career record of 209 league goals for Sunderland has yet to be surpassed. He also scored 15 goals in 33 FA Cup ties.

Buchan enjoyed a long and successful career as a football journalist, travelling all over the world reporting on his beloved England. In 1951 he launched *Charlie Buchan's Football Monthly*, a periodical whose sales mirrored his popularity on the football field. In 1956 he retired from the *News Chronicle* and at last his wife had him all to herself. The pair were on holiday together in the south of France in the summer of 1960 when Buchan died from a heart attack. He was sixty-eight.

The papers the following day all carried news of his passing. The *News Chronicle* described him as 'that rare combination – the complete footballer and the perfect gentleman'. While another called him 'The Man Who Was Too Good' and said he didn't win more England caps because his abundant skill mystified his team-mates.

Few of the eulogies mentioned his war record with the Guards. It was an unfortunate oversight. Nothing Buchan achieved in his footballing life gave him as much satisfaction as the three years spent as a guardsman. 'It was tough,' he remembered shortly before he died, 'mighty tough, but I know now it did me all the good in the world. I was proud to belong to the Grenadier Guards.'

CHAPTER SEVEN

Edgar Mobbs

E*dgar Mobbs was a natural leader although his streak of unconventionality didn't always go down well with those in authority. A brilliant winger for Northampton rugby club, Mobbs didn't receive the recognition he deserved at international level because of disputes with the RFU. Yet among his peers he was admired and respected and when war broke out in 1914 he raised his own sportsmen's battalion and then led them into battle.*

'How are all at home?', Edgar Mobbs wrote to his sister on 25 July 1917. Outside his dingy and claustrophobic dug-out, the war on the Ypres Salient continued on its barbarous way. 'I have lost my MO [medical officer], the enclosed is a letter from him it may interest you to read. We are off again tomorrow morning at 5am, so must away. Look out in the papers in a few days' time and think of me and *pray* for me.' It was Mobbs' last letter home before the beginning of the Third Battle of Ypres at 0350 hours on 31 July.

Lt-Col Mobbs, commanding officer of the 7th Battalion, Northamptonshire Regiment, addressed his men and issued their orders on 30 July. They were to capture an area of high ground at the south of the salient named Tower Hamlets.

Mobbs remained at Battalion Headquarters as the Northamptonshires went into battle. Gradually reports filtered back to him about the progress of his men. The faces of the runners staggering into HQ told their own story – it was bloody murder out there. The Germans had moved a machine-gun into no man's land and the 7th Battalion had walked into a murderous fire. A short while later another runner appeared; what was left of the battalion was trapped in the mud of no man's land, soaked from the torrential rain, and cowering from the menace of the machine-gun.

All the officers were dead or wounded and the attack was on the point of disintegrating. Mobbs was in an unenviable position. As commanding officer should he remain at HQ, or should he join his men and lead the attack himself against the troublesome machine-gun? Convention suggested he should remain where he was. But Mobbs had a reputation for doing the unconventional.

Edgar Mobbs was born in 1882 and attended Bedford Modern school. He was a reasonable rugby player but hockey was his preferred sport. When he left school in 1900 he didn't play rugby again for another four years, until he joined his local village side, Olney, as a scrum-half. In 1905 he was spotted by Northampton and they invited him to play at Franklin's Gardens. His career at his new club didn't start auspiciously – he was dropped after a couple of matches and wasn't selected for the game against the touring All Blacks, led by Dave Gallaher. Perhaps he thought about a return to Olney. Instead, he accepted an offer of a match for the first XV, but on the wing.

It took Mobbs just one match to discover he had found his true position. He became a permanent fixture in the Northampton XV, a terror for opposition wings with his powerful hand-off and muscular 6ft, fourteen-stone, physique. Laurence Woodhouse, writing in the periodical *Rugby Football*, described Mobbs' unorthodox style: 'Every limb seemed to be employed, as it seemed, independently when he ran. He was distinctly a high-stepper, his knees being very much raised when he was going. This laborious action of his rather deceived one as to the pace he was actually travelling.'

At the start of the 1906–7 season he was appointed vice-captain and in the same year he captained East Midlands for the first time. Leadership came naturally to Mobbs and Northampton made him captain of the club in June 1907. Once entrusted with the captaincy, Mobbs quickly gained a reputation for outspokenness, a repute that grew as his standing in the game increased. Shortly after Mobbs became Northampton's captain, he gave an interview to the local paper, the *Independent*, in which he aired views that have been passed down through successive generations of players, whatever their club:

> 'In the match against Exeter I did not play, but sat on the members' stand, and if some of the people on that stand knew what fools they made of themselves by their shouting and talking that day, they would never express an opinion on football again.'

Mobbs was acting the polemicist again at the end of 1907 when Northampton, along with Leicester and Coventry, found themselves in front of an RFU inquiry answering charges of professionalism. The clubs had to produce their books and, although they were in perfect order, Northampton were reprimanded because, in the words of the *Northampton Mercury*, they had 'provided their players with tea and cigarettes in the dressing room at Franklin's Gardens after the matches … Mr Goulding [the club's honorary secretary] was given to understand that cigarettes must not be given, although tea may be provided.' Mobbs was furious with the RFU for the heavy-handed way they had handled the affair. He demanded a statement exonerating Northampton from all charges.

Perhaps Mobbs' disquiet with the RFU delayed his England debut. The newspapers had called for his inclusion in the team in 1908 but to no avail. He had to wait until the visit of Australia to Blackheath in early 1909 for his first cap.

He made a dream start, scoring a try after just two minutes. The *Evening Standard*'s E H D Sewell wrote that 'the movement started at half-way, and it was close to that line that Tarr first gave the ball to Mobbs, who ran outwards, and drawing the nearest opponent, returned the ball to Tarr. The way in which Mobbs kept his position to receive the ball again from Tarr, in spite of most obvious attempts at obstruction, was striking proof that in him England had found a real player of the game.'

For the remaining 78 minutes the tourists took control, winning 9–3. Mobbs was dropped the following week when the team to play Wales in Cardiff in the opening Championship match was announced. No explanation was given to Mobbs as to why he'd been dropped. He had scored a good try and was hailed in all the newspapers as one of the few pluses in an otherwise mediocre England display. Perhaps the honest, if tactless interview, he gave to a local paper when he arrived back in Northampton handed the selectors their motive. 'The whole idea of our side was wrong,' he said. 'We ought to have gone into it with the intention of attacking instead of which we defended. I suppose most of us will be kicked out of the team for the next match.'

Mobbs' cynicism wasn't misplaced and when the RFU revealed their XV for the Wales match, it contained only eight of the players who had performed against Australia. But fortune favoured Mobbs on this occasion when Tom Simpson, selected in his place, pulled out through injury and the call went out for him to join the side in Cardiff.

Mobbs was on the losing side once more but this time he made a favourable impression on the selectors, being picked out as 'our best threequarter' by Rowland Hill, secretary of the RFU. By the end of the season Mobbs was the only member of the England backline who had played in all five internationals, either on the left or right wing. He scored his second try in the 22–0 win against France at Welford Road – always a thrill for a Northampton man to score at Leicester – and crossed the line for scores in the win over Ireland and the 18–8 defeat to Scotland. The Calcutta Cup match against the Scots was played at the Richmond Athletic Ground in Surrey, although the RFU had hoped at the start of the season to stage the match in their impressive new stadium in Twickenham. Building delays, however, scuppered that idea and it wasn't until Wales came to London in 1910 that Twickenham was proudly displayed as the new home of English rugby.

The 1909–10 season proved even more unpredictable for Mobbs than the previous one. Although Northampton reeled off eight successive wins early on, Mobbs found himself more closely marked than ever before. After the match against Bedford one reporter wrote that 'Mobbs was receiving as much attention from Bedfordians as the Prime Minister is receiving from the Suffragettes'.

Mobbs continued his good form, however, and was selected to play for England in the 1910 International Championship against Ireland, a match that finished 0–0. On 3 March he replaced Adrian Stoop as captain of England when they played and beat France in Paris. It was his seventh cap but Mobbs knew it would be his last. The captaincy, it seemed, had been the selectors' way of giving the condemned man a final meal before they wielded the axe. Just a few days before he was dropped from the side to play Scotland in the final match of the 1910 season, Mobbs told his old friend Tommy Mitton: 'My international career is finished. They made me captain against France, and you'll find the England selectors will not choose me again.'

Mobbs was only twenty-eight when he was dropped from England. His comments to Mitton suggest he knew why he was being discarded. He'd scored four tries in his seven appearances and contemporary accounts of his England exploits show he wasn't out of his depth at international level. In all probability Mobbs was shown the door in such an abrupt manner because his face didn't fit at Twickenham, a ground the RFU had taken possession of at the start of the 1910 season. Mobbs wasn't an establishment fellow, nor was he the sort of obsequious yes-man the RFU wanted around them. He was far too outspoken for the self-important committee men in charge of English rugby, and they were keen to get rid of Mobbs, but not before they had given him a 'golden handshake' to counter any accusations that the fans' favourite had been dealt a shoddy hand. Stoop returned for the Scotland game and Mobbs was no more.

Mobbs' last season at Northampton was 1912–13, his sixth as captain, and one that again saw him at odds with the RFU. South Africa, led by Billy Millar, had arrived in Britain in the autumn of 1912 and soon discovered that RFU-style English hospitality wasn't all it was cracked up to be. After the post-match dinner following South Africa's win against Northampton, Mobbs apologized for the manner in which they had been treated for much of the tour. His speech was reported in *The Truth* magazine:

'Betwixt mob oratory and Mobbs oratory there is no great gulf fixed. He roundly attacked the Rugby Union for the miserable, miserly manner in which it was treating the visitors. Tea or coffee after dinner forbidden; the team brought up from Portsmouth by the midnight train and landed in London at 3am ... they were treated like naughty schoolboys, everything being made as unpleasant as possible by reason of petty meanness simply because some infatuated noodles on the Rugby Union were afraid that the amateur status of the visitors might be imperilled. Wherefore it was mighty plucky of Mobbs to give tongue at the dinner.'

There were probably not many RFU faces present at the Northampton Town Hall on 29 May 1913 when the club threw a retirement party for Mobbs. He was lauded as the club's greatest ever player, his 177 tries evidence of the impact he had made in his nine seasons at Franklin's Gardens. Albert Orton, the club's match secretary, said by way of tribute: 'Wherever he led, everyone would follow. Rugby Football tended to bring to the surface all that was good in a man – courage, resolution, sacrifice, unselfishness and forbearance.'

When war was declared just over a year later, Mobbs was thirty-two and perfect officer material, or that was what he thought. The recruiting officer thought otherwise, and rejected his application for a commission. Mobbs stormed out of the recruitment office, muttering under his breath, 'my country will want me yet'. He enlisted as a private on 8 September but continued to harbour dreams of becoming an officer. He mooted the idea of forming a Sportsmen's Battalion among his friends and former team-mates. When it was announced in mid-September that all rugby was indefinitely postponed, he circulated his idea among the local clubs and asked for volunteers. By the end of the month he had 400 recruits to join the Sportsmen's Battalion, of whom 264 were accepted as meeting the requisite standards of physical fitness and age. 'D' Company, 7th Service Battalion, Northamptonshire Regiment, or the 'Mobbs' Battalion marched off to Shoreham to undergo several weeks of military training, with Mobbs now a Lieutenant.

The regiment remained in England for nearly a year, arriving in northern France in September 1915, just in time for the Battle of Loos. The British launched their attack on 25 September across the coalfields of Loos and broke through the Germans' front line, moving towards the second line at Lens. However, the British needed reinforcements and when they turned to them they discovered they were too far back to give the attack fresh impetus so that as the reserves rushed to the front they tangled with the men withdrawing. In the Official History the situation is described thus: 'It was like trying to push the Lord Mayor's procession through the streets of London, without clearing the route and holding up the traffic.'

During this confusion the Germans counter-attacked and threatened a breakthrough of their own. Tenacious British defence repulsed the attack but when they tried to relaunch the offensive on 13 October the Germans were better prepared and inflicted heavy losses on the British. Bad weather brought the fighting to an end, by which time the two sides were back where they had started three weeks earlier. The only difference was that 50,000 British and 48,000 French lay dead.

The Northants were one of the battalions held in reserve and as Mobbs described in a letter to his sister, Olive, on 26 September they were rushed into the battle the day after the initial attack.

> 'We got to this place at 3am this morning after a march all night of nineteen miles with full packs – Next day, Saturday, am writing this in a railway carriage with guns on all sides of me. We are at it now and under shellfire, it is like hell let loose, the wounded are passing all the time. We have broken the German line and it is the biggest fight of the war, you will read all about it in the papers. We have taken three lines of trenches and we the Northants are pressing on behind as supports to two army corps. We hope to get into the German trenches tonight.'

A few hours after he had written this letter 'D' Company went into action for the first time. Casualties were heavy and for a lot of the men their war lasted only a few hours. Mobbs admitted to his sister in a letter written shortly after they had been relieved that 'I am sick of having to write to all the mothers, etc, about their children, but one has to do it.'

In early October a Northampton paper printed a letter from the Reverend Sydney Groves, who was at Loos and, as a Northampton native, had taken a particular interest in his local regiment. He tried his best to sound upbeat but what he had seen had clearly left him shaken. 'I am afraid they have had a pretty bad time of it. I must say it was very hard luck on them after a long march and quite unprepared and unaccustomed to the trenches to be rushed into what will probably prove to be the fiercest battle of the war.'

By March 1916 Mobbs had been promoted to Major and was in temporary command of the battalion while Lieutenant-Colonel Skinner was being treated for illness in hospital. In fact, Skinner never recovered his health and returned to England in April, handing Mobbs permanent command of the battalion and the rank of Lieutenant-Colonel. The same month he wrote a cheerful letter to Olive from their new position at Messines in Belgium, proud of his promotion but even prouder at his encounter with a senior officer a few days earlier.

'I had the Corps General round my lines yesterday, found he played for Blackheath in the old days so we soon got friendly, he said are you "MOBBS?", I said "Yes, Sir," then we started – Well I must away, but love to Father and all, yours ever, the "CO".'

The jolly nature of the letter might have been an attempt to conceal the strain of commanding a battalion that had come through a bad spell in the trenches. In the twelve days before Mobbs wrote the letter he had lost seventy-three men, nearly all to shellfire. At the beginning of May Mobbs was sent on a week's leave on the orders of his General who had told him he was 'a little run-down and overworked'.

The first serious examination of Mobbs' military leadership skills came three months later when his regiment took part in the Battle of the Somme. The Northamptonshires had missed the first month of the campaign, but their presence was required in August for an attack on the village of Guillemont. It was the village that a week earlier had claimed the life of Jack King, a rugby contemporary of Mobbs who'd won twelve England caps.

Mobbs avoided the fate of King, but only just. The daylight attack commenced on 18 August and during the advance Mobbs was wounded by some shrapnel that lodged itself in his shoulder-blade, causing severe stiffening in his back. Against his wishes, Mobbs was taken to a casualty clearing station and, after a brief stop in a Rouen hospital to remove the shell fragment, was invalided back to England.

His stay in England wasn't a peaceful one, at least for the army medical authorities. He presented himself at a Medical Board on 8 September and was disgusted to find himself declared unfit for duty. Less than two weeks later he wrote a letter to the Board, in the politest possible terms, asking for another examination. To his delight he was declared fit to return to the front on 7 October, the medical report stating that 'the shrapnel wound has now quite healed. It causes him no discomfort.' The scar, noted the report, was 'on the right side of the spine at about the level of the second dorsal vertebrae'.

Back in the trenches with his boys, Mobbs found two months in England had dulled his battle hardness. In a letter to Olive on 30 October 1916, he did his best to reassure her he was readapting to trench life.

'I have arrived safely and gone to a new line, so have been very busy moving. The weather has been bad and the trenches are rather full of water, but one has got to put up with it ... Everyone out here was very pleased to see me back, but I must say I don't like the shelling. I expect I shall get used to it again.'

The Regiment was indeed delighted to have their CO back with them, not just because of his leadership skills and sense of humour but because he had achieved a reputation for immortality from which the men drew comfort. In an earlier letter home Mobbs had written: 'They tell me out here nothing would ever kill me, I do my best to keep everyone cheerful, it is the only way.'

The next couple of months were the most trying of the war so far for Mobbs. The battalion was in trenches at Vimy Ridge, moving back to Loos in November, and for most of that time Mobbs suffered from ill-health related to the wound on the Somme. He was confined to his bed over Christmas with bronchitis, brought on by the shrapnel wound and aggravated by those constant companions of trench warfare, the wet and the cold.

He was reunited with his regiment on Boxing Day and on 3 January came news of his Distinguished Service Order, awarded in the New Year's Honours List for his outstanding leadership of the 7th Battalion, Northamptonshire Regiment. The DSO, coming on top of two Mentioned in Despatches in 1916, cemented his reputation in the eyes of his men as a CO without equal, and did much to raise his spirits after a depressing few months.

Mobbs' decoration coincided with a spell in a quiet sector for the battalion but that ended violently at the beginning of April 1917 when the Northamptonshires were caught up in the Vimy Ridge offensive. On 11 April, two days after four divisions of Canadian troops had captured the Ridge, one of the few hills on the Flanders lowlands, Mobbs wrote home. He was brutally candid to his sister.

'Still going strong but "some" fighting. I had the bad luck to lose my Second-in-Command today, Major Millard, he was killed early this morning, also my runner who came from Harpole. I was only six yards away from him at the time. We have got the Hun "set", so I expect you will see all about it in the papers. I shall not be able to stand the strain much longer, so they'd better soon finish the war off. We have not been out of the front lines for twenty-one days, no bath or anything. This is private, I was hit in the hand in two places last week but did not leave the trenches, they are quite alright again now, only skin wounds. Another attack tonight, so must away.'

The shock of losing two close comrades had clearly unsettled Mobbs. The death of the runner must have been particularly traumatic because of its proximity. Mobbs might well have suffered minor shellshock but he would certainly have been showered with bits of the unfortunate soldier. Mobbs was now under great duress, losing comrades on a daily basis and in desperate need of a rest from the front line. Yet when he faced his greatest test he passed it admirably, refusing to disclose his hand wound to the medical officer and continuing to command the battalion. The idealistic Mobbs, who had enlisted with such vigour in 1914, was growing increasingly war-weary, his earlier enthusiasm a victim of the German guns, but his courage and sense of duty remained intact.

There was no respite for Mobbs and his men as the summer replaced spring. On 7 June the battalion took part in the battle for Messines Ridge in the Ypres Salient. The battalion took heavy casualties and Mobbs was twice wounded. The first wound was fortunate in that the shrapnel that hit him was flat instead of jagged. The point of impact was just above his heart, so although he suffered shock and severe bruising, there was no deep penetration. Mobbs insisted on continuing to lead from the front. A few minutes later he was caught in a shell blast that killed his orderly and left him trying to staunch the blood from a piece of shrapnel that was embedded in his neck. Once more he composed himself and took command of the battalion, allowing himself to be examined only when he was satisfied the battalion had done all that had been ordered of them.

The neck wound was serious enough for Mobbs to return to England for a spot of recuperation but on 26 June he returned to the Western Front, one of the dwindling band of original members of 'D' Company, the Sportsmen's Battalion.

Even amid the din of battle Mobbs could hear the rain from battalion HQ. He held the runner's note in his hand and read it once again. Unless the machine-gun could be silenced the dwindling band of survivors pinned down in no man's land would remain trapped. There was no alternative. Mobbs would lead a bombing party to destroy the gun position. He took Second Lieutenant Berridge with him and stepped outside into the downpour.

Mobbs briefed his junior officer on his orders once more: take three or four men and draw the fire from the machine-gun. Mobbs, accompanied by his batman, disappeared into the grey, cold dawn.

The pair slithered into no man's land, dragging themselves across the mud that encrusted their uniforms and made the task even more exacting. Clutched in Mobbs' hand was the grenade he hoped would get rid of the German machine-gun. As they edged nearer to the German lines they heard the sound of rifle fire, answered by the chatter of the machine-gun. Berridge had done his task, now it was the turn of Mobbs.

When he got to within forty yards of the gun, Mobbs scrambled to his feet and sprinted towards the gun. He covered ten yards without being seen but then one of the gun crew tapped the gunner on his shoulder and pointed in the direction of Mobbs. Just another few feet and Mobbs would be close enough to hurl the grenade. The German swung the gun round and squeezed the trigger.

Mobbs was slammed backwards by the impact of the bullet. His batman, just a couple of yards behind his officer, braved the attention of the machine-gunner and dragged him into a shellhole. He tried to stem the blood gushing from the wound to Mobbs' neck. Mobbs, unable to speak, grabbed a pencil and paper from his tunic pocket and, taking care not to get any mud on the paper, wrote down the gun's grid reference for the British artillery. He added a postscript: 'Am seriously wounded.' He handed the message to his batman. He took a couple of deep breaths and dashed out of the shellhole. Within a matter of seconds he had been shot by the same machine-gun.

It would be comforting to think Mobbs died quickly in the shellhole. He probably did, slipping away quietly as the blood drained out of his body. Perhaps he found another piece of paper and managed, amid all the rain and mud, to write a final letter to his sister. If he did, it was never found, and nor was his body. He lies under Flemish soil, along with 42,000 other British soldiers who disappeared in the mud of Flanders before the battle ended in November.

Mobbs' Sportsmen's Battalion died with him on the Ypres Salient. The 7th

Northamptonshires suffered so many casualties, 246 killed or wounded, that they were later amalgamated with another regiment. When the war ended only eighty-five original members of the 264 men who had enlisted with Mobbs in September 1914 returned home. The Sportsmen's Battalion marched together for the last time on 17 July 1921 when they formed the centrepiece of a memorial procession in Mobbs' honour. Thousands of people lined the streets of Northampton as the survivors of 'D' Company placed a wreath at the foot of Mobbs' statue and saluted the man who had led them with such gallantry.

CHAPTER EIGHT

Arthur Harrison

A rthur Harrison joined the Royal Navy as soon as he was old enough. He made just two appearances for the England rugby team in the 1914 season, but showed some of the courage later seen by his shipmates when war broke out. In 1917, volunteers were needed for a dangerous mission. Harrison came forward and found himself involved in one of the most daring raids in the history of the Royal Navy.

Arthur Harrison was a nondescript England international. He won his two caps in 1914, in an era when the coruscating talent of Cyril Lowe, Cherry Pillman, Ronnie Poulton-Palmer and Willie Davies illuminated English rugby. Harrison lumbered round the field in their wake, puffing and panting, always a yard off the pace. Second row has never been the most glamorous of positions. In today's rugby vernacular they're described as grafters, work-horses, the boys in the engine room. Any of these would have suited the bulldog-jawed Harrison perfectly.

When war broke out Cyril Lowe became a pilot, Pillman an officer in the Dragoon Guards. Harrison was a junior officer in the Royal Navy. Even at war, it seemed, he was overshadowed by his more charismatic team-mates. But Harrison has a distinction that no England rugby international has, and, one can say with almost complete certainty, none will ever emulate. He won the Victoria Cross. The second row 'donkey' turned himself into a lion.

Harrison might perhaps have had a few more caps had he not been married to the Royal Navy. As it was, he didn't make his debut until he was twenty-eight and his appearances in England's Grand Slam season of 1914 were restricted because of naval duties. Harrison's heart was the navy and it was this devotion that won him the VC and cost him his life.

One of the first sights Arthur Leyland Harrison would have seen when he entered this world on 1 February 1886 was the bristling moustache of his father, twitching above him as he cradled his son in large, sandpaper hands. Lt-Colonel A J Harrison of the 7th Royal Fusiliers no doubt had ambitions for his son to follow him into the army, but instead Arthur joined the navy on leaving Dover College and, on 15 May 1901, he was sent to the training ship *Britannia*.

So began a distinguished career that saw him climb as steadily up the ranks as he did the rigging aboard *Britannia*. On passing out as a midshipman his captain described the sixteen-year-old Harrison as 'zealous and energetic'. In April 1904 a report called him 'zealous and reliable', and two years later he was promoted Sub-Lieutenant, with the attached report describing him as 'physically very strong ... most reliable and capable'. In 1908, having successfully passed pilotage, gunnery and torpedo exams, he was promoted to Lieutenant and given his first command, Torpedo Boat No 16. His superior officer wrote twelve months later that Lieutenant Harrison was 'Hard working, able ... and a very fine type of character'.

Somewhere between the exams, the assessments and life on the high seas, Harrison found time to shoehorn some rugby into his schedule. His size made him an obvious candidate for the second row and it would have suited someone as unassuming as Harrison. The second row of a hundred years ago didn't seek much out of life; a bit of pushing, the odd jump in the line-out, if they were lucky a scrum-half might inadvertently stray into their path who could be squashed, but it was tacitly acknowledged that running with the ball was something above and beyond the call of duty. E H D Sewell, rugby correspondent for the *Evening Standard*, described Harrison in the RFU Internationals Roll of Honour as 'strong and tireless ... his game was the sturdy, bustling type'.

The Royal Navy always came first in Harrison's life but rugby was a welcome distraction, made all the sweeter because naval rugby in the years immediately before the First World War was as strong as it had ever been. The half-back pairing of Francis Oakeley and Willie Davies made their debuts in 1913, the same season that prop Norman Wodehouse won the last of his fourteen caps. The strength of naval rugby, and the similarly robust state of army rugby, led to the revival of their traditional fixture. After a period of abeyance it was brought back in 1907 and the Royal Navy won the first four. Many warships boasted their own teams, some of whom were as strong as the army's best regimental XVs, and it came as something of a shock therefore when the Army won in 1911.

The Navy reasserted their superiority in the following two years but the presence in Army ranks in 1914 of a trio of talented Scots internationals, Scobie, Usher and Robertson, was the cause of many a corrugated brow within the Navy team. It was a foul March day that greeted both sides at the Queen's Club in Kensington. A Scotch mist hovered over the ground and the rain did its best to dampen the enthusiasm of all involved. King George V was introduced to the two teams beforehand and then took his place in the stand. During the war that was soon to engulf the world, the King impressed his people by striking German princes off the roll of the Garter and changing the name of the royal house from Hanover to Windsor. On this occasion he contented himself by refusing the use of an umbrella. It was a gesture that was noted by the *Daily Telegraph* correspondent: 'It rained during the match but His Majesty sat in the open, and did not use his umbrella. Spectators behind the King made it quite evident that the consideration thus shown for them was much appreciated.'

The match he saw was worthy of the presence of a king. It produced a record number of points and the skill on display was outstanding, despite the conditions. There was uncertainty about who scored the Army's final try because, as one newspaper wrote, 'by this time the players were so clothed in mud and mist that identification was doubtful'. What wasn't in doubt, however, was the talent at work within the British game.

The Army won 26–14 and *The Times* considered that 'seldom has a better game of clean, hard football been played'. The Army's score equalled that of the Navy's record in 1909 and their superiority stemmed from the strength of the pack, five of whom were internationals. 'There was hardly a penalty and only one brief interruption for a try,' continued *The Times*, 'yet the vigour of the play was such that had not every man been as hard as nails he would have been in the dock for repairs.'

Harrison's introduction to the King before the Services match had been unnecessary. The two had met three weeks earlier at Twickenham when His Majesty attended his first rugby match since his succession in 1910. The opponents were Ireland and it was thought – at a time when the Home Rule question was causing tension between the two countries – that it would be seen as a conciliatory gesture if both the King and Prime Minister Herbert Asquith were present among the 40,000 spectators.

Harrison was the only new cap in the England side. The selectors wanted some more bulk in the side. In the opening match of the Five Nations, the English forwards had been pushed around by a heavier Welsh pack. The Irish, led by the bellicose Belfast doctor William Tyrrell, would be equally intractable unless measures were taken. Harrison was brought in and there was a recall for his namesake, 'Dreadnought' Harrison, a Royal Marines officer, last capped in 1909, but a prop forward of such gargantuan proportions that his team-mates named him after the new British battleship.

Ireland opened the scoring after seven minutes with a dropped goal from Lloyd. Wing Jimmy Quinn extended the visitors' lead to 7–0 after a rare mistake from Harrison's naval team-mate Willie Davies. The error, however, focused the mind of the fly-half and thereafter he took control of the game in tandem with Oakeley. The pair engineered a try in the corner for Andy Roberts, the left wing, and just before the interval the diminutive Cyril Lowe ducked under the arms of Quinn for a second try to narrow the gap to 7–6.

The English pack had spent the first half drawing the sting from the Irish forwards and after the break they were noticeably slower and more sluggish. England's backs showed their class, scoring further tries through Lowe and Davies, with No 8 Cherry Pillman getting the fourth. 'The English forwards,' said *The Times*, 'stiffened in the scrummage by the inclusion of the Harrisons, did better than against Wales. They were no match for the Irish at dribbling but they never let them get away from the scrummage.'

Ireland had the consolation of scoring the final try through Jackson but England's 17–12 victory was deserved. The King departed in good heart. So did the crowd, Englishmen and Irishmen alike, sharing a joke, spinning a yarn, forgetting about the troubles across the water. As Asquith drove through the crowd on his way back to Downing Street he must have wished he could bottle up some of the goodwill and sprinkle it over the Home Rule imbroglio. 'Rugby,' as *The Times* pointed out in Monday's edition, 'is a game in which all classes combine, it knows no divisions, political or other.'

Unfortunately for Harrison and the rest of the England team the bonhomie that had been so evident before, during and after the Ireland game was conspicuous by its absence in Paris. England had beaten Scotland comfortably in their penultimate match to secure the Triple Crown. Harrison returned to the side after missing the Scottish match because of naval duties. A win against a French side that had never beaten England would result in a second successive Grand Slam. France had lost their other matches that season against Wales and Ireland. They would probably have lost to the Scots, too, but the SRU refused to play France because of the crowd unrest that had marred their win in Paris the previous year.

England won the match comfortably, 39–13, despite conceding the opening try to Toulouse flanker Capmau. In the second half they cut loose, outscoring France five tries to one, with all the tries coming from the threequarters. In the opinion of *Sporting Life*, however, the key to England's win was the superiority of the forwards, in skill and stamina: 'They worked the scrums infinitely better than did the French eight ... The Frenchmen were excellent while they were fresh, but the victors gradually and surely wore them down.'

All of which, though, was incidental to the correspondent of *The Times*, whose spluttering indignation reflected his paper's peculiar brand of imperial smugness on which its readers fed. 'The match was unfortunately marred by two things – the rough play by one or two of the French team and the exceedingly bad behaviour of the large crowd of spectators. We have come to associate chivalry with the name of France but if the behaviour of the spectators is typical of French crowds they have learned very little by the lesson of playing rugby football.' W R Johnston, the Bristol full-back, might well have shared the sentiments of *The Times* journalist. He was knocked unconscious by a late tackle from Pau centre Pierrot. The rest of the players, however, were more interested in a night on the town in Paris. If they bore any resentment towards the French it probably soon disappeared in one of the estaminets off the Boulevard St-Germain.

Four months later, when Britain and France declared war on Germany, there was little trace of animosity among the fifteen players as they rushed to enlist. Perhaps they thought that if they could survive an obstreperous French rugby crowd, a spat with the Germans would be a picnic. They were wrong, of course. Before the end of the war, six would be dead, including Ronnie Poulton-Palmer, who had scored four tries in the win in Paris.

Harrison was the last of the six to die. When he was killed in the early hours of 23 April 1918 he became the twenty-sixth England international to give his life for his country. Only Scotland, who lost thirty players, suffered more grievously than England.

The popular refrain in Britain during those first giddy weeks following the outbreak of war was 'It will be over by Christmas!' This prompted a rush to the recruitment stations, lest any fun be missed. Earl Kitchener, Secretary of State for War, called for 200,000 volunteers in the first month of war. He got 300,000, of whom twenty-eight were current rugby internationals. Their enthusiasm was astonishing.

Perhaps Harrison could have done something to rein in such exuberance. By the end of August, as record numbers charged through the doors of recruiting stations – between 25 August and 5 September, 174,901 men enlisted – Harrison had been in action for the first time. The sight of Harrison and his crewmates fishing the corpses of British sailors from the North Sea might have made some appreciate better the reality of war. The Battle of Heligoland Bight on 28 August was the first major naval engagement of the war. The British were the aggressors, attacking German destroyer patrols operating from their base on Heligoland, to the west of Denmark. The British raiding force consisted of two light cruisers, twenty-five destroyers and three submarines. They would lure the Germans out into the open sea where two more submarines and two battlecruisers would be waiting to finish the job. German naval intelligence, however, got wind of the raid and formed a plan that turned them from hunted to hunter. When the two British light cruisers, *Fearless* and *Arethusa,* attacked, the Germans led them into a trap where they had a strong cruiser force waiting to blow the Royal Navy ships out of the water. The commander of the British forces saw the trap bearing down on him and called for help just as the first broadside ripped into the *Arethusa.*

To the rescue steamed Admiral Beatty and his three 'Lion'-class battlecruisers. Known as the 'Big Cats', the cruisers comprised *Princess Royal, Queen Mary,* and Harrison's ship, the *Lion.* The *Lion* was the flagship of the Grand Fleet's battlecruiser force in the North Sea. Built in 1912, it had a crew of 1,061, a top speed of twenty-nine knots and was the first battlecruiser to boast eight 13.5-inch guns.

The arrival of Admiral Beatty's force turned the battle the way of the British. The German light cruisers, *Köln*, *Mainz* and *Ariadne*, were sunk, as was a destroyer, and three more light cruisers limped back to port. The *Arethusa* had suffered serious damage but was towed home.

Harrison next saw action at the Battle of Dogger Bank in January 1915, by which time two former England team-mates, James Watson and Francis Oakeley, had gone down with their ships. The *Lion* took a fearful pounding and was forced to withdraw from the battle.

Harrison escaped injury on the *Lion*, and during the next fifteen months cropped up frequently in the wartime internationals, staged around the country to boost the morale of the public and raise money for the war effort. Any time Harrison was able to enjoy a run ashore, he would have his boots tucked under his arm, as Sewell recalled when he wrote his obituary: 'Lt-Commander A L Harrison was very much to the fore in the scratch games played at the Old Deer Park, Richmond, and it goes without saying that though past the age at which men receive their first National Cap, he was so fit he would have played many times for England but for the war.'

On 31 May 1916, Harrison was one of the 70,000 sailors involved in the Battle of Jutland. It was the biggest naval engagement of the war, the first and only time that the British Grand Fleet was to engage the German High Seas Fleet. When the battle finished early on the morning of 1 June, however, no one was entirely sure who had won. The British had lost more ships, fourteen to the Germans' eleven, but the Germans had withdrawn from the battle and, to Jellicoe, this meant the day belonged to the Royal Navy. In reality, the outcome was a minor tactical triumph for the German navy but, significantly, one that had failed to wrest strategic control of the North Sea from the British.

What was incontrovertible was the damage caused to the prestigious 'Lion'-class battlecruisers. The 'Big Cats' were mauled, with the *Lion* again singled out for treatment by the enemy gunners. At 1600 hours she had a turret destroyed but she continued to engage the Germans and was still in action later that evening. Harrison was mentioned in despatches for his conduct during Jutland.

Shortly after the *Lion* lost her turret, the *Queen Mary* came under fire. At 1625 hours she was hit by a broadside from the *Derfflinger*. A massive explosion rent the air and within two minutes the *Queen Mary* had disappeared beneath the waves, taking with her 1,300 sailors.

Although the Royal Navy declared the Grand Fleet operational on 2 June, the German fleet was crippled for many months. Jutland had caused a rethink in naval tactics, the German Navy in particular adamant that it would never again engage in a battle of such gigantic proportions. As a result Harrison's war entered the doldrums. After three major engagements, 1917 offered him little in the way of excitement. There was a welcome flurry of rugby matches, a chance to blow off steam and meet old team-mates. But the only thing he was sinking was beer.

Then in late 1917 he saw a memo pinned to the officers' mess in Scapa Flow. It was brief and to the point. Volunteers were wanted for a 'show' against the Hun. There were two stipulations: all men must be single and athletic. Intrigued, Harrison put his name forward.

He heard nothing for a few weeks. Then, one day in late January 1918, he was told to report to HMS *Hindustan* at Chatham Docks in Kent. Another volunteer, Able Seaman Wainwright, put himself forward in order to escape the drudgery of life aboard *Superb* in Scapa Flow. He recalled arriving at Holborn station and finding dozens of other sailors waiting for the train to Chatham, standing around in groups and trying to find out if anyone knew for what exactly they had volunteered.

When Harrison and the other officers arrived they were met by the commander of the 'show', Vice Admiral Keyes. In after years he recalled those moments: 'It was very interesting to watch their reaction when I told them that the enterprise would be hazardous, and finally said the best chance of escape I could offer them after it was a German prison until the end of the war. With one exception only, they appeared to be simply delighted and most grateful for the honour I had done them in offering such a wonderful prospect!'

Keyes weeded out those officers who had conveniently forgotten they were married. He also discarded half a dozen he deemed unsuitable for the operation because of their temperament. He needed officers who were cool and reliable because 'the command might well pass rapidly'. Why might the command pass rapidly? No one told them. Instead they were handed over to infantry instructors from the Middlesex Regiment and shown the 'dirty work' of close-quarter fighting. How to 'point and parry' with a bayonet; the skills needed for trench raiding and how to kill a man with a rifle butt. Some of the men found themselves issued with pistols and cutlasses. The sailors soon discovered that three cutlasses made an ideal wicket for a game of deck cricket aboard *Hindustan*.

As the intensity of the training increased so the volunteers found themselves attacking an elaborate replica of a harbour mole. All Keyes would tell the men was it represented 'a position in France'. It wasn't until the end of March that the cloak of secrecy was lifted. The 'position in France' was actually a position in Belgium. It was the Zeebrugge Mole, one of the most heavily guarded ports in Europe. It was home for at least thirty-five German torpedo craft and thirty submarines, all of which had been laying waste to British shipping for the past few months. The Government wanted something done about it. The public's morale was at a low ebb following the horrific losses at Passchendaele in 1917, and news of British ships being sent to the bottom of the sea was not making things any better.

Keyes devised a plan to prevent the submarines leaving their pens in Bruges. To do this would mean blocking the entrance to the eight-mile ship canal that led from the port of Zeebrugge to the pens. If this was done the submarines and torpedo craft would be trapped in the port for several months.

A snag did present itself, however, when he took the plan to the Admiralty. The canal mouth was guarded by the mole, a giant stone pier that at the time was the largest in the world. It was nearly two miles in length and curved round from the coastline as if it were putting out a protective arm to shelter the canal. The Germans had turned the mole into a fortress. Displaying the same diligence and attention to detail that made their trenches the envy of soldiers on the Western Front, the defenders of Zeebrugge exploited the mole's daunting structure.

Using the railway that ran across a viaduct, linking the shore to the mole proper, the Germans brought up an assortment of artillery guns. The main mole was 1,850 yards long and 80 yards broad with a 16-foot seawall for protection. This seawall, 10 feet thick, guarded a road which narrowed and eventually led to a 360-yard extension. At the extremity of this extension was the lighthouse.

Ranged along the extension was a formidable arsenal. Commanding the approach route to the harbour with an unimpeded arc of fire were four 4.1-

inch and two 3.5-inch guns. A Very cannon had also been installed to illuminate the harbour with powerful flares. Halfway along the extension, and behind these guns, the Germans had built two anti-aircraft emplacements and a shelter trench running across the mole with a machine-gun position. The garrison of the mole lived in two large sheds made of reinforced concrete with barbed wire around the outside. The men inside were pleased with their lot. Not so far south their compatriots had to contend with the squalor of trench warfare. In Zeebrugge, all the home comforts were provided. In addition, the chances of having to fight were negligible. Not even the British would be crazy enough to attack the mole.

Back in Chatham Keyes gathered Harrison and the other officers and explained the objective of the raid. Three outdated cruisers, *Thetis*, *Intrepid*, and *Iphigenia*, would be sailed into the mouth of the ship canal and scuttled. There was, of course, he continued, a bit more to it than that. Before the blockships arrived on the scene, the mole would be stormed by a combined force of Royal Marines and sailors. This was the 'show' for which they had volunteered. The purpose of the assault was to distract the garrison on the mole so the ships could be scuttled before being blown out of the water. The assault would be launched from a cruiser called *Vindictive*, another obsolete vessel that had been destined for the naval scrapyard before Keyes chanced upon her.

HMS *Vindictive* had been modified to suit the needs of the men who would storm the mole from her decks. In the words of one sailor, *Vindictive* now had a 'strange Noah's Ark look about her'. Barricades had been constructed on the main deck and the storming parties would shelter behind these until near to the mole. Then they would move up on to a raised deck that was the same height as the raised parapet. Once alongside the mole, sixteen gangways would be lowered from the port side of the *Vindictive* and the men would charge down these on to the mole.

Keyes went on to reveal the answer to a puzzle that had baffled and angered the entire population of Merseyside in recent weeks: the fate of the two Mersey ferries, *Iris* and *Daffodil*. They had been withdrawn from public service earlier in the year. 'Needed to assist the war effort' was all the Navy would say. In fact, the two ferries would help the *Vindictive* transport the storming parties across the Channel to Zeebrugge.

The men gathered round Keyes were impressed. Such assiduous planning hadn't always been a characteristic of Britain's military commanders during the war. It looked as if every potential problem had been obviated. Keyes could even announce that a smoke screen would be laid down a few minutes before the raid started. This would be the responsibility of Wing-Commander Brock, son of C T Brock, purveyor of wondrous fireworks. With everything in place the raiders could do nothing but sit and wait. For the raid to succeed the right sea conditions were essential, particularly the tide. If the *Vindictive* arrived at the mole at low tide the parapet would tower above them, out of reach of the gangways but not the German guns.

Eventually, after two aborted attempts earlier in the month, the raiders slipped away from the Kent coast at 1653 hours on 22 April. As Keyes bade his wife farewell, she reminded him that 'Tomorrow is St George's Day and St George can be trusted to bring good fortune to England.' With this in mind, Keyes signalled a message to the fleet shortly after they had set sail, wishing them good luck and reminding the men of the significance of 23 April. Alfred Carpenter, captain of the *Vindictive*, signalled back, 'May we give the dragon's tail a damned good twist.' He later admitted that for a captain to send such a brazen message smacked of impertinence but that 'impertinence was in the air that afternoon'.

On board the *Vindictive,* there was also an air of insouciance. Able Seaman Wainwright recalled in after years that: 'Most of the time was passed with impromptu concerts and dances and I doubt if any there thought of the serious mission … after supper had been served, everybody snatched an hour or two's sleep.'

At 10.30pm a hot chicken broth was served to the men. This was the last chance for the raiders to be alone with their thoughts and think of loved ones back home. Some stood by themselves on deck staring out to sea, while others sought solace in the company of their mates and drank their soup, laughing and joking. At 11pm the order was quietly passed among the men to ready themselves. Down below the decks of *Vindictive*, Staff Surgeon James McCutcheon and his team of medical staff went through for the final time the treatment procedure.

A quarter of an hour later the mainbrace was spliced, although few of the men accepted the rum on offer. 'A clear head and steady eye,' said Wainwright, 'were more beneficial.' At 11.20pm two small warships, *Erebus* and *Terror*, and three destroyers began bombarding Zeebrugge, as they had for the past few weeks. The Germans on the mole, the majority of whom were relaxing in the sheds, looked up for a moment and then carried on with what they were doing. Another British bombardment, nothing out of the ordinary.

Aboard the *Vindictive, Iris* and *Daffodil,* the order 'Action Stations' was quietly passed among the men. W C Childs, a Lewis gunner aboard *Vindictive* and one of the men in Harrison's storming party, remembered that 'Chums were saying goodbye in case they did not survive the action'. At 2325 hours the smoke screen was laid down by coastal motor-boats along an eight-mile stretch of coast. Then the boats began spraying the mole with machine-gun fire. The Germans, thinking it was an act of British bravado, didn't send out any of their vessels to investigate. It was only at 2345 hours, when a sudden change in the direction of the wind sent the smoke screens back out to sea, that the Germans became aware of the raiding party bearing down on them.

The swirling smoke made communication impossible between the British vessels and when the *Vindictive* emerged through the last trails of smoke four minutes before midnight, Captain Carpenter's eyes scanned the mole for distinguishing features. The storming party was to be deposited on the mole so that they were practically on top of the German artillery battery. Before the machine-gun emplacement had time to open fire, the raiders would be in among the artillerymen.

When the Germans saw the three ships they unleashed a tornado of gunfire against the invaders. Childs, atop the *Vindictive* with his Lewis gun, must have felt like a pea-shooter taking on a rifleman. 'It seemed like hell let loose,' he wrote later in a letter to a friend. 'The shrapnel and pieces of funnel caused havoc among the men, and the air was full of the cries of the wounded and dying. The Huns were hitting us every time they fired.'

The Germans couldn't miss. Carpenter later estimated that as he steered the *Vindictive* towards the mole they were no more than 50 yards from the German artillery battery. Carpenter, a man whose phlegm and good humour never once wavered during this infernal night, described the *Vindictive*'s approach to the mole as a 'truly wonderful sight. The noise was terrific and the flashes of the mole guns seemed to be within arm's length.'

That wasn't such a bad guess. The *Vindictive*'s gunners were doing their best to defend their ship but two 7.5-inch howitzers, one 11-inch howitzer and half a dozen pom-pom guns were simply inadequate. One of the gunners later told Carpenter that he opened fire at 200 yards and continued to fire until close to the mole. 'How close?' Carpenter enquired. 'Reckoning from the gun muzzle, I should say about three feet.'

The *Vindictive*'s gunners, perversely, were to be envied. At least they didn't feel as powerless as Harrison and the other members of the storming parties. All they could do was crouch behind the flimsy barricades and pray. Their prayers did them little good. German shells and machine-gun fire ripped into the *Vindictive*. By the time she was alongside the mole, Captain Halahan, commander of the naval storming party, was dead, as were the two senior officers of the Royal Marines. Command would have fallen to Harrison, but he was also dead, a piece of shrapnel having ripped open his jaw. Or that was what his men thought as they carried him down to the dressing station.

At one minute past midnight on St George's Day, the *Vindictive* was alongside the mole. That maelstrom of gunfire that had greeted the appearance of the ship had blasted to bits all but two of the gangways. But, led by Lt-Commander Bryan Adams, the only detachment commander still standing, the storming party swarmed on to the mole. One of the marines later described to the *Daily Express* what happened in those hellish few minutes: 'With a cheer and a cry of "Over you go, boys!" our men landed on the first ledge of the mole, but we lost heavily, for the shellfire directed against us was terrible … a number of German sailors swarmed up to attack us, but they found themselves in front of British bayonets, and with a shout our men charged them. This was more than Fritz could stand.'

Adams realized at once they had been landed in the wrong place. They were 300 yards shy of the German artillery battery. This was bad news. Instead of landing right on top of the battery, which posed the most serious threat to the progress of the blockships, they were now behind it and between them and their target was the trench and machine-gun emplacement.

As Adams was formulating a new plan, the men on board *Iris* were trying to get on to the mole. In place of gangways the raiders intended to use scaling ladders to climb over the mole's parapet. But a three-knot tidal stream pressed against the mole and formed a cushion of troubled water that pushed back against the side of the ship. Unable therefore to position the ladders in place, two officers took it upon themselves to perform acts of extraordinary courage. Lt Claude Hawkings ordered half a dozen of his men to hold on to the ladder while he climbed to its top. Once there the men swung him towards the top of the parapet. Incredibly this bold plan worked and Hawkings clambered over the wall and began securing the ladder. As he did so, he was set upon by a gang of Germans. Hawkings was last seen defending himself with a revolver, and his body was never recovered.

Watching all this was Lt-Commander George Bradford, whose brother had been awarded the Victoria Cross earlier in the war. He scrambled up the derrick and took hold of the grappling anchor. Then, with the agility and daring of a trapeze artist, he swung on the end of the derrick until he was within reach of the parapet. He made a desperate lunge for the parapet wall and just managed to haul himself over. He began to fix the grappling anchor to the mole but a burst of machine-gun fire lifted him off his feet and sent him plunging back over the wall into the sea between the *Iris* and the mole. Petty Officer Hallihan leapt into the water in search of his officer. Neither re-emerged. George Bradford was awarded a posthumous VC.

The official despatches described this period of the raid as 'very trying'. For Adams and the remnants of the storming party taking cover on the pathway of the mole it could probably have been summed up in slightly stronger terms. Adams knew he had to act with alacrity. The timings had been worked out with pinpoint precision. The three blockships would pass the mole at twenty-five minutes past midnight. If they couldn't destroy, or at least distract, the German battery, the blockships would be sunk and the raid would be a failure.

Adams led his men along the parapet towards the machine-gun positions. They came first upon a concrete observation post. Childs was one of those in the vanguard. 'Some Germans made a rush for it. In making a point with my bayonet at one of them, my blade finished up like a corkscrew.'

With the occupants of the observation post now longer posing a threat, the machine-gun emplacement was the next obstacle in their path. It was a formidable barrier, made all the more menacing by the Very cannon that lit up the end of the mole and made them easy prey for the machine-gunners. Adams made a sweep back along the parapet, collecting as many reinforcements as he could find. Then, stopping in his tracks, he looked in amazement in the direction of the *Vindictive*. A man was making his way along the parapet, albeit on legs that looked unsteady. The shape and gait was that of Harrison, Adams' good friend. But wasn't he dead?

The shell fragment that had shattered Harrison's jaw made talking a chore, but he explained briefly he had been merely knocked unconscious. On coming round, Harrison had pushed aside the attentions of the medics and made his way on to the mole. Adams briefed his senior officer on their position. Harrison told Adams to return to the *Vindictive* and bring back any lightly wounded and those men from the *Daffodil* and *Iris* who were still clambering off their vessels.

The sight of Harrison cheered the survivors. If there was one man to get them out of a hole it was Lt-Commander Harrison. No officer was as well respected. Not only was he a former rugby international, but he had led the men in physical training during the weeks in Chatham. The men would follow him into the jaws of Hell, or in a charge against an enemy gun emplacement.

The German machine-gunner could hardly miss Harrison. A man that big, half dazed, silhouetted by the Very lights, was an easy target. Carpenter described Harrison's last moments in his memoirs:

'Gathering together a handful of his men, Harrison led a charge along the parapet in the face of heavy machine-gun fire. He was killed at the head of his men, all but two of whom were also killed.'

These men were Able Seamen Eaves and McKenzie. Eaves hoisted his commander's body on to his back and started back along the parapet. A burst of fire cut him down. He rose, badly wounded, and tried once more to bring in his officer. He was hit again and this time his wounds proved too much even for such a gallant gentleman. Eaves was taken prisoner but survived the war.

McKenzie, all 5ft 3in of him, deployed his Lewis gun magnificently. He had been beside Harrison when he led the charge and had seen his commanding officer killed, but he continued to work his gun until it was blown out of his hands by German bullets. Left grasping just the stock and pistol grip, McKenzie smashed it into the face of an advancing German and then pulled out his pistol and finished him off. Then he beat a retreat towards the ship. 'All I remember was pushing, kicking and kneeing every German who got in the way.'

Harrison's sacrifice hadn't been in vain. While he had been leading the charge towards the machine-gun, the blockships had passed the end of the mole. All three had run the gauntlet of battery fire and made it through the other side. The lead ship, *Thetis,* became entangled in the obstruction nets that guarded the canal mouth and couldn't be scuttled in the right spot. But she had removed the obstruction net and the remaining two ships, *Intrepid* and *Iphigenia*, were scuttled in the canal entrance.

With the blockships scuttled, the sound of the recall cut through the din of battle and the storming parties retired to their ships, carrying their wounded with them. All the while the storming parties had been fighting their way along the mole, the *Vindictive* had been pounded by fire from the mole and from three German destroyers docked at Zeebrugge. Her upper decks, as one survivor told the *Daily Express* a few days later, were 'slippery with blood and all around lay dead, dying and wounded … it was horrible; but our men behaved magnificently'.

The Germans continued to pour fire into the *Iris, Vindictive* and *Daffodil* as they left the mole. Fate was particularly unkind to those aboard *Iris*. As they crammed below decks in search of hot soup, a shell tore into the side of the ship, killing seventy-five and wounding dozens more. Below decks, said one marine, 'was simply choked with dying and wounded'.

At 8am on 23 April, the raiding party limped into Dover Harbour. They were welcomed with unfettered euphoria. But to the survivors this was not the time for back-slapping. 'It upset us a bit,' admitted Childs, 'for we were all beginning to feel the reaction of the night's work.'

In Zeebrugge there was considerable upset among the Germans. The Kaiser himself came to view the mole and a captured British marine officer explained to him how the raiders had carried out such an audacious plan. Even the German press was impressed. The *Cologne Gazette* admitted the raid showed 'considerable strength and gallantry'. British reconnaisance planes took photographs of the canal the next day and the sight of the *Intrepid* and *Iphigenia* lying in the canal entrance were proof to the British that the raid had been an unmitigated success.

The reality, unfortunately, was somewhat different. The Germans sent divers to inspect the position of the two blockships and were pleased to discover that the obstruction they caused would not prove a serious disruption to the passage of the submarines. On 24 April, Admiral von Schroder sent a general report to Berlin in which he said that 'Submarine warfare would be neither obstructed nor delayed by the English onslaught'.

The following day UB16 went out in search of victims in the North Sea, leaving from Zeebrugge.

But if the raid failed to produce much in the way of tangible results, it proved invaluable in terms of propaganda and boosting the morale of the nation. The newspapers lavished praise on the raiding party, and the King and Queen expressed their thanks by visiting the wounded on 30 April. The King asked Marine James Cowgill, who had been on *Iris*, what it had been like: 'It was very, very bad, sir, but worth it.'

Men continued to succumb to their wounds for several days after the raid. When the official casualty figures were released they made grim reading. One hundred and eighty-eight men had been killed, while a further sixteen were missing, presumed dead. In addition, 384 men had been wounded. The number of dead rose by one, a week before the Armistice, when McKenzie, still recovering from his wounds, contracted Spanish flu and died.

Harrison was awarded the Victoria Cross for his actions during the raid. His mother collected her son's medal from the King in May 1919. The official citation read:

> 'This officer was in immediate command of the Naval Storming parties embarked in *Vindictive*. Immediately before coming alongside the mole, Lieut-Commander Harrison was struck on the head by a fragment of shell which broke his jaw and knocked him senseless. Recovering consciousness, he proceeded on to the mole and took over command of his party, who were attacking the seaward end of the mole. The silencing of the guns on the mole head was of the first importance, and though in a position fully exposed to the enemy's machine-gun fire, Lieut-Commander Harrison gathered his men together and led them to the attack. He was killed at the head of his men, all of whom were either killed or wounded. Lieut-Commander Harrison, though already severely wounded and undoubtedly in great pain, displayed indomitable resolution and courage of the highest order in pressing his attack, knowing as he did that any delay in silencing the guns might jeopardize the main objective of the expedition, i.e, the blocking of the Zeebrugge-Bruges Canal.'

In 1921 Carpenter published his account of the raid and remembered

Harrison in words that, although they now seem slightly facetious, at the time pandered to a need among the public to mask the brutal reality of a war that had ruined a generation of young men.

> 'Harrison's charge down that narrow gangway of death was a worthy finale to the large number of charges which, as a forward of the first rank, he had led down many a rugby football ground. He had "played the game" to the end ... with Harrison's death the Navy lost an officer who was as popular and as keen as he had been invaluable to the success of this particular operation.'

On 22 April 1968, seventy-five survivors of Zeebrugge gathered in Belgium to remember the courage of their comrades who had died on the mole. Fifty years later, and after another world war, death was by then no longer described in sporting euphemisms. Instead the veterans spoke in simple but moving terms about their part in the raid. One told *The Times*: 'An officer said I should make out a will and get things straight. Instead, I went out and got married. I thought she might just as well have the pension. Anyway, I came back and my wife is with me today. But all my pals died.'

CHAPTER NINE

Aubrey Faulkner

*T*he South African all-rounder was one of the most talented *cricketers of his generation. He fought for the British in the Boer War and achieved international recognition on the cricket field before the outbreak of the First World War. He served with the Artillery for four years and survived. But war had worn down Faulkner mentally and life in the 1920s gradually began to lose its appeal.*

Aubrey Faulkner looked over the radio microphone at Jack Hobbs, and grinned. 'These young fellows today don't know how marvellous it is to be young enough to get on with things.' Hobbs smiled: 'I can't complain, I've had a good innings with plenty of good times.' Faulkner, interviewing 'The Master' in September 1930 to mark his recent retirement from Test cricket, congratulated his friend. 'You're lucky. The majority of us aren't so fortunate. What a pity we can't stay young!'

A week later Aubrey Faulkner took his own life. He was forty-eight. The premature death of one of South Africa's greatest cricketers has never been adequately explained. The hint had been there, during the Hobbs interview, that like other great cricketers such as Albert Trott and Arthur Shrewsbury, Faulkner was finding it hard to come to terms with a body that was no longer indestructible. But the spectre of old age would not have cowed Faulkner. This was a man who had fought in two wars, won the Distinguished Service Order and a chestful of other gallantry awards. Everybody who knew Aubrey assumed he was fearless. He had seen action during the First World War, when he spent four years in the Royal Field Artillery. He had survived intact but had the war levied its revenge twelve years later? Did Faulkner kill himself because in the end he could no longer outrun the horrors of the past?

The life that ended in such piteous circumstances had begun in Port Elizabeth on 17 December 1881. Little is known about Faulkner's early days. He went to the Wynberg Boys' High School in the Cape, but his schooldays were blighted by an alcoholic father. At times his drunkenness turned violent and Faulkner was once forced to beat him up to protect his mother.

The confrontation left Faulkner with a lifelong distrust of alcohol. He became a teetotaller in adulthood, and when he opened his cricket school in London he refused to countenance the idea of installing a bar so cricketers could slake their thirst. He feared it would attract layabouts to whom cricket was of secondary importance.

After leaving school, Faulkner moved to Transvaal where he was 'engaged in secretarial work upon the Rand' in the late 1890s. When freed from the confines of the office he would dash to the Old Wanderers ground in Johannesburg on the off chance of a net against some of the senior players. He was a rather plump teenager, but his enthusiasm couldn't be faulted. Sometimes, in fact, he buzzed around the seniors too much and one or two came to consider him a gadfly. He might have been banished forever, were it not for his ability as a cricketer.

Jimmy Sinclair, who in 1898–9 against the MCC had scored South Africa's first century, grew sick in one practice of this overweight youth who sent down a succession of leg-breaks, either overtossed or pitched outside leg stump. He told Faulkner to go and play with the juniors in their net. Faulkner slunk away to bowl at those he considered inferior. Ten minutes later he slipped unobtrusively into the queue of bowlers waiting for Sinclair. With the unshakeable confidence that was later to characterize his Test career, Faulkner pushed one through a bit faster and knocked down Sinclair's stumps.

Faulkner soon shed his puppy fat and by the time he reached adulthood stood 6ft tall with a powerful physique. His development as a cricketer was interrupted by the outbreak of the Boer War in 1899. His distinguished and lengthy service in the First World War eclipsed his involvement in the South African war, but when he enlisted in 1914 he gave his previous military experience as six months in the Imperial Light Horse. An account of Faulkner's life, written shortly after his suicide, said he served in the war as a gunner whose unit was attached to the Light Horse.

Towards the tail end of the war in 1902, Faulkner played a lot of cricket in Cape Town. But it was back in Johannesburg in 1903 that he began to be noticed by the cricketing fraternity. At Easter that year he played for Transvaal in the Currie Cup competition in Port Elizabeth. He was now an adequate provincial player but no more. His critics told him he must improve his technique. His run-up to the wicket, they said, was wrong. While his batting stance with both shoulders facing the bowler was too open. Faulkner might have been tempted to consider altering his style were it not for Reggie Schwarz.

Schwarz returned from England in 1904, having won a cricket blue at Cambridge and played rugby for England. He came home with a broadened mind, although what he had learned at Cambridge was of little interest to Faulkner. Schwarz had managed to wrest the secret of the 'wrong 'un' or 'googly', as it's better known, from its inventor, Bernard Bosanquet. It was the seminal moment in Faulkner's career.

The 'googly', still an effective weapon a hundred years later, is an off-break bowled to a right-handed batsman with the action of a leg-breaker. Once Schwarz had shown Faulkner the mechanics, he went away and perfected the art, becoming more proficient than his mentor and paving the way for a mesmeric entry into Test cricket. Just three years later, the legendary C B Fry said of Faulkner's destruction of the English batsmen at Headingley:

> 'His length was impeccable. He was dangerous and deceptive in the air. In an age when few batsmen believed it was possible to spot the "wrong 'un" from the action of the bowler's hand he only needed a little connivance from the wicket to be almost unplayable.'

When Pelham Warner brought an England XI to South Africa in 1905–6, Faulkner had the same unerring control over his 'googly' as he did over his leg-break and top-spinner. He had a deceptively short run-up – even then it still caused his critics to wince – but he managed to send the ball through the air much quicker than the average bowler of his type.

England had been sending sides to South Africa since 1888–9. The thought had never occurred that they might one day lose. It wouldn't have crossed the minds of Warner's side as they sailed towards the Cape. In the previous four tours England hadn't lost a game. Warner had made his Test debut on the 1898–9 tour and scored an unbeaten 132. He could hardly contain his excitement at the prospect of more easy pickings.

His illusions were rudely shattered. Before the Test series had even started, England's undefeated reign in South Africa was at an end. They lost by 60 runs to Transvaal at the Old Wanderers. Faulkner knew the ground like the back of his hand. He took six wickets in the match and scored 63 not out in the second innings. His display won him a Test call-up for the first Test. Faulkner was in luck. The venue was the Old Wanderers.

The South African selectors picked four leg-break bowlers. By the end of the series Bernard Bosanquet was not a popular man with his countrymen. One or two wanted him to stand trial for breaching the Official Secrets Act. The tourists had lost the series four Tests to one and the spinning quartet of Faulkner, Schwarz, Gordon White and Bert Vogler had routed the Englishmen.

Faulkner enjoyed his best match on his debut at the Old Wanderers. In England's second innings he finished with figures of four for 26. He had reined in the visitors' batsmen who had threatened at one stage to set an impossible run-chase for South Africa in their second innings. Faulkner ripped out the heart of their batting but the home side still needed 284 for victory.

They were 239 for nine when captain Percy Sherwell joined Dave Nourse at the crease. The two knocked off the winning runs, with Nourse finishing unbeaten on 93. South Africa had won their first Test. Pelham Warner took defeat gracefully, although in his memoirs there was a dash of pique as he reflected on the defeat: 'Men were shrieking hysterically, some were even crying, and hats and sticks were flying everywhere. For half an hour after it was all over, thousands lingered on and the whole of the SA XI had to come forward on the balcony.'

In 1907 South Africa toured overseas for the first time. They played three

Tests in England but rain ruined two. The only result came in a low-scoring encounter at Headingley where England won by 53 runs. Warner remarked later that 'The South Africans, if they did not win the rubber, left a great name behind them.' The name was Faulkner, outstanding even in a losing team. On a damp Leeds pitch, he made the ball slash knife-like off the pitch. He accounted for Haywood, Tyldesley, Braund, Jessop, Arnold and Lilley for 17 runs. England were all out for 76.

England bowler R E Foster wrote a paean for Faulkner in the 1908 *Wisden*: 'His performance at Leeds is surely the greatest that has been achieved in this unorthodox style of bowling.' What made Faulkner so hard to play, Foster went on to explain, was the way in which he gave the appearance of bowling a common leg-break, only to make the ball rise from the pitch with accelerated velocity. Then of course there was the dreaded 'wrong 'un'. Foster, an astute judge of the bowling art, surmised that the spin of the ball was imparted solely by finger and wrist action. In time, he said, great batsmen might soon begin to spot the 'wrong 'un'.

Faulkner, however, was not a man to wait for the opposition to catch up. He was barely down the gangplank after returning from England before he was back in the nets expanding his bowling repertoire. Such attention to detail was largely unheard of in an era that regarded too much practice as ungentlemanly. This was poppycock to Faulkner. He wasn't the most naturally blessed of cricketers but he decided to compensate by determination, patience and perseverance. 'With these tools,' wrote the *Johannesburg Star* in 1930, 'he worked and fashioned a style entirely his own. He constructed his own theory of successful play, and tried it out by ceaseless practice.' Consequently, not only his bowling improved, but he turned himself into a successful all-rounder.

Faulkner's batting had up to now been overshadowed by his bowling exploits. He had always been competent with the bat. Now he set about reinventing himself as a genuine Test all-rounder. He succeeded. Harry Altham in his *History of Cricket* wrote: 'Faulkner was a magnificent batsman. Though rather cramped at the start of an innings, he was a master of foot work and one of the greatest exponents of the hook stroke.'

Faulkner's all-round talents were at their zenith in 1909–10 when England arrived for a five-Test series. In the first Test at the Old Wanderers, always a happy hunting ground, he scored 78 of South Africa's first innings total of

208. England batted and Faulkner took five of their wickets. A century in the second innings was followed by a further three wickets as South Africa won by 19 runs. It was a formidable display, and there was more to come.

England were beaten in the second Test in Durban. Faulkner scored 47 in the first innings and finished with bowling figures of six for 87 in the tourists' second innings. Although the Englishmen fought back to win the third Test in Johannesburg, Faulkner scored 76 and 44, and took six wickets. In the fourth Test at Cape Town he had the honour of hitting the winning runs in an unbeaten 49. England claimed a consolation victory in the fifth Test but Faulkner frustrated them to the bitter end, scoring 99 in the second innings.

Gordon White played alongside Faulkner throughout that series. In *The History of South African Cricket,* he wrote about his former team-mate: 'I have played against many first class cricketers in my time, but if, as is often the case, one were asked to choose a World XI, Faulkner could never be left out. Not only was he a great batsman, but he took innumerable wickets in Test matches. It is said that Faulkner was not always himself at the start of his innings, but once he had played himself in, he had so many strokes that he was able to score all round the wicket.'

Faulkner was now feted by his countrymen as the best all-rounder in the game. Few Englishmen quibbled with such a view, but Australians asked how such an opinion could be formed when he hadn't tested himself Down Under. Faulkner and his fans had their chance when South Africa embarked upon their inaugural tour to Australia in 1910–11.

Faulkner soon discovered that his peculiar brand of spin wasn't suited to Australian pitches. Wickets didn't come as easily as they had back home or in England. Batting, however, was a different matter. In the five Test series he scored a record 732 runs, a series aggregate not surpassed until England's Herbert Sutcliffe scored 734 runs in Australia in 1924. In the second Test in Melbourne he cracked 204. One cricket correspondent reported that 'he made the iron spikes of the boundary fence ring like a tuning fork'. There was also a century in Adelaide, three half-centuries in Sydney, an 80 in Melbourne and 92 in the final Test at Sydney. Faulkner's average for a series that South Africa lost 4–1 was 73.

It was through such masterly performances that Faulkner earned selection in Pelham Warner's World XI, chosen to take on the Martians in his book *Cricket Reminiscences.* In a team that included immortals such as W G Grace,

Victor Trumper, Jack Hobbs, Frank Woolley, Sidney Barnes and K S Ranjitsinhji, Faulkner was given the nod. 'If the wicket is really sticky I shall play Mr Faulkner, vice Lockwood, as this would give us another batsman and a googly bowler.'

Faulkner never managed to scale such heights again as those he reached in Australia in 1910–11. He turned thirty in 1911 and his powers began to decline. When South Africa next toured England in 1913, Faulkner was already there, playing league cricket in Nottingham, and he didn't appear in any of the Tests. He didn't play his last Test, however, until 1924, when, in his forty-third year and living in England, he accepted an invitation to represent South Africa in the second Test at Lord's. Just about the only memorable feature of the match for Faulkner was the venue. That aside, it was not the way that he would have wished to finish his Test career. England won by an innings and 18 runs. Faulkner scored 25 and 12, and failed to take an English wicket in 17 overs.

It was one of the few low points of a stupendous career. He was arguably the most gifted all-rounder of his generation. In 25 Tests he had taken 82 wickets at 26.58 runs apiece and scored 1,754 runs – an average of 40.79.

The question now was what next. His cricket ability had atrophied during the war years, yet life without cricket for Faulkner was barely tolerable. He had been teaching irregular verbs and a straight bat to little boys in a Surrey prep school, but that didn't stretch his coaching powers.

His ambition was to open an indoor cricket school. That had been his dream during the war, on the few occasions when he dared think of a future beyond a Royal Field Artillery Battery. In 1925 he rented a disused garage in Richmond, Surrey, and installed two nets. He began to spread the word that if anyone fancied improving their game they knew where to come. One or two popped their heads round the garage door, then a few more, until the trickle became a steady flow.

Six months after opening the school – the first of its kind in England – demand began to outstrip supply and Faulkner was forced to up stumps and move to bigger premises. He rented a vacant bus garage in Walham Green, large enough for four nets, changing room, a restaurant and offices.

The success of the school was down to the dedication of Faulkner. He had set himself high standards as a player and he now expected his pupils to push themselves equally hard. He also possessed the priceless gift for any aspiring coach, what are now called man-management skills. 'Some he goaded on with almost parade ground methods,' recalled Tom Reddick, who was coached by Faulkner in his teens. 'The more timid he encouraged and led with a much lighter rein, and no change or correction was ever suggested to a pupil unless accompanied with a sound explanation as to the whys and wherefores.'

He also employed unconventional methods. Walter Robins, then a Cambridge University player, turned up at the school seeking a cure for his high backlift. Faulkner stretched a slim plank of wood across the net to check Robins' backlift and bowled at him for hours on end. Every time the net reverberated to the sound of willow on wood, Faulkner would bellow 'Too high' and the next ball Robins made sure he played with a lower backlift.

Robins went on to play for England, as did many others who passed through Faulkner's production line. Douglas Jardine captained England in the notorious 'Bodyline' series against Australia in 1932–3. Freddie Brown was another future England captain whose skills were honed in the unlikely surroundings of a South London bus garage. Ian Peebles, Doug Wright and K S Duleepsinhji enjoyed fruitful Test careers after Faulkner had tightened a few nuts and bolts.

Pelham Warner would pop in to the school if he was passing and watch his old rival at work. He later wrote in his autobiography, *Long Innings*, that Faulkner had 'a considerable influence at this period on our [England's] cricket … He was a great coach, who encouraged his pupils and was neither too rigid nor too theoretical. He encouraged and did not crab, imparted a pleasant atmosphere, and made the practices great fun. He knew everything there is to know of the various departments of the game, and his book *Cricket: Can it be taught?* was a masterpiece.' Warner wrote the foreword for the book, which was published in 1926. It was a no-frills instruction manual that contained detailed analysis of the techniques needed to be a success. There were also several photographs of a rotund Faulkner practising what he preached.

His portliness didn't prevent him turning his arm competitively when called upon, albeit reluctantly at times. William Pollock, a county cricketer who became cricket correspondent for the *Daily Express*, remembered an encounter with Faulkner in a charity match in the late 1920s: 'In two overs Faulkner sent me down about twelve different kind of balls, hardly any one of which I got the bat against, and at last, probably fed up with me, bowled me neck and crop with a very quick off-break for which I was hours late.'

In 1928 Faulkner was inveigled into appearing in a match to mark the opening of Essex's new ground at Chelmsford. Faulkner hadn't played cricket outdoors for over two years and was concerned that the middle-aged man he now was might become the object of the crowd's ridicule. The invitational XI, however, had such faith in Faulkner that they concealed his identity from the Essex players. They didn't want their secret weapon launched until the time was right. After half an hour standing at slip, Faulkner was brought on to bowl. He took seven wickets and left the Essex team in a frightful kerfuffle. Dudley Pope, a highly regarded young batsman, was one of his victims. Muttering profanities as he trudged back to the pavilion, Pope glanced the way of his tormentor: 'I don't know who you are, sir, but my word, you bowl a bloody good wrong 'un.'

By 1929 the school was flourishing, yet Faulkner continued to push himself relentlessly. The previous year he had married Alice Butcher at a registry office. After the ceremony they had brought a bottle of champagne back to the school. Faulkner broke his self-imposed alcohol ban momentarily, enjoying a glass, but he was back coaching in the nets by the afternoon. Bob Wyatt joined the school's staff in 1929, a year before he captained England for the first time. It was a chastening experience. 'I never remember being so tired. We worked from 10am to 7.30pm, each pupil being allowed fifteen minutes in the net. Aubrey was anxious not to waste time. So we were not allowed to walk to the batsman's end and give advice; we had to conduct our tuition from halfway.'

Although the number of pupils passing through the school each year showed no signs of slowing, Faulkner began to fret about financial matters. To alleviate his anxiety he redoubled his efforts in the nets, never turning away a student. A degree of ambidexterity allowed him to bowl with either arm, so when his right became stiff, he would switch to the left. Tom Reddick, now on the coaching staff, noticed a change in Faulkner. 'He looked tired and began to worry over things that never disturbed him before.'

Faulkner also began to be troubled by illness. At the tail end of 1929 he spent some time in hospital. A corollary of this poor health was depression. On the cricket field he had been regarded as implacable, now he became tetchy.

Any mental problems Faulkner might have suffered would have been exacerbated by his personality. He had always been something of a loner, even though he had many friends. A brusque exterior fended away those he didn't wish to know better, but the few he admitted to his inner circle found him sensitive, witty and intelligent. But Faulkner rarely opened himself completely, even to his wife. He was, after all, a Victorian at heart, and such men didn't care for displays of public emotion.

Even his war record was a subject he didn't like to discuss. When Reddick asked what he had done to merit a DSO, he flicked the question away as if it were a legside long-hop:

> 'I was never quite sure. But whenever an order was received to fire, I insisted on immediate response from my battery. I never found out how many Turkish wickets we took, but our enthusiasm certainly pleased the colonel.'

Such modesty distorted Faulkner's army service. He had served in what were rather blithely dismissed at the time as the 'sideshows' of the First World War, Macedonia and Palestine. Yet his battery was heavily involved in operations in Salonika in 1916 and 1917, and in 1918 Faulkner took part in the Battle of Armageddon, the biggest British offensive that year outside the Western Front. The British soldiers on the Western Front disparaged those further east, calling them 'The Gardeners of Salonika'. Men posted from France to Salonika arrived flushed with joy at their good fortune. Within a few weeks their hopes for a 'cushy' number had been squashed like one of the thousands of mosquitoes that plagued the British army in Salonika.

One Irish officer who served in Salonika regarded it as a hellish place, its miseries unknown to those in France and Belgium. 'We had to contend not so much with the malice of the enemy, as with homesickness, dearth of leave, surfeit of bully beef, absence of feminine society, the attentions of mosquitoes, flies and other insects, dysentery, septic sores and malaria.'

Disease accounted for more British soldiers in Macedonia than enemy action. At one time or another 400,000 troops served in Salonika, yet the official figure for men falling sick was 481,000. The cause was recurrent malaria. G Ward Price, who was a war correspondent in Macedonia, wrote a book about his experiences after the war and devoted a large chunk to the curse of the mosquito. 'Your symptoms are a high temperature combined with a chilly feeling; you can't stand the sight of food. You probably have a headache; you tremble all over, and you simply have to go to bed and shiver and sweat alternately until the attack is over. This sort of thing repeated several times leaves you very thin and weak.'

For the soldiers, unfortunately, bed wasn't always an option. There was a war going on. The British were in Macedonia to help the Serbs and French fight the Bulgarians. In the autumn of 1915 Bulgaria had invaded Serbia and Britain and France answered a call for assistance from the Serbs. The co-operation of the Allies wasn't entirely on account of poor, down-trodden Serbia. They saw it as a chance to erect a barrier across Germany's direct road to Turkey, thus preventing two hostile powers mastering the whole of the Balkan Peninsula. Germany was quite content to let Britain and France redirect thousands of soldiers from the Western Front to the Balkans. They came to call Salonika 'the greatest Allied Internment Camp' of the war.

Faulkner had joined up in September 1914, just a few weeks after the outbreak of war. He arrived at the Nottingham recruitment office in search of a commission. He had with him a reference that would have pleased any red-blooded recruitment officer. Francis Lacey, Secretary of the MCC, vouched that Faulkner was of 'good, moral character'. The interviewing officer concurred: 'Except that he is thirty-two years of age, I recommend him in view of having served for six months in the Imperial Light Horse.' He joined the Worcestershire Regiment as a Second Lieutenant, but a short while later transferred to the Royal Field Artillery.

After several months training in England, Faulkner sailed from Avonmouth in June 1915 to Alexandria in Egypt. From there he embarked for Salonika, arriving in October. Once off the troopships the British wasted no time in advancing north into Macedonia to help the Serbs beat off the invading Bulgarians. But they were too late. They headed inland only to discover the Serbs retreating across the Albania mountains. The British withdrew and decided on a defensive strategy while they readied themselves for an offensive in 1916.

Faulkner, like thousands of other fighting soldiers, found himself digging an entrenchment camp around the perimeter of Salonika. Gradually, throughout the spring of 1916, the Allies inched northwards towards the

Greek frontier, a tortuous advance hampered by the lack of roads and railways in the primitive countryside. Here they dug in and prepared for an autumn offensive against the Bulgarians.

All the while, conditions for the soldiers were becoming more unpleasant. Faulkner was in the 57th Brigade and their war diary during the summer of 1916 recorded the travails. On 14 July: 'Great heat [the temperature regularly topped 100 degrees] and sickness continues. Units on average have 20 per cent of their strength off parade. Training restricted to the early hours of the morning and late in the afternoon.'

Faulkner transferred to the 67th Brigade in August 1916 but there was no respite. On 26 August, the diary was devoted to the water shortage:

'The question of water both for horses and for drinking is getting very serious. The horses do not get enough to drink owing to the scarcity of the water and the large number of units that have to use it, and they are seriously falling away in condition on account of this. Drinking water for the men is only to be obtained from wells which are picketed by the 28th Div. RAHQ was informed of this and we asked to be allowed to draw water from the well.'

Faulkner was now on the Struma Plain. The Struma River ran through the plain, considered one of the most fertile stretches of ground in Europe. Which is why it was also considered one of the most dangerous malarial belts anywhere in the world. To the British Tommy, it was known as 'The Valley of Death'. The soldiers' only defence against the mosquitoes was a daily five-grain dose of quinine. It was as effective as using a cricket bat to fend off enemy shells. Ward Price guessed that the mosquitoes were 'scarcely able to believe their good fortune' when thousands of British soldiers marched onto the Struma Plain. 'With infuriating high-pitched buzz ... the mosquitoes alighted on every square inch of exposed anatomy, and caroused from dusk to dawn.'

Faulkner went down with malaria on 2 September. He was admitted to hospital but was discharged in time to participate in his first major action of the war, the start of the Allies' offensive against the Bulgarians. While the Serbs, French and Russians launched a full-scale assault against the town of Monastir on 13 September, the British attacked some heavily fortified villages on the other side of the Struma River, tying up several thousand Bulgarians who otherwise would reinforce Monastir.

For nearly three weeks, Faulkner commanded 'D' Battery of 67th Brigade in a series of artillery barrages against the Bulgarians. The biggest was on the last day of September when his Brigade bombarded the village of Zir. Ward Price witnessed the fury of the British artillery. 'Three hundred and thirty 6-inch shells had fallen into the village in the last five minutes. Then Zir slowly emerged again, but smashed and battered into a shape that its oldest inhabitant would not have recognized.'

The next day the Bulgarians launched a counter-attack and for several hours Faulkner's battery was subjected to 'constant shelling' by enemy guns. He endured the punishment, perhaps unconsciously adopting the philosophy of Winston Churchill who, in 1916, wrote that 'meeting an artillery attack is like catching a cricket ball. Shock is dissipated by drawing back the hands. A little "give", a little suppleness, and the violence of the impact is vastly reduced'. Two days later Faulkner directed his battery's fire on to the village of Jenikoj, before laying down a creeping barrage under which the Royal Munsters and Royal Dublin Fusiliers advanced to take the village.

During the winter of 1916–17 there was a period of enforced inactivity for both sides as a bitter winter made any movement impossible. In May 1917 Faulkner, now with the 57 Brigade, was in Yenikoi, Greece, still playing cat and mouse with the Bulgarian artillery. On 24 May, Faulkner's battery came under a prolonged spell of bombardment. He was reported in the war diary as saying 'there were some very large detonations to the right of D/57'. That wasn't the most noteworthy entry in the diary that day, however. In among the high explosive shells Faulkner had heard an 'unusual sound [which] on bursting was not as loud as an ordinary burst'. Every ear in an artillery battery was attuned to such a noise for it meant only one thing. Gas. Faulkner and his men frantically donned their masks, but no more such shells came their way.

In August 1917 Faulkner was posted to 67th Brigade to command 'A' Battery. The following month the Brigade moved out of Greece and embarked for the Palestine Front. British and Turkish troops had been fighting each other for control of Palestine since 1915, but for much of that time there had been nothing but stalemate. The British, however, wanted to make a decisive breakthrough and in June had appointed General Allenby to revivify the campaign.

Faulkner's first action in Palestine was in November when his Brigade took part in an offensive that pushed the Turks back from the Beersheba-Gaza line they had held for two years to a line south-west of Jerusalem. The British continued their thrust towards the holy city until, on 11 December, Allenby rode into Jerusalem at the head of a triumphant Allied army. The fall of the city was of little importance to the Germans but it was a shot in the arm for the British, whose morale had been badly shaken by the scale of losses during the battle for Passchendaele and the disappointment at Cambrai.

Faulkner wasn't one of those entering Jerusalem in December clinging to Allenby's riding breeches, although on 6 January he attended a Thanksgiving in the city at St George's Church. He was back at the end of the month, three days of leave allowing him time to explore in greater depth.

The first six months of 1918 were quiet for Faulkner. Allenby had been plotting a final, massive British offensive to drive the Turkish forces from Palestine but events elsewhere forced him to delay. At the end of March 1918 Germany launched the Kaiserschlacht Offensive along the Western Front and Allenby was ordered to send 60,000 of his best troops to help stem the German tide. Reluctantly, he was forced to postpone the attack until autumn.

A cloud of ennui descended upon the British troops. With no infantry advances to support they had little to do except send over the odd salvo to keep the Turks on their toes. As boredom began to afflict the men, so did sickness. Faulkner was admitted to hospital on 2 June. He returned to his battery six days later, to learn that he had been awarded the Distinguished Service Order for his conduct in Egypt and Palestine. At least that gave him something to write about in his letters home. On 21 June Faulkner fell sick again. This time the war diary gave the cause, malaria. He rejoined his battery eight days later but he was clearly suffering from the illness he first contracted two years earlier.

The Brigade organized a Sports Day on 5 September in an attempt to dissipate the men's lethargy. Faulkner was on the organizing committee and they even went to the trouble of printing a programme. The event opened with a 100-metre sprint and included the sack race, tug of war, wrestling on horseback and vaulting. The Open Mile was scheduled to take place at 1430 hours, but was cancelled for lack of entrants. Fighting the Turks was a duty, running a mile for the sake of it was just plain stupidity.

The sports were a much-needed distraction but by now the men knew the months of waiting were nearly at an end. Troops, horses and guns had all been arriving at the front for the past few weeks and by mid-September Allenby was satisfied everything was ready. The Turks, while they had been waiting for some sort of assault, had no idea that facing them across the shimmering heat of the desert were 57,000 infantry, 12,000 cavalry and 540 artillery guns. It was the biggest British offensive of 1918 outside the Western Front, and it was a resounding success.

The Battle of Megiddo, also known as the Battle of Armageddon, began at dawn on 19 September. By late afternoon the Turkish HQ at Tel Karm, 25 miles behind their front lines, was in British hands, as were 7,000 prisoners and 100 guns. Faulkner's battery supported an advance made by the token French colonial force involved in the action. For the next four days they continued to throw their weight behind infantry advances as the Turks retreated towards Damascus. A week after the initial attack, the British had accepted the surrender of 50,000 Turkish soldiers. On 1 October Damascus fell and by the end of the month Turkey had ceased hostilities.

The Battle of Megiddo had brought Turkey to its knees. It was a triumph for Allenby and the British High Command, but as ever the real credit belonged to the soldiers on the front line. In the months before the battle they had suffered greatly from heat, insects, disease and boredom. It had reached the stage where the men craved action. Anything was better than sitting on their arses, swatting flies and dreaming of supping a pint in their local. The monotony had led some of the men to seek a more comfy time in the hospital. Yet when called upon after months of inactivity they delivered a powerful knockout punch to the Turks. This was noted by the brigade war diarist after the battle: 'Health of men – good. At the beginning of the month whilst the Bde was in rest, admissions to hospital, chiefly with recurrent malaria and diarrhoea, were above the average. In action, admissions to hospital were practically nil.'

Faulkner was sent on three weeks' leave in late October and with fortuitous timing he was in England when Turkey threw in the towel. He was given a UK posting, and another decoration, the Order of the Nile, fourth class, awarded by the Sultan of Egypt for his part in the Battle of Megiddo. If

Faulkner hadn't been so abstemious he might have celebrated with a quiet pint.

In the parlance of the time, Faulkner had enjoyed a 'good war'. A DSO, an exotic Egyptian medal to impress the ladies, and twice mentioned in despatches. Few other international cricketers could boast of such a record. But where the war had given, it had taken. Faulkner's medals were pinned on a chest much shrunken from the one that had been measured in the recruiting office four years earlier. Recurrent malaria had weakened him considerably, while a constant diet of bully beef and biscuits had also added to his ailing physical appearance. As he strolled down the street in his major's uniform, few would have guessed that this scrawny, haggard-looking officer was in fact only thirty-seven.

There were also mental scars. Faulkner had suffered during the war, but how much he kept to himself. One can speculate as to how the effect of shelling would have frayed his nerves, but speculation can often fall wide of the mark. Perhaps the most graphic way to convey some idea of what he endured is to quote from a book that was published in 1945 called *The Anatomy of Courage*. Its author was Lord Moran, a medical officer in the First World War, who later became physician to Winston Churchill. In his book, Moran drew on his experiences in the trenches to examine courage in all its various forms and suggest how armies might best preserve the courage of their soldiers. He had faced bullets and bayonets during the war, but had no doubt that 'the acid test of the man in the trenches was high explosives; it told each one of us things about ourselves we had not known till then.' With chilling frankness he then described how his first experience of shellfire had left fragments of fear embedded in his subconscious. 'The war had never been the same since, something in the will had snapped … once it happened it was always there, and every shell that fell near the trench seemed to be but the beginning of a new cataclysm. At the time I do not think I was much frightened, I was too stunned to think. But it took its toll later. Even when the war had begun to fade out of men's minds I used to hear all at once without warning the sound of a shell coming. Perhaps it was only the wind in the trees to remind me that war had exacted its tribute.'

Maybe Faulkner, standing in the nets coaching his pupils, was sometimes reminded of a narrow escape in Salonika by the fizzing of a ball as it sailed back past his ear from the bat of a straight drive. If he was, he kept such flashbacks to himself. Although his occasional mood swings hadn't gone unnoticed, none of his friends considered him suicidal. The day before he died Faulkner was reported to have been in 'good spirits'. His wife had suggested a short holiday in Paris the following week. To her delight he had agreed.

Thus the final bout of depression that led to Faulkner's death seems not to have crept up on him like one of the barrages he used to lay down for the infantry, but instead tore him apart suddenly, like a stray shell from an eighteen-pounder.

On the night of 9 September 1930, Faulkner hadn't arrived home by the time his wife went to bed. She was used to his long hours and wasn't unduly worried. But when she woke the next morning and it was plain he hadn't returned she became alarmed.

As she was making her way to the school in search of her husband, Mr Mackenzie, the secretary of the school, was opening up the premises. Almost at once he smelled gas. The trail took him to one of the bat-drying rooms, used to dry bats in the process of the manufacture. He found Faulkner slumped on the floor, his mouth over one of the gas radiator jets. When the police surgeon examined the body at 9.45am, he estimated that Faulkner had been dead no longer than four hours.

At the inquest a few days later, the coroner asked Mrs Faulkner if her husband had ever before threatened to take his own life. 'Only once, definitely,' she replied. 'In exactly the same way as he did do it – by gas.' She also reported the breakdown in his health and that it had left him very depressed and 'temperamental'. She agreed with the coroner's suggestion that perhaps Faulkner had found the business affairs of the school too much for a man in his health. The coroner concluded that: 'He killed himself while in a state of unsound mind.'

His death shattered the cricket community. Pelham Warner, who had enjoyed so many tussles with Faulkner in England and South Africa, said: 'I am terribly grieved; the news was a fearful shock to me. Faulkner was a wonderful cricketer – one of the greatest in the world – and as a man he was one of the finest friends I have known.' Jack Hobbs was equally stunned: 'I can hardly believe the news. He was very cheery when we were speaking together over the wireless last week. He was a delightful personality and a wonderful cricketer.'

Faulkner's achievements have become shrouded in the fog of time, but his Test record bears comparison with the great all-rounders. He scored 1,754 runs and averaged 40.79, superior to Ian Botham, Imran Khan, Kapil Dev, Richie Benaud, Learie Constantine and Keith Miller. Only the greatest of them all, Sobers, can boast a better batting average. But Faulkner could point to a bowling average superior to that of the West Indian legend. His 82 Test wickets cost him a parsimonious 26.58 runs each.

Faulkner rose to prominence through his bowling prowess. Although he was proud of his batting feats, nothing gave him greater pleasure than winkling out a batsman with one of his googlies. And if, on that bleak September morning as he slipped into unconsciousness, his mind drifted back to the past, one can only hope that the images he saw were not of twisted, charred bodies on a battlefield, but of glories won on the cricket field, and the tribute once paid to him by W G Grace: 'When bowled well at the pace of Faulkner, the googly is the most difficult ball to play that was ever sent down the length of a cricket pitch.'

CHAPTER TEN

Herby Taylor

Herby Taylor remains one of the greatest batsmen in the history of Test cricket. He made his debut for South Africa in 1912 but some of his best years were then lost to the First World War. Taylor served first as a gunner and then as a pilot. He came through the horrors intact and returned to the crease determined to make up for lost time.

Herby Taylor stood on the balcony and addressed the delirious Johannesburg crowd: 'In recent years we have had a steep hill to climb, and I think today we have reached the top, and can always now look forward to giving other sides a good fight in the Tests.'

Taylor had the crowd eating out of his hand. Their adulation belonged to him. The other ten players who had taken part in the victory over England were incidental to the celebrations. Taylor's innings of 176 had won South Africa the match. The *Cape Times* succinct headline the next day encapsulated its readers' feelings: 'TAYLOR'S TRIUMPH'. The England captain, F H Mann, called it a 'magnificent innings ... he realized the responsibility that rested upon himself and he won the match for his side'.

Taylor's innings in the first Test of the 1922–3 series against England reinforced the widely held view that he was the greatest batsman South

Africa had produced. His footwork was immaculate and he was able to adapt his technique to suit the matted pitches of South Africa or the grass wickets of England and Australia. His durability was equally impressive. He was thirty-three when he butchered Mann's English bowling attack. He made the last of his forty-two Test appearances in the 1931-2 series against Australia and New Zealand. Even at forty-two he was able to despatch the likes of Bill O'Reilly, Clarrie Grimmett and Tim Wall to the boundary ropes.

His claim that South Africa had 'reached the top' in 1922 might have been slightly premature but Taylor's batting performances were the inspiration for future generations. His example provided the scaffolding for the construction of a much sturdier batting order in the late 1930s that included Alan Melville, Bruce Mitchell, Dudley Nourse and Eric Rowan. In 1998, John Woodcock, the highly respected former cricket correspondent of *The Times,* selected Taylor among his hundred greatest players of all time. And this despite the fact that he lost the prime years of his cricketing life – generally considered to be the late twenties for an opening batsman – to the First World War.

Researching Taylor's war record was as exasperating, one imagines, as bowlers found it trying to remove him from the crease. He followed one of his South African team-mates, Aubrey Faulkner, into the RFA [Royal Field Artillery] and displayed similar courage. Unfortunately, Taylor's army service record has been lost and so details of his enlistment are not known. He served initially with the Special Reserve of the RFA, but was attached to 147 Brigade at the end of 1916. This brigade served on the Western Front throughout 1916, and was heavily involved in providing artillery fire before and during the opening phases of the Battle of the Somme on 1 July.

In January 1917 Taylor was awarded the Military Cross. Unfortunately 147 Brigade's war diary, otherwise intact, is missing the month of January 1917, so the circumstances surrounding his MC remain a mystery. However, at the start of 1917, the Brigade were still on the Somme. They were near Mesnil, a village about a mile from the trenches and an area in which British troops were advised not to dawdle. The road from Martinsart to Mesnil was the main artery into the battle zone and the Germans shelled it heavily and frequently. The shells that screamed over Aveluy Wood left huge depressions in the road that unnerved even the strongest of men. The poet Edmund Blunden wrote in his memoirs of a night he accompanied a transport limber along the road to the front line. The limber slipped into a crater and had to be unloaded. As Blunden helped unload it, 'his flesh crept at the delay in such a deadly place'.

The citation for Taylor's MC, published in March, read:

> 'For conspicuous gallantry and devotion to duty. He carried out the observation for wire cutting under very heavy fire with conspicuous success.'

There was no major offensive in this area in January 1917, so the wire-cutting that Taylor observed was probably the prelude to a raid on enemy trenches by the infantry, the purpose of which would have been to bring back a prisoner for interrogation. Wire-cutting by the artillery was an imprecise art at this time. The failure to cut the German barbed wire prior to the first day of the Battle of the Somme had taken a terrible toll of the British infantry. They were cut down as they searched frantically for a way through the barbed wire entanglements in no man's land. The failure to cut the wire, as much the fault of the shells themselves as the men who fired them, led the British to introduce a new type of percussion fuse in 1917.

But in January Taylor and his comrades would have been using the old methods. This involved firing a shrapnel shell that burst about 20 feet above the ground. The theory was that the bullets from the shell would destroy the wire entanglements. That was the theory. The reality was different. The success of the shrapnel shell was dependent on the accurate setting of the time fuse but these had, as Major James Marshall-Cornwall, an intelligence officer on the GHQ Staff, later admitted, '… a lot of manufacturing faults … they didn't all burn the right length and, I'm afraid, a lot of the half-trained gunners of the New Army didn't set the fuses exactly accurate. The fact was that many of the shells burst too high and the bullets dropped into the ground, or the fuse didn't work and it buried itself into the ground so the wire was left.'

As an observation officer, Taylor's job would have been to report back to the battery commander the effect of the shelling on the wire. Second Lieutenant Kenneth Page served on the Somme with the artillery and remembered the problems of wire-cutting: 'It wasn't an easy thing to do. You had to do it very slowly and very deliberately. You would go plugging away at one short stretch of wire … the tendency was for a gap to get cut here and then a gap got cut a little way along there.'

Taylor clearly took his observational duties above and beyond the call of duty. One can infer from the citation that as the British began shelling the enemy wire, the Germans retaliated with a barrage of their own. Taylor, however, ignoring the shells that fell around him, crawled out into no man's land to check the accuracy of his brigade's fire. This required not only great courage but also nerves of proverbial steel. As an artilleryman himself, Taylor would have been fully aware of the lethality of the shells screaming overhead, both in terms of their explosive content and their tendency to drift wide or drop short of their intended target, which in this case could well mean on top of him. He nonetheless conquered his fear and, judging from the wording of the citation, his subsequent report contributed to the success of the wire-cutting.

Towards the end of March 1917 the Brigade left the Somme and marched north towards Vimy Ridge to assist an assault by Canadian troops on a strategically important position that overlooked the town of Arras, but Taylor missed this particular scrap. Two days earlier 147 Brigade's war diary had noted that: 'Second Lieutenant Taylor, MC, left to join the RFC [Royal Flying Corps].'

Taylor was probably relieved to get out of the trenches. He might not have been so eager had he known what was going on in the clouds above him as he departed for England to become a pilot. The RFC called it 'Bloody April'. Over 150 aircraft were brought down with 316 airmen killed or posted as missing. The life expectancy of new pilots fell to just seventeen days. The Germans had a new Albatross aircraft, superior to anything the British possessed at the time, and in the hands of a genius like Baron Manfred von Richthofen, it blasted the inexperienced RFC pilots out of the sky.

Taylor, paradoxically, probably owed his life to the efficiency of the Germans. The scale of British losses so appalled MPs and the public that guidelines were introduced that stipulated all new pilots must spend a certain amount of time in the air before being posted to France on active service. Although some preposterously undertrained young pilots were still sent to France in the latter half of 1917, it had gradually dawned on senior RFC officers that there was no benefit to be gained by continuing such a policy.

Taylor's service records in the RFC indicate that he never flew any combat missions over the Western Front. He spent 1917 in England and then, on

4 April 1918, three days after the Royal Flying Corps had merged with the Royal Naval Air Service to form the Royal Air Force, he joined 194 Training Squadron. In July he joined 14 TDS (Training Depot Station) as an instructor and in September went on a pilots' course in southern England. This might have been on the instructions of his commanding officer after Taylor was involved in an embarrassing incident one summer weekend. He had flown down to Devon to visit some friends but was forced to ditch the plane when he ran out of oil. He made an impromptu landing on the shores of the Bristol Channel, although the plane ended up in the water. He was dragged to safety by some startled bathers, one of whom was a cricket fan. When he realized he was in the presence of Herby Taylor, nothing became too much of a problem and attention was lavished upon him until the RAF came to retrieve their missing airman.

Taylor was discharged from the RAF in May 1919, shortly after his thirtieth birthday. He remained in England for a few months and took the opportunity to improve his technique on the grass. He turned out for various guest XIs that summer as the sport made its way back into the public's consciousness. Playing for Lionel Robertson's XI against the Australian Imperial Forces, he made 19 and 16.

When Taylor finally returned to South Africa in 1920 few people thought he could recapture the form of the pre-war years. Taylor was thirty-one. He hadn't played first-class cricket for over six years. One of his great strengths had been his footwork. This was complemented by superb reactions. He was able to decide how to play a ball a split second quicker than most other batsmen. Few cricketers possess this enviable quality of making batting appear easy. But Taylor's career had been quiescent for six years. Wouldn't such gifts have been blunted by the passing of time?

Taylor's pre-war fame had been built almost entirely on his duel with England's Sydney Barnes in the 1913–14 Test series in South Africa. In the 1912 Triangular series against England and Australia, when he made his Test debut, he had struggled on the grass wickets of England, making only 194 runs in six Tests. The transition from the matted pitches he had been brought up on to those of grass proved hard for a young batsman still feeling his way in Test cricket. But when Johnny Douglas brought his England team over in 1913–14 Taylor felt much more confident on a surface whose vagaries he knew.

Taylor respected the skills of Barnes, but he didn't fear him The cataplexy that afflicted other batsmen in the presence of Barnes never got a hold of Taylor. He relished the challenge of facing the man who at that time was regarded as the world's best. The irascible Englishman bowled leg-breaks and off-spinners at medium pace. He could also roll one for a top-spinner that was, according to Taylor, 'very difficult to detect'. If the conditions were right Barnes would open the bowling and the vicious away-swingers he was prone to send down took the outside edge of many an opening bat.

After his travails in the Triangular Tournament, Taylor had sought the help of South Africa's spinning quartet of Aubrey Faulkner, Bert Vogler, Gordon White and Reggie Schwarz. They bowled hundreds of deliveries to Taylor in the nets and by the time Barnes had arrived in South Africa, he was ready for him.

> 'I'd learnt to watch a bowler's finger movements as he delivered the ball. This made me quite confident that I would be able to handle Barnes … but I doubt very much if anybody took me seriously. In those days you only had to mention Barnes' name to have batsmen scurrying for cover.'

In the first Test at Durban, Taylor's assiduity had its reward. Barnes took 5 for 57 as South Africa were dismissed for 182, of which Taylor scored 109. Despite Barnes' bowling figures, *The Times* wrote that 'the feature of the first day's play was undoubtedly the innings of 109 by Mr H W Taylor, the South African captain. To score 109 out of a total of 182 in a Test is a performance which speaks for itself.' At the post-match banquet, Johnny Douglas called Taylor 'one of the greatest players South Africa has produced'.

But the century masked the inadequacies of Taylor's team-mates. Herbert Strudwick, the England wicketkeeper, said Barnes had made them look ordinary. Remove the joist, said the English, and the house would collapse. Taylor was out for eight in the second innings and his side crumpled to 111. England had won by an innings and 157 runs.

Barnes and Taylor squared up to one another in the second Test and it was the South African who had to be helped back to his corner. He scored 29 and 40 and Barnes got him twice, plus a further fifteen wickets, to finish with extraordinary figures of 17 for 159. In the third Test Taylor could claim a points victory. He scored 70 and Barnes, although he took eight wickets in the match, didn't count Taylor among his victims.

Taylor now felt he was on top in the personal contest with Barnes, even if South Africa had lost the first three Tests. The method he employed to nullify the threat of Barnes was simple.

> 'I kept my eyes glued to the ball in his hands as he ran up to the wicket. And just before he delivered it I would switch my eyes to about a yard above his head to catch any finger movement as the ball left his hand. It was no use picking up the ball after it has left the hand of a bowler like Barnes because you would have no idea of what it would do off the pitch.'

The two met again in England's nineteenth match of the tour. It wasn't a Test. Rather, Natal hosted the tourists in what was meant to be a relaxing game between the third and fourth Tests in South Africa's most English of cities. It turned into cricket's equivalent of a showdown between the two toughest gunslingers in the land. And it was Barnes who was run out of town.

The two sides had met earlier in the tour and Taylor had helped himself to 83 runs in the absence of a sick Barnes. England batted first in the return match and slumped to 132 all out. Taylor then scored 91 to give Natal a first innings lead of 21. The only other Natalian to make double figures was Chapman, with 11. England made 235 in the second innings to set the home side 215 to win.

Natal lost two quick wickets and Taylor was joined at the crease by Dave Nourse. 'From the start he was in the soup against Barnes,' Taylor recalled many years later. 'Somehow he survived the few overs to lunch. He and I took a couple of sandwiches and went and sat apart from the others. "Herby," he confided in me, "I can't play this blighter. That darn top-spinner of his is impossible to spot."'

After the interval Taylor shielded Nourse from Barnes as much as possible. But in doing so he exposed himself to the Englishman's potency. On 49, he edged one to slip. It was put down. 'His wrath was something to behold,' said the South African. Flustered, Taylor now decided to put into practice the old cricket adage that attack is the best form of defence. In the next three overs he struck Barnes for 32. Barely able to contain his rage at such impudence,

Barnes snatched his cap from the umpire and stormed down to the boundary ropes where he bubbled with rage and indignation.

At the start of his fourth over, Barnes suddenly exploded in fury. 'Taylor!' he screamed, hurling the ball to the ground, 'it's always Taylor.' The focus of Barnes' apoplexy stood mouth agape at the other end of the wicket. 'Without another word, he stalked off the field, while Johnny Douglas pleaded with him to carry on. We were later told that Barnes had stormed into the dressing room, whipped off his shirt, and had a nice wash-up. Then he stretched himself out and drank several whiskies!'

Nourse had never been so pleased to see Barnes' backside disappearing up the pavilion steps. With his nemesis gone, Nourse settled down and compiled a steady half-century. Then he suddenly took a wild swing at Wilfred Rhodes and was caught on the boundary. 'For Heaven's sake, Dave,' said Taylor, as Nourse passed him on his way to the dressing room. 'Why did you do that?' Nourse nodded his head in the direction of the pavilion. 'That *!# is coming back! I saw him getting ready on the verandah.'

The return of Barnes was to no avail. Nourse and Taylor, who was dismissed on an even hundred, had steered Natal to a deserved win against the tourists.

In the fourth Test, Barnes kept a lid on his temper and twice took the wicket of Taylor but not before he had scored 93 in the second innings. It was a subdued knock, lasting three hours and 25 minutes. The *Johannesburg Star* wrote that it 'was not characterized by his usual attractiveness. His strokes included only four 4s, no fewer than 60 of his runs being singles.' But it was the consolidating innings required by his team. It enabled South Africa to set England a target of 313. When bad light brought a halt to play on the final day, the tourists were in trouble at 154 for five.

The drawn fourth Test was the only relief for South Africa in the series. They lost the fifth and final Test, even without the menace of Barnes, who was, according to whoever one chose to believe, either unfit or sulking over a financial squabble with the South African cricket authorities. Taylor's last innings of the series brought him 87 more runs, a result, said the *Star*, of 'splendid wristwork … he rapidly settled down and treated the crowd to an exhibition of ideal batmanship'.

Taylor's wristwork complemented his footwork. Both had been perfected in his bedroom as a young boy, much to the despair of his mother. 'I would draw chalk lines all over the floor,' he explained. 'Had it not been for my father she would probably have put a stop to the whole project.'

Taylor didn't resort to chalk in 1920, but the technique that had brought him 508 runs against England in 1913–14, at an average of 50.8, needed to be reshaped after the disruption of the war. By 1920–1 the fluency had begun to return to his game. He scored 150 for Natal against Orange Free State in his first Currie Cup match since 1913 and when Australia arrived the following season for a three-Test series scores of 47 and 80 in the second Test did much to restore his self-belief.

It was F H Mann's XI that experienced the full force of Taylor's Second Coming. After his aforementioned 176 in the first Test, his regeneration continued through the second Test, where he made 68 in a partnership of 155 with Bob Catterall, and into the third Test, in which he scored 91 in a match that was ruined by rain.

In the fourth match of the rubber, Taylor displayed the same obstinacy that had driven Barnes to distraction. In the second innings he and Dave Nourse saved the game for South Africa with a defiant partnership. Nourse later wrote of Taylor: 'One enjoys watching Taylor even more from close range than from the pavilion. One is able to see more definitely the precision of the timing of his strokes and what daring he employs. Only a batsman gifted with an exceptional eye can, with all the apparent confidence in the world, despatch a good length ball on the off stump to a vacancy at mid-wicket and seem as though he intended it to go there all the time.'

Taylor made 102, his third century of the series, in the fifth Test, although South Africa's total of 234 was a long way short of the 344 they had been set to win by England. The tourists had won the series by two Tests to one, but South Africa had indubitably the player of the series. He had scored 582 runs at an average of 64.66.

Taylor was never again able to find such consistency. In 1924 he led South Africa to England for a series against an XI that contained two debutants in the first Test, Maurice Tate and Herbert Sutcliffe, who showed such confidence that South Africans wondered if they had swum as children in the River Styx. The tourists were outplayed and lost the series 3–0. In the first Test at Edgbaston they suffered the indignity of being dismissed for 30. Taylor top-scored (after extras), with seven. He scored only 197 runs in the series and his captaincy was criticized by the South African newspapers.

A move to Johannesburg in 1925, however, gave his career fresh impetus and he helped Transvaal win the Currie Cup in 1926 and 1927. When England toured in 1927–8 he played with more freedom than he had for several years. The reactions had slowed, but he still scored 412 runs in the series, including a century in the victory in the fourth Test. A young fast bowler called George Bisset took 7 for 29 in England's second innings of the final Test to level the series at two apiece.

For the first time in Taylor's international career he was not regarded as South Africa's sole match-winner. Freed from such pressure, Taylor began to bat with greater confidence and by 1929, when South Africa toured England, he was able to show his talent to a new generation of English cricket fans.

Seventeen years after he had first come to England – and now aged 40 – he hit 121 in the fifth Test in a fourth-wicket partnership of 214 with 'Nummy' Deane*. He came to the wicket when his country were reeling at 20 for three – his one concession to middle age was to come in lower down the order – and in his first few overs he scratched around nervously. 'He did not start his subsequently magnificent innings as if he were destined to improve it,' wrote *The Times*. 'But after the interval we were privileged to watch an exhibition of batting which, whatever criteria he adopted, must be described as altogether admirable. The technical excellence of the strokes was faultless.' In the course of the partnership, which lasted nearly two and a half hours, the ball was lifted off the ground by the bat only twice. As the venerable correspondent of *The Times* sat entranced by what he saw he was reminded of the words of Taylor's old adversary: 'The Taylor seen in the afternoon was the Taylor whom Barnes is said to have selected as about the best batsman to whom he has ever bowled, confident, free and masterful.' Taylor played his last Test on the 1931-2 tour to Australia and New Zealand. It was a tour that made him feel very old. He was forty-two; no one else was above thirty.

The South Africans were put to the sword by the Australians. Taylor spent a lot of the time in the field, as the home side compiled a series of massive scores. But at least it gave him an opportunity to marvel at the majesty of Don Bradman. In the fourth Test Taylor made 78 and 84. Bradman scored 299 not out.

He played the last of his forty-two Tests against New Zealand in the first

* This remains a record fourth -wicket partnership for South Africa in Test cricket.

series ever played by South Africa that didn't involve England or Australia. South Africa won the two matches comfortably, although Taylor scored just nine in the first Test and missed the second through injury. Only Frank Woolley of pre-First World War players remained in Test cricket longer than Taylor.

His contribution to South African cricket had been immense. Not only had he scored 2,936 Test runs at an average of 40.77, but he had also captained them eighteen times, a record surpassed only by Hansie Cronje, who singularly failed to live up to the high standards cherished by Taylor. His impact stretched far beyond the boundary ropes of Kingsmead and Old Wanderers. Through his masterly batting displays, Taylor sowed the seeds of ambition in the minds of a new generation of young South African batsmen. In 1935 South Africa won their first Test in England and by the end of the decade, the likes of Bruce Mitchell, Dudley Nourse and Eric Rowan could hold their own against England and Australia.

Although he had stepped down from international cricket Taylor returned to Natal for a final flourish. If Taylor needed reminding of his advanced age he got it when he found himself batting with Dudley Nourse, son of his old team-mate, 'Dave'. For Nourse, it was an instructive period in his development. 'I was privileged to bat as partner to that master of footwork,' he later wrote. The old master could also show his pupil a thing or two about wiliness. 'I was enjoying myself hugely against a bowler who had just been brought on and having scored three boundaries that over, I was quite delighted with life.' Taylor, however, had become noticeably more agitated after each successive boundary. At the end of the over he strode down the wicket to Nourse. 'Don't be an utter fool. Why do you want to hit the chap to the boundary so often in one over? Do you want to take our bit of bread and butter away? Don't make it quite so obvious, please. Milk him slowly, otherwise the source of profitable runs will dry far too quickly … and I want a taste of it before they remove him.'

Nourse learnt quickly from his tutor and in December 1935 he scored 231 against Australia in Johannesburg. Nourse returned to the pavilion for lunch on 179, having surpassed the 176 Taylor made against England in 1922. Taylor came up to the dressing room and warmly congratulated Nourse. Then he took him to one side and whispered: 'Now that you have the highest Test score made by a South African in this country, go on to break the record of 204* in a Test match by a South African. If you don't, young man, I will dust your pants for you.'

Taylor retired from first-class cricket at the end of the 1935–6 season, shortly before his forty-seventh birthday. During a first-class career that spanned more than a quarter of a century, he had scored 13,105 runs at an average of 41.86.

Taylor adapted to his new life as successfully as he had adapted his technique to the different pitches of the world. Cricket is littered with the tragic tales of former players who found themselves cast adrift in a sea of depression after they retired from the game that had consumed so much of their early life. Taylor encountered no such problems. In the years before the Second World War he owned a share in a Durban sports business. In the 1950s he worked for a firm that distributed marble and lime. He also wrote a number of coaching manuals for schoolboys and taught cricket at Hilton School in Natal. In 1971 he produced a booklet on batting techniques, perhaps hoping that an eager young schoolboy might be encouraged to teach himself some of the shots, as he had been similarly inspired seventy years earlier when he had found an article written by C B Fry in a *Boys' Own* comic.

Taylor died two years later at his home in Rondebosch aged eighty-three. The next day at his old stamping ground, Kingsmead, players from Natal and Western Province stood in silence as a mark of respect before play began. On the same morning, the front page of the *Cape Times* carried news of Taylor's death alongside a photograph of the former Natalian batsman. The headline asked simply, 'South Africa's Greatest?' Two generations of South Africans nodded their heads.

* Aubrey Faulkner's 204 made in the second Test against Australia in Melbourne in the 1910–11 series.

CHAPTER ELEVEN

Cyril Lowe

Cyril Lowe was 5ft 6in and weighed about 8 stone, but he is one of the greatest wings ever to play rugby for England. What Lowe lacked in physical stature he made up for in willpower and courage, and he rarely missed a tackle. During the First World War Lowe became one of the most celebrated pilots in the Royal Flying Corps, shooting down at least nine German planes. Despite some terrifying ordeals, Lowe put it all behind him after the war and returned to the England team.

The South Africans didn't know quite what to make of Cyril Lowe. They may even have felt a little insulted. What were England doing fielding a slip of a lad against them on this their first appearance at Twickenham? Cyril Lowe was a twenty-one-year-old student when he made his international debut in 1913. England had trouble finding a shirt that fitted him. There weren't too many 5ft 6in, 8-stone players around at the time, even on the wing.

If the Springboks thought the pipsqueak would be a pushover they soon came to realize that he relished the physical side of the sport. Lowe's opportunities to attack during the 9–3 defeat by the tourists were scarce but in defence he nailed anyone who came near him. He also went looking for victims, making frequent raids infield to tackle the South Africans.

The Twickenham crowd warmed to this stout-hearted little winger. Over the course of the next ten years Lowe came to be regarded with great affection. His breeding was impeccable – Dulwich and Cambridge University – and his plucky defiance caught the imagination of the English public who in 1913 felt themselves menaced by the domineering Germans. If Lowe could stand up to a bigger bully then so, they reasoned, could Britain.

It surprised no one that when war between the two nations erupted in August the following year, Lowe was in uniform by the end of the month. It was apparent he intended to take his courage and cussedness to war. Lowe enlisted initially in the Army Service Corps as a Second Lieutenant and was posted to the First Reserve Horse Transport. He was responsible for the supply of horses and vehicles for use by soldiers at the front. It was an essential task, one of those unglamorous jobs that didn't carry much prestige, but without which the whole war machine would have spluttered and eventually ground to a halt. Now at least he knew what it felt like to be a prop forward. Although he appreciated the importance of the Service Corps, Lowe decided it wasn't for him. After all, he was a wing-threequarter, one of the glamour boys, and he wanted a role in the war that was more quixotic.

The obvious choice would have been to join a frontline infantry regiment, the Guards, perhaps. His height, however, was the barrier that prevented him going down that avenue. Anyone under six foot would be laughed off the Guards' parade ground.

There might also have been another reason why he desisted from joining the infantry. At the start of 1915 Lowe had married Ethel Watson. He was rather keen on his new wife and he intended to grow old with the woman eight years his senior. It struck Lowe, as he scanned the increasingly long casualty lists in the newspapers, that life in the trenches offered him little prospect of reaching middle age. Rarely did a month go by when he didn't recognize the name of a former team-mate or adversary posted as killed or missing.

Instead, Lowe applied for a transfer to the Royal Flying Corps (RFC). They had been at the Western Front since the start of the war but the scope of their operations had been limited by the shortage of suitable aircraft. Perhaps Lowe thought that life in the RFC, while not cushy, offered him a somewhat better chance of survival.

Unfortunately for Lowe, as he contemplated a career change, the RFC was welcoming a new field commander in France. General Hugh Trenchard had his feet under the desk in August 1915, and immediately he adopted a more aggressive approach to the aerial war. There were to be more offensive patrols over German lines. He waved aside – with the wilful arrogance that led him to be despised by many combat pilots – the concerns of some high-ranking RFC officers about the inferiority of the British aircraft in comparison to their German counterparts. For Trenchard, it was the quantity of the planes that mattered not their quality. It wouldn't be long before the average life expectancy of a new RFC pilot arriving in France was seventeen days.

It was fortunate for Lowe that he transferred to the RFC when he did. He received adequate training in all aspects of aerial combat while at Instruction School in the first half of 1916. It was at this time that the Germans started to inflict fearful losses on the RFC, shooting out of the sky the obsolete British planes that chugged their way into enemy territory. From late 1916, the scale of the casualties compelled the RFC to send to France under-prepared young men, often straight out of school. Trenchard, in one of his more overweening moments, labelled German pilots as 'floating meat'. At the end of 1916 it was an apter description of British pilots.

Lowe was posted to 11 Squadron in France in October 1916. He arrived to find morale at its lowest ebb. The previous month the RFC had lost sixty-two men with thirty-six wounded and a similar figure captured. There were a lot of new faces in 11 Squadron's mess that month. Lowe's status as an England rugger wing might have led to a couple of free drinks in the bar but most of the old stagers probably didn't expect him to be around for long. A few weeks, perhaps. Christmas, if he was lucky. Lowe was introduced to his observer, Masters, and then to his aircraft, the FE2b. It was a cumbersome old kite, used for reconnaissance patrols over enemy lines. Masters operated the camera, which was fixed to the outside of the cockpit. Behind him, slightly elevated on the petrol tank and with the engine and radiator immediately at his back, sat Lowe. Communication between Lowe and Masters was through sign language. The roar of the Beardmore engine precluded any chatter.

Lowe had been with the squadron less than three weeks when he was hit by anti-aircraft fire over German lines. The damage was superficial. The engine wasn't hit and Lowe managed to land the crippled plane at his own base. He and Masters probably made their report and then headed to the mess for a stiff drink and a game of cards. Card games were popular among the pilots. One new recruit remembered walking in upon a game to see sums changing hands in excess of £50 [equivalent to approximately £1,000 today]. 'What does it matter?' one of the players smiled sardonically, when he saw the look of incredulity on the face of the newcomer. 'We shall all be dead in a week, we're being swatted like flies.'

This fatalism increased throughout the winter of 1916–17 as losses continued to soar. A shift in German tactics added to the depression among the RFC. Where previously they had been content to wait for the British to fly over their lines – 'let the customer come to the shop', as the lethal and legendary Baron Manfred von Richthofen would say – they now realized their machines were so superior to the British they could afford to be more intrepid. In December 1916, seventeen of the twenty-seven downed British planes crashed behind their own lines.

Lowe, however, was still alive and able to usher in the New Year in 11 Squadron's mess. The question he and every other pilot asked himself was whether he would be around to see it in in 1918. If the answer was to be no, they mused, then please God let it be a merciful end. It was thoughts such as these that haunted all pilots whenever they contemplated their own mortality.

The death they feared above all other was being shot out of the sky, alive and unable to do anything to save oneself, as the plane plummeted earthwards. It took a fighter aircraft about five minutes to fall 10,000 ft. There was no recourse to a parachute. The Air Board had looked into the matter but concluded coldly that: 'The presence of such an apparatus might impair the fighting spirit of pilots and cause them to abandon the machine which might otherwise be capable of returning to base for repair.' Such crass disregard for the pilots' lives – the Air Board seemed to care more about the machine than the man – flew in the face of the pilots' opinions. One, Arthur Gould Lee, said that 'to know you had a sporting chance from a break up or a flamer would make you much braver in a scrap'.

To an extent Lowe was in a more enviable position than Masters, his observer. At least he had a certain amount of control over his own destiny. With the FE2b engine situated directly behind Lowe, there was a good chance that if the engine was riddled with bullets, one or more would penetrate Lowe. Masters, however, seated a good deal further forward, would probably be left alive, but powerless, as the plane fell out of the sky, with his pilot slumped over the controls. One RFC officer recalled looking at the wreckage of an FE2b that had crashed into the ground from 4,000 feet: 'Mac [the pilot] was looking peaceful and quite normal, being shot through the back … but Everingham looked as though the end had not come quite so peacefully. He was not shot, but had been broken by the fall.'

When Lowe and Masters climbed into their FE2b shortly before 8am on the morning of 24 March 1917, they would have put such thoughts to the back of their minds. Lowe was still in the pink, having been promoted to flight-commander the previous day. It was to be another routine reconnaissance patrol, just one of the dozens performed by 11 Squadron following the withdrawal of the German infantry to the Hindenburg Line earlier in the month. They spent more than two hours observing enemy positions and taking photographs.

Also in the sky that morning was Unteroffizier Jorke of Jagdstaffel 12 in an Albatross. He couldn't believe his luck when he spotted the FE2b. He manoeuvred himself behind the British plane, exploiting its blind spot, and opened fire.

The initial burst of gunfire startled Lowe. He wouldn't have heard the bullets tear into the soft fabric of the FE2b. He would just have seen a splatter of bullet holes appear on the wing, like the first raindrops of a spring shower. The second burst from Jorke was more accurate and Lowe felt a stab of pain in his right shoulder as a bullet ripped through his flying suit.

As Lowe wrestled with the controls, Masters opened fire with the Lewis gun and forced Jorke to break off the attack. He retired to a safe distance, observing the noblesse oblige that still governed the air war, and watched the pilot of the FE2b struggle to bring his aircraft under control.

Despite the immense pain he must have been in from the gunshot wounds to his right shoulder, Lowe landed the plane at Croisilles behind British lines. Masters walked away without a scratch. His pilot, however, was taken straight to hospital.

For the next month Lowe recuperated in France. He returned to England on 19 April, and, having failed two medical boards that summer, was pronounced fit to return to active service on 23 August 1917. Lowe remained tethered in England until April 1918. He spent the intervening period with 28 Squadron, learning the skills needed to become a fighter pilot in a single-seater squadron. He'd had limited opportunity to shoot down German aircraft while with 11 Squadron, but his two confirmed victories before he was brought down demonstrated he had the aptitude to become a fighter pilot.

On 18 April 1918, Lowe – now a captain – was back in France. He arrived at 24 Squadron three days after they had taken possession of a new mascot, Jim, a beautiful and energetic red setter. It was a cosmopolitan squadron. If Lowe wanted to spend an evening discussing South African rugby, Barton and Southey were only too happy to oblige. Lowe was particularly fond of Southey; he was even smaller than himself. There was also Lambert, an American, and two Canadians, Crossen and MacDonald.

The disparate nature of the squadron did nothing to dilute its operational effectiveness. Lowe soon found he was among men who enjoyed flying as much as he did. On 23 April he led 'B' Flight on an observational patrol. With him were Mark, Lindeburg, Farrell, Palmer and Harrison. Lambert wrote later that: 'They met ten enemy fighters who seemed to want to start an argument. The men of B Flight were never prone to dodge an argument, regardless of the odds. Mark dived on the nearest EA [enemy aircraft], fired two short bursts and watched him crash while Lowe hit another and sent him down out of control.'

May was a good month for Lowe. On 9 May, he shot down two Albatross Scouts, although one was classified as an indecisive combat, as opposed to a decisive combat in which the enemy's plane was confirmed wrecked. Lambert recorded what he saw: 'He [Lowe] was on the tail of a blue and red machine. A few short bursts and that one turned over and started to spin. I did not have time to watch it but someone else saw it almost to the ground still spinning out of control. A few seconds later Lowe pounced on another Albatross and, with a long burst, drove him down, damaged.' A week later Lowe claimed another indecisive. On 19 May he received orders to provide an escort on the following day for a squadron of bombers.

The sun was just peeking its head above the skyline when Lowe climbed into the cockpit of his SE5a. As he made his final preparations he glanced across at Lt Mark and gave the thumbs up. Mark grinned back at him. They had known each other less than a month but already Lowe trusted him more than any of the team-mates he had known during his two seasons in the England XV.

With Lowe and Mark were eleven other pilots from 24 Squadron, including Lambert. The outward trip was a picnic. The DH4 bombers dropped their loads east of Chaulnes at 8.15am. A similar run back and they would be tucking into bacon and eggs by 10am. As they turned to go home seven Fokker biplanes swooped down on them from out of the sun. Seconds later six Fokker Triplanes – derisively labelled 'Tripes' by the British – joined the ambush. 'Soon everyone was busy,' recalled Lambert. 'Planes everywhere, diving, climbing, banking, rolling and falling; some with long plumes of black smoke and flames trailing behind; some on their backs and some on their wing-tips; some in headlong dives, followed by a tremendous burst of flame. Twenty-six fighter planes trying to destroy each other, fifty-two machine-guns spouting bullets at a rate of 500 or 600 per minute. The crackle of these guns could be heard above the roar of the engines and the shriek of the bracing wires, vibrating in speeds of 150 to 200 mph.'

Lowe's reaction to the ambush was as savage as it was swift. Supported by Lt Mark, he went for the seven biplanes that had attacked with the sun at their backs. He fired a short burst of thirty rounds at the first Fokker he trapped in his sights, but another German latched on to his tail and he was forced to break off the attack as bullets lacerated the flimsy fabric. Lowe's SE5a caught fire but he didn't flap. Weaker men would have panicked.

When a plane caught fire at 17,000 ft the chances of survival were slim. Lowe dived in a calculated attempt to extinguish the flames, pursued all the while by the German whose sense of chivalry had been overpowered by his bloodlust.

Mark, meanwhile, had problems of his own. He had attacked one of the seven Fokkers but inexplicably a section of his top right wing started to break away. He turned west but at speeds of 140mph the fabric continued to be torn from his wing, strip by strip. The wooden structure of his plane was being exposed like the ribs of the dead soldiers rotting on the battlefield below him.

Mark's plane was barely airworthy. He should have limped back to base. But when he saw Lowe, in a nosedive 1,500ft from the tops of the trees, he went to his aid and drove the attacker from his tail. As Lowe fought to regain control of his plane, the German turned on the crippled intruder, determined he would not be denied a kill.

It didn't bother him that his prey was helpless, 'floating meat' to pinch a Trenchard expression. Mark had no ammunition left and his plane was incapable of outrunning the Fokker. His brain was his only weapon; he used it to out-think his attacker and make good his escape. He began to circle slowly as if he was going to land on German-held soil and accept defeat.

The Fokker pilot took the bait. He watched from above, expecting Mark to land and hand himself over to the watching infantry. As the German pilot relaxed for a moment, perhaps totting up in his head his new tally of victories, Mark dived suddenly in a last desperate attempt to foil his rival.

Lambert, the American pilot, described what happened next: 'Lowe, having manoeuvred out of his predicament, climbed back to about 2,000 feet. He then saw Mark going down in a steep dive over Wiencourt with the EA pumping bullets into his tail … in spite of having a boiling engine, his Aldis sight fogged and only one gun, Lowe attacked and fired about sixty rounds at medium range. Some of his bullets got home, apparently, because the German went down and was seen to land behind a small clump of trees.'

Lowe and Mark escorted each other back across British lines. Mark's plane disintegrated on landing, but he was able to scramble clear before it burst into flames. Lowe landed to see if he was OK, then climbed back into his plane and returned to Conteville to make his report. Major Robeson wrote in the squadron's log that evening that the pair had rescued each other in 'appallingly difficult circumstances'. He recommended both for a Military Cross. It was gazetted the following month, and the citation ended by saying:

'The action of both these officers, in practically unmanoeuvrable machines, in coming to the rescue of each other in turn, showed courage and self-sacrifice of a very high order.'

At the end of 1916 Dr James Birley had been asked by the Air Board to investigate the increase among pilots of mental breakdowns. He conducted an extensive study of combat pilots and produced a report that divided a pilot's life into seasons. In the spring he learned to fly and fight, and gained experience, although often at the expense of his own life.* But if he survived, he entered the summer of his career. His confidence, self-assurance, skill, initiative and determination were at their zenith. But when the summer passed, autumn came, and with it a gradual deterioration in the pilot's health.

---

* Three-quarters of pilot casualties in 1917 and 1918 were sustained by men who had less than three months of active service experience

Lowe was enjoying the summer of his career. His terrifying encounter with the Fokkers had done little to quell his ardour. On 6 June he saved Lambert's life when he shot down a Fokker 'Tripe' that had attached itself to the American's tail. Lambert only discovered his saviour when they were being debriefed: 'Lowe said that at the start of the fight he had seen a "Tripe" on the tail of an SE5 which seemed to be having trouble. He had driven off the EA and stayed with it, firing bursts at very close range. The Fokker fell into a spin and Lowe watched it crash to the ground. I gave Lowe a pat on the back, thanked him and told him who was in the SE.'

Following the debriefing the men filed out into the warm summer sunshine and spent the rest of the afternoon relaxing. Some of the men wrote letters home, others read, a couple played ping-pong. Lambert found a chair and 'anchored myself to the end of that Nissen hut and just sat there in the sun until tea time. I was not alone for long. Several others came along to do the same thing. There was always some deep thinking done in that spot.'

Supper in the mess was usually more riotous, particularly after a good day's hunting. 'A lot of kidding and boisterous horseplay took place,' remembered Crossen, one of the Canadians. 'Good humour prevailed … when victories were to be celebrated the orchestra (Lindeburg on accordion; Foster on piano [the more he drank the louder came the piano]; Palmer on mouth organ; Southey on tins; and Daley on drums) would be led by Hallan, who had some theatrical experience prior to the war. Whatever the orchestra played a good time was had by all.' 'Life was good,' reflected Lambert, 'but there was an element of fear deep in every man there. But very few allowed this to come to the surface. Most of us faced the fact: "What is to be, will be."'

On 7 June Lowe claimed his seventh confirmed kill – another Fokker triplane – although any satisfaction he felt evaporated when he saw one of his flight plunge to earth in flames. It was only when he returned to base that he realized it was Dawe, a reserved but experienced English pilot. Southey, the South African pilot, ruminated on his death fifty years later: 'I wonder if he had a presentiment? The afternoon before … he just sat there brooding in his chair and was very quiet. He appeared to be under stress and seemed to bite his tongue as he sat there.'

Dawe had been a popular pilot and the pilots drank to his memory in the mess that evening. The next day he was forgotten. It was a callous attitude but a necessary one. To mull too long over the death of a comrade was to invite into one's mind the demons of self-doubt. As Thomas Hardy wrote of the First World War: 'More life may trickle out of men through thought than through a gaping wound.'

Within two days Dawe's bed was taken by a new pilot. He was blooded on 9 June when three flights from the squadron made a dawn patrol well inside enemy territory. It was too early for the Germans. They were not yet up in the sky and the squadron returned safely to base just after 6am, disappointed but eager for some breakfast. 'As we started for the orderly room,' remembered Lambert, 'someone shouted, "Last man in the mess buys the drinks." Every man for himself and devil take the hindmost! We burst into the shack like a herd of bull elephants. Chairs flew in all directions, one section of tables was overturned and a few dishes were broken. Surplus energy was what we all had and we had to expend some of it.'

Lowe continued to patrol throughout June, but he didn't claim another confirmed victory until 25 June when he shot down his eighth German. The next day he was hit once again by anti-aircraft fire. His propeller was damaged but he landed unhurt. The action was the culmination of an exemplary month's flying. He was rewarded with a Distinguished Flying Cross, the citation of which ran:

> 'This officer has destroyed five enemy planes and driven down two others out of control. On one occasion he attacked two enemy triplanes, although at the time only one of his guns was serviceable; he shot down one of the machines in flames. On another occasion, while leading a formation of eight scouts he engaged a hostile formation of twenty-six machines. Having shot down a Fokker biplane he went to the assistance of one of our scouts and drove the enemy machine down to 500 feet; at this low altitude half of a blade of his propeller was shot off by fire from the ground.'

The citation, gazetted at the start of August, took into account the Fokker Lowe had forced down out of control on 1 July. It was the last of Lowe's confirmed victories. Although he was officially credited with nine the actual figure was probably at least twice that number. As he himself commented many years later: 'In those days, everyone was claiming a shoot-down, even infantrymen in the trenches, so many of mine could not be officially verified.'

Lowe took temporary command of 24 Squadron in July while Major Robeson went on leave. When he returned, Lowe was granted eleven days' leave in England. He was back with the squadron on 6 August, two days before the Allies launched their mighty offensive that became known as the Battle of Amiens.

Lowe was in command of B Flight, supporting the Canadian Corps. Their orders were to bomb and strafe the German infantry as the Canadian troops attacked. The squadron's log recorded the day's events: 'We put in a very heavy day in our old area in the valley of the Luce. Enemy AAMG (Anti-aircraft machine-gun) defence was very hot, all the squadrons working low lost heavily. We were ten machines short at the end of the day.'

The squadron's work on 8 August was nothing out of the ordinary for them. They had been concentrating on low work for the past month, reporting on the movement of enemy troops and transport, attacking observation balloons and strafing German trenches. The men hated it. The risks were inordinate and if some had been enjoying the summer of their flying career, it began to appear that for several pilots the days were growing shorter and autumn was approaching. Lambert, on the evening of 9 August, reported that: 'The nerves of almost every pilot in the squadron were about shot. Most had been doing this work for three weeks. No one complained but one had only to look into the face of a pilot and watch his actions. The story was there.'

Lambert was shot down a couple of weeks later but survived. Lowe's good fortune continued until October when he contracted Spanish flu. The aerial war by then was petering out and Lowe didn't miss much in the way of action as he sweated and shivered in his bed in the RAF Hospital, Hampstead. Unlike an estimated 70 million people worldwide who succumbed to the influenza epidemic, however, Lowe made a complete recovery.

Fourteen months after the armistice international rugby resumed. About time, thought Lowe. The previous year had dragged interminably. A year in an RAF Technical Training School was enough to break the dullest of men; for an experienced fighter pilot like Lowe, a veteran of dozens of dogfights, the banality of the School was excruciating. Rugby was the salve he required.

Lowe's rugby talent had come to the fore in his first year at Cambridge. At Dulwich he dabbled in a multitude of sports, breaking various athletic records, and representing the college in football, cricket and boxing (in which he fought in the Public Schools' Championship). When he went up to Cambridge he was soon installed in the 1st XV. When they defeated London Scottish in November 1911 the *Observer* reported that he 'skimmed along the surface of the quagmire, and sidestepped and feinted with grace and quickness which would have baffled any defence ... even old stagers and great heroes of other days were inclined to be carried away in their eulogies of Lowe'.

He continued to develop until the England selectors could no longer ignore the praise lavished on his narrow shoulders by the newspapers. On the morning of the 1913 Varsity match, E H D Sewell, writing in the *Evening Standard*, said: 'Lowe possesses two qualities that are inseparable from really great, as apart from merely good, three-quarters. These are hands and pace ... the pace that is governed by a seemingly born knowledge of football.'

Having made his debut against the Springboks in 1913, Lowe played in every England match until war interrupted. Now, with hostilities over, his name was the first the selectors jotted down as they picked the XV to face Wales in the first match of the 1920 Five Nations.

Lowe, John Greenwood and Sid Smart were the only survivors from the England XV that had beaten France in 1914 to win the Grand Slam. Six of that side had fallen in the war. It must have been a profoundly moving experience for the three to take the field. Did they look around half expecting to see Ronnie Poulton-Palmer, that imperious and insouciant centre, with his lop-sided smile and shock of wavy blond hair? Had the German sniper noticed the colour of his hair as he squeezed the trigger five years earlier? And where was Arthur Harrison and that massive backside of his, jutting out of the scrum, as he shoved with all his might? No one knew where his body lay.

England lost 19–5. It was all depressingly familiar for Lowe, standing in splendid isolation on the wing. He hardly had a whiff of the ball all day. The correspondent of *The Times* took up the cudgels on his behalf: 'Lowe ought to write a book entitled *English centres I have known*. Once again he was starved and neglected ... it is terribly sad that the most dangerous wing in the four countries should always be so starved.' It had always been so. How Lowe had come to score eight tries during the 1914 Five Nations* was a mystery no one

---

* A championship record that was never beaten – although equalled by Ian Smith of Scotland in 1925 – before the Five Nations expanded to include Italy in 2000.

could fathom, least of all P G Wodehouse.

The comic writer was an enthusiastic rugby fan and, sharing with Lowe the same alma mater, Dulwich College, he took a special interest in the England wing. When Lowe still hadn't received a pass after his first three caps, Wodehouse picked up his pen in indignation. The result was 'The Great Day'.

> I can recollect it clearly,
> Every detail pretty nearly,
> Though it happened many, many years ago.
> Yes, my children, I, your grand-dad
> A reserved seat in the stand had
> On the afternoon when someone passed to Lowe.
>
> I had stopped to light my briar,
> For the wind was getting higher,
> When a thousand voices screamed a startled 'Oh!'
> I looked up. A try or something?
> Then sat gaping like a dumb thing.
> My children, somebody had passed to Lowe!
>
> His astonishment was utter.
> He was heard to gulp, and mutter,
> 'What on earth has happened now, I'd like to know?'
> And incredulous reporters
> Shouted out to the three-quarters:
> 'Do we dream? Or did you really pass to Lowe?'

The following season was a considerable improvement, for England and Lowe. The side was beginning to come together. Lowe was now the only player to bridge the pre- and post-war XVs. He was still only twenty-nine but he felt like an old man. Around him he had whippersnappers such as Tom Voyce, Wavell Wakefield, Ronnie Cove-Smith and Cecil Kershaw. England won the Grand Slam, and Lowe at last began to see some ball. P G Wodehouse, busy writing *Indiscretions of Archie*, might even have been tempted to dedicate another ode to Lowe. He deserved it. The English right wing scored tries in the wins against Wales, Ireland and France. But it was his all-round play that was most impressive. The *Observer* reported that against Ireland, Lowe 'found his way to the line hopelessly barred. He doubled back and in doing so stumbled but regained his footing cleverly and, with the Irishmen almost on him, dropped a delightful goal with the left foot.'

Lowe had a number of balls to juggle during 1921. Something noted by his instructor at the RAF Cadet College. 'He worked under disadvantage,' he commented, 'as continually taken away to play and instruct rugby.' Nevertheless, when Lowe took a refresher course with 24 Squadron in February he scored 93 per cent. 'Exceptional,' wrote the examiner.

Lowe was commending himself to his superiors in other ways, too. When the RAF played the Army in the 1921 Inter-Services game, in the presence of King George V, he led his side to a record 26–3 victory. Senior RAF officers' moustaches bristled with delight as he crossed the Army line four times. The third try, wrote the *Daily Mail*, 'was a gem of opportunism and elusiveness. By swerve and feint and sidestep he ran through half the Army side closely massed.'

Lowe didn't play any more rugby for the rest of the year. It was an enforced lay-off, caused, first, by a broken arm as he attempted to start his car in June. Barely had he been passed fit when he dislocated his collar-bone in an RAF game in October. The injury unsettled the correspondent of the *Evening Standard*, who prayed he would pass muster for the 1922 Five Nations. 'An England team without Lowe,' he wrote, 'would be like *Hamlet* without the moody Prince.'

Lowe was given the all-clear for the Championship and he scored three tries in a season in which England lost to Wales, beat Ireland and Scotland, but drew with France, the first time they had failed to defeat the French in twelve matches.

The following season was Lowe's last for England. Fittingly, he ended his international career as he had begun it ten years earlier: with a Grand Slam. But it hadn't been easy. The England side of 1913 had romped to the title, dropping just four points en route. The gap in standard had narrowed. *The Times* said that England 'has had to play three undoubtedly hard games ... [and] has fairly earned her Championship'.

Lowe, although he hadn't played badly, was beginning to feel the pace. He was now thirty-one and the lightning speed he once relied on was on the wane. The *Times* correspondent, his iron hand wielding a velvet pen, alluded to it in his report: 'The age and war-weariness of some of the leading English players caused a certain amount of anxiety – their skill, of course, was not in question.'

Lowe announced his retirement from international rugby at the end of the 1923 season. He had won twenty-five consecutive caps and scored eighteen tries,* despite not getting his first try until his sixth match. He had also won four Grand Slams, appearing in every one of the sixteen possible matches, the only player from any country to have achieved such a feat in the ninety-year history of the Five Nations.

The *Daily Express*'s valediction depicted Lowe as an athlete who combined grace with power and skill with steel. He was rugby's answer to Nijinsky: 'A little giant, strong and beautifully built, a track sprinter for speed, a dancer for balance. He could be baulked. That was merely a challenge. He would check, perform what we would call his "hesitation waltz", double inside, and, as likely as not, drop a goal.'

The *Times* had been right to describe Lowe as weary, but wrong to attribute it to the war. Lowe had fallen out of love with rugby because he didn't like the way the game was being played. 'I got very few passes and consequently I gradually began to absorb a policy wrong in any game,' he wrote later, 'and became a defensive rather than an offensive player … I confess I look back on the later games I played with little pleasure, because as time went on chances of scoring tries became rarer and rarer.' He concluded his article in the *Evening News* with a word of advice for young rugby players: 'I think that in many ways wing-threequarter is the most uninteresting position on the rugby field. I would rather have been a forward or a centre.'

Lowe retired from the RAF in 1944 at the age of fifty-three and with the rank of Group Captain. His service record read like a book as thick as Wodehouse's *Right Ho! Jeeves*. Not as humorous, of course, but his conduct had been as impeccable as Bertie Wooster's faithful butler. He had commanded No 1 Squadron in Mesopotamia during the 1920s; led reconnaissance patrols over the Palestine coast of the Mediterranean in the

---

* This stood as an English try-scoring record until 1990 when it was surpassed by Rory Underwood. He and Lowe had much in common. Underwood was also a winger and an RAF pilot. In eighty-five Tests from 1984 to 1996 he scored forty-nine tries for his country.

Herby Taylor (front row, second from left) does his best to blend in with the rest of South Africa's tour party to Australia in 1931-2. Every player, except Taylor, was aged under 30. He was 42 and celebrating twenty years as a Test cricketer.

COURTESY OF GLEN HUNTER/WANDERERS CRICKET STADIUM

ABOVE: Cyril Lowe (middle row, third from the left) with the England XV that beat Scotland 8-6 at Edinburgh on 17 March 1923. In the 1923 season England won their fourth Grand Slam title.

RUGBY FOOTBALL UNION ARCHIVE

ABOVE RIGHT: The cosmopolitan nature of No24 Squadron in 1918 can be seen in this rare photo as the pilots relax between patrols. (From left to right, sitting): Crossen, Macdonald (both Canadians), Lowe (English), Johnson (American), Farrell (English) and unknown.

RAF MUSEUM HENDON/*OVER THE FRONT* MAGAZINE

BELOW RIGHT: British SE5s and German D7s engage in a dogfight over France in 1916. With no parachutes, and at heights of 15,000ft, pilots were a special breed whose courage was matched by their extraordinary nerve.

HULTON ARCHIVE

ABOVE: Perhaps it was pre-match
nerves that caused Fred Harvey
(middle row, far right) to look so
glum on the day of Wanderers' win
against Bective Rangers in the 1911
Leinster Cup Final.

TERRY LONG/WANDERERS FOOTBALL CLUB

LEFT: Four rugby union internationals
have won the Victoria Cross and
three have been from the Wanderers
club in Dublin. Robert Johnston and
Tom Crean in the Boer War were
followed by Fred Harvey in 1917.

PORTORA ROYAL SCHOOL, ENNISKILLEN

ABOVE: Arnold Jackson crosses the line to win the 1500m gold in the 1912 Stockholm Olympics. Four years later to the day, Jackson was one of his battalion's few survivors from a disastrous attack on the Somme.

ASSOCIATED SPORTS PHOTOGRAPHY/
NORMAN BARRETT

ABOVE RIGHT: A rare photo of Jackson (far right) training in 1912, here with his Oxford team-mates. The look on his face suggests he would rather be supping a pint in his local pub.

HULTON ARCHIVE

BELOW RIGHT: In early November 1917 a senior British officer visited the Passchendaele battlefield. He broke down and wept when he saw conditions: 'Good God,' he sobbed, 'did we really send men to fight in that?'

HULTON ARCHIVE

ABOVE: A bruised but defiant Pieter van der Bijl hits out on his way to his maiden Test century against England in the 1939 'Timeless Test' in Durban.

LEFT: Like father, like son. Well, nearly. Vince van der Bijl (left) would have followed his father into the South Africa Test XI were it not for their sporting isolation during the 1970s and 1980s.

ABOVE LEFT: The tail of a Blenheim bomber can be seen above the burning Cologne power station that was targeted by the RAF in 1941. Bill Edrich won a DFC for his part in the daring daylight attack.

IWM PHOTOGRAPH

ABOVE RIGHT: The 'Terrible Twins' of Edrich (left) and Denis Compton walk out to bat for Middlesex during their incredible 1947 season.

HULTON ARCHIVE

RIGHT: England manager A J Holmes (left) takes notes as Compton, Norman Yardley and Edrich plan that night's celebrations following another Test victory against South Africa in 1947.

HULTON ARCHIVE

ABOVE: A shy Blair Mayne (fourth from the left) does his best to look inconspicuous after being caught on camera during the 1938 British Lions tour to South Africa.

COURTESY OF JOHN KANE

LEFT: Blair Mayne at his happiest, in the desert with the SAS in 1942. This quiet, bashful and cultured man loved war and talked of going on raids looking for 'some good killing'.

COURTESY OF JOHN KANE

ABOVE: Mayne (centre, standing) supervizes a rather chaotic SAS scrum during a break from training at their base in Scotland in 1944. Fortunately, their fighting was better than their rugby.

COURTESY OF JOHN KANE

RIGHT: Johnny Cooper (far right) and other SAS 'Originals' salute a statue of Mayne, erected in Newtownards in 1997 to commemorate probably the greatest soldier in the regiment's history.

COURTESY OF JOHN KANE

1930s; and served in Suez and Cyprus in the 1940s. In the UK he had commanded 43 Squadron for three years from 1927 to 1931. During that time it became renowned for the acrobatics it performed at airshows. Lowe – war hero and England international – was the star turn, and when the nine aircraft appeared tied together in three flights, the spectators would crane their necks and try to pick out his plane.

He spent two years in the 1930s as Chief Flying Instructor at the RAF College, Cranwell, passing on skills learnt in one war to young pilots who would find them useful in a second war. That he had an indirect hand in defeating the Luftwaffe would have pleased Lowe greatly.

Lowe's life, both in the RAF and on the rugby field, was characterized by an iron will and determination. Maybe his small build was the propeller he used to drive himself forward; as if he felt he was compensating for his physique with a mental strength greater than that of a man twice his size. It would be wrong to say Lowe had no fear; few, if any, men can claim to be fearless. Every time he and his fellow pilots climbed into their cockpits they faced a lonely struggle with their imagination. Fear had been pushed to the back of their minds but if they removed the chocks and let it roll forward it would destroy them, either when they were 17,000 feet above the ground, or as they lay in their beds at night.

Lowe's ability to conquer his nerves was perhaps his greatest achievement of the war, more so than all the planes he shot down or the medals he won. There must have been times when he was frightened out of his mind but he stuck it out.

Shortly before he died in 1983, aged ninety-one, Lowe said, 'If you set your mind to do something … you can do anything.' It could serve as his epitaph.

CHAPTER TWELVE

Fred Harvey

*F*red Harvey won just two caps for Ireland at the start of the last century and suffered criticism on both occasions. The newspapers said he didn't have the nerve for international rugby. But during the First World War Harvey showed there was nothing wrong with his nerve, as he won a Victoria Cross and Military Cross serving as a mounted soldier with the Canadian Calvary.

What on earth did the Wanderers rugby club put in the beer a century ago? It was some brew. Tom Crean and Robert Johnston whiled away many a long Dublin night in the clubhouse in the 1890s, a few years before they were awarded the Victoria Cross during the Boer War. Among the next generation of Wanderers players who supped from their bar stool was Fred Harvey. Like his illustrious predecessors, Harvey was capped by Ireland, although his international career was mediocre in comparison to Johnston and, in particular, Crean. Hesitant on the rugby field, perhaps, but Fred Harvey on the battlefield was a formidable proposition. The Victoria Cross he won in 1917 should never have been awarded. That is not a slight on Harvey, for rarely have such acts of prodigious courage been performed. But in the first moments of the charge that led to his VC, Harvey should have been shot dead. That he wasn't owed as much to the outrageous boldness of Harvey as to the incompetence of the Germans.

Frederick Maurice Watson Harvey was born in 1888 into a religious household. His father was a vicar but with three hardy sons there wasn't always an air of reverence pervading the vicarage. All three boys were enthusiastic sportsmen and might well have been present when Ireland and Tom Crean beat Scotland 5–0 at Lansdowne Road in 1894 on their way to their first ever Triple Crown.

Fred was educated at the Portora Royal School in Enniskillen. It was a happy period in his life. He enjoyed the popularity that was a concomitant of being a talented sportsman, excelling in rugby, athletics and boxing. His brothers also helped in giving Fred some status. Being the youngest of three brothers has its drawbacks, bruises and hand-me-down clothes among them, but all is forgotten when one of your big brothers is capped for Ireland. Fred went one better. Both his brothers were capped when he was a schoolboy.

Arnold, who later became the Bishop of Cashel, won the first of his eight caps in 1900 against Wales. His penultimate appearance was in 1903 against England, the only match in which he played alongside his middle brother, Duncan. 'Lank' – as Fred was known to his family – was probably not allowed the weekend away from school to go and watch the match in Dublin, but he must have felt a surge of pride when he heard Ireland had won 6–0.

'Lank' liked to think his rugby talents were more refined than his brothers', although such seditious thoughts were kept to himself. They played in the pack, relying more, in the eyes of Fred, on brawn than brain. He was a scrum-half, although his accomplished ball skills made him an option just about anywhere in the back line.

In 1906 Fred played in the Wanderers XV that won the Leinster Cup. It was the fourth time the club had won the trophy but their first success in twelve years. The last occasion had been in 1894 when Crean and Johnston had featured so prominently. The 3–0 victory against Monkstown pleased none but the most dedicated Wanderers' fan. It had been a match devoid of quality. The *Irish Times* lamented the shoddy handling skills, commenting that 'seldom has so little back play been seen in a contest of this kind, and what there was of it was poor'.

The next season Harvey made his international debut. He was just eighteen years and seven months and still a schoolboy. Double mathematics, however, would have been infinitely preferable to the pasting meted out to the Irish XV by Wales. Over 30,000 fans filed into the Cardiff ground to see the demolition. Among the onlookers was the Irish ladies' hockey team who had performed a lap of honour prior to the kick-off following their defeat of their Welsh counterparts the previous day.

Harvey was selected at fly-half with T H Robinson, the only other Wanderers representative, at scrum-half. Robinson had a dreadful match, so bad, in fact, that he never played again for Ireland. Harvey laboured valiantly but he was playing behind an out-of-form scrum-half and a feeble scrum, according to the *Irish Times*: '[Wales] shoved the Irishmen almost as they liked, while in getting possession they were successful in almost every occasion.'

Wales led 6–0 at half-time. After the break they wiped the turf with the Irish. Wales' scrum-half Percy Bush was superb, 'the dominant factor, the predominant partner and he played the Irish himself,' wrote the *Athletic News*. He scored one of the four second-half tries as Wales ran up a record 29–0 score. 'One never saw an International side so thoroughly demoralized and upset,' the *Athletic News* opined. 'They seemed stupefied by the brilliance of their opponents.'

The *Irish Times* did its best to dust the match in search of any fingerprints of comfort. On the evidence of the game they concluded that Harvey had been 'playing against terrific odds and … [was] practically unable to do anything during the entire game … but he may content himself with the knowledge that he never once flinched, and we sincerely trust he has profited by his experience'.

At least the humbling by Wales brought to an end the 1907 Championship. Ireland slunk home to recover from the indignities they had suffered. When the new season rolled around it was impossible to know whether Harvey had profited by his experience. He had emigrated to Canada. It would be a touch mischievous to suggest Harvey fled Ireland to escape the ramifications of such a heavy defeat. More probable was a desire, like a great many other Irishmen in the early twentieth century, to explore the rest of the world.

Little is known of Harvey's movements in Canada during this period. He lived in Fort Macleod, Alberta, and he may well have acquired his later love for horses during this time. But sometime in late 1910 he returned temporarily to Ireland. Perhaps he felt it safe to return after three years. He wasted little time in digging out his boots and taking his place in the Wanderers XV. He wasn't selected for an Ireland trial match in early 1911, but on the same Saturday he helped his side beat Old Wesley 19–11. He was, said the *Irish Times*, 'easily the best back on the home team'.

Ireland started the 1911 Five Nations with wins against England and Scotland. Wales, however, beat them 16–0, extending a winning streak against the Irish that had begun with the 1907 victory. Harvey, meanwhile, had continued to impress with his performances for the Wanderers, being employed in various backline positions. Such versatility hadn't gone unnoticed by the Ireland selectors. When, on the eve of the match in Cork against France, full-back W P Hinton cried off sick, Harvey was mooted as a possible replacement. C Thompson and R A Wright, however, were the preferred choices. Both were wired, both were unavailable. Harvey, fourth choice, had no other commitments that day. Despite the fact that he had scant experience of playing full-back he was asked to make his way to the Mardyke Road ground.

It was a gorgeous Cork afternoon when the match got under way. Maybe it was the sun that got in Harvey's eyes as the French right winger, Faillot, ran at him. The *Irish Sporting Illustrated* was not impressed with Harvey's defensive abilities: 'It looked as if he had him safe. Harvey, however, misjudged the pace at which Faillot was travelling, and when he finally "went out" for him, the Frenchman had slipped past him along the touchline.'

That was the only French try of the match. Ireland's forwards played with greater cohesion after the break and scored 17 points during a fifteen-minute purple patch and the final score of 25–5 reflected the lopsided nature of the second half. It was a victory nearly as comprehensive as Wales's win against Ireland four years earlier. The *Sporting Illustrated*, however, refused to allow the scoreline to mask what it considered a poor display by Harvey: '[He] was not a success. It was a difficult trial to put him through, and it must be remembered that he had never played in that position before. Those, however, who are acquainted with his play in club games, were quite confident he would be a success in any position. True he only made one bad mistake, but that might easily have cost us the match.'

Club rugby was the stage on which Harvey performed best. On the two occasions he played for Ireland he had trouble remembering his lines although, admittedly, in his second performance he was the understudy forced to play a lead part at the eleventh hour. The month after the France game, Harvey was back in the spotlight with the Wanderers in the final of the Leinster Cup, a role that was far less daunting than representing Ireland.

Their opponents were Bective Rangers, the reigning champions, and the favourites in most people's eyes. Harvey was in the centre, alongside fellow international R V Jackson. It was a good pairing, too good for Bective, who lost 9–0. The *Irish Times* reported that 'the Wanderers' threequarters all played well, and in saying Jackson and Harvey were the pick of them, it's impossible to separate the two. Jackson was perhaps more brilliant, but Harvey got through more work. Both of them had much to do with winning the game.'

A few weeks later Harvey returned to Canada. He wasn't particularly sorry to leave Ireland. He didn't dislike the place but a young woman had caught his eye in Fort Macleod and Harvey was determined to woo her. Her name was Winifred Lillian Patterson and she was the daughter of a Superintendent from the NorthWest Mounted Police. Maybe she was the reason Harvey learned to ride. There was no indication during his schooldays that he had a passion for horses but in the years leading up to the First World War he became a proficient rider. If his motivation to become a horseman had been to impress a lady it paid off handsomely. He married Winifred in 1914.

The peal of the bells had barely time to fade before Britain declared war on Germany. Harvey enlisted the following year and joined the Canadian Mounted Rifles at Fort Macleod. In 1916 he was commissioned, and later that year he was transferred to the Lord Strathcona's Horse. The Strathcona's were a nascent regiment, raised for service in the Boer War and recruited largely from the Royal-West Mounted Police. Like many colonial regiments that had fought in South Africa, the Strathcona's had performed with such courage that they became an established unit of the Canadian militia.

Although Harvey didn't join the Strathcona's until the latter half of 1916 he had missed little action. It had been planned that the regiment would be deployed during the Battle of the Somme – to the concern of Brigadier-General Seeley, commander of the Canadian Cavalry Brigade – who later wrote of their intended mission: 'I tried to make myself believe that the operation was possible, though my reason told me it was not so.' Seeley was correct in his analysis and, fortunately for the Strathcona's, the chiefs of staff soon realized that the Somme and cavalry were incompatible. They were pulled from the attack and spent the summer of 1916 kicking their heels in reserve.

The first couple of months of 1917 continued in equally dispiriting fashion. Some of the men, Harvey among them, began to wonder if they would ever get to grips with the enemy. In 1915 the regiment had served on the Western Front as infantrymen at the request of High Command. They had been reconstituted as a mounted force in February 1916. The more disgruntled members of the regiment had begun to propose a return to the infantry. That would be preferable to spending day after day grooming their horses and polishing their boots.

Their disquiet ended in March when they received orders to return to the Somme from their training area on the French coast. The regiment established headquarters at Moland, six miles east of Peronne. On the morning of 24 March the Canadian Cavalry Brigade formed along a twelve-mile frontage and advanced beyond positions held by the British infantry. The Royal Canadian Dragoons were first into action and by nightfall had taken several important positions. That night the Fort Garry Horse captured two villages and on 26 March the Strathcona's entered the fray, capturing the village of Equancourt.

The following morning, the villages of Longasvesnes and Lieramont were taken by the Dragoons and that evening the Strathcona's and the Fort Garrys were asked to attack the last of the Brigade's objectives, the villages of Saulcourt and Guyencourt. A heavy snowstorm delayed the attack and it wasn't until shortly after 5pm that the Fort Garrys penetrated the defences of Saulcourt. Attention now turned to Guyencourt where it was known the Germans had heavy defences.

Harvey was in command of the leading troop, with orders to gallop over a ridge approximately half a mile to the left of the village and then swing right round behind. Brigadier-General Seeley had reconnoitred the position earlier that day, but the falling snow hampered his observations. Although he declared himself satisfied that the attack should go ahead, he later confessed that 'perhaps owing to the frequent snow squalls, I had not discerned the line of thin but strong wire running from the north-east corner of Guyencourt straight back to the German second position'.

Harvey and his troop (approximately thirty-six men) got over the ridge with few casualties. The Dubliner might have taken to riding late in life, but he was now as accomplished on a horse as those men under his command who had learned to ride almost before they could walk. He galloped on in front of his men round the back of Guyencourt and saw the wire that his Brigadier had missed earlier in the day. Seeley watched as Harvey rode up and down the wire: 'He turned about and galloped back, waving to his men to follow his movements,' recalled Seeley. 'I saw him galloping straight towards me, looking to his left and right, and wondered what on earth he was going to do, for I could see a little trench … with one machine-gun.'

The machine-gun was probably a Maxim 08/15. To the German soldier it was a work of art. To the Allies it was the 'Devil's Paint Brush'. The gun's manufacturers would have burst with pride if they could have heard such a compliment. The Maxim 08/15 was an improvement on the Maxim MO8, which had been the choice of the German army in the early days of the war. The new improved version fired 500 rounds per minute and normally had a three-man crew but it was possible for one gunner to operate it. Harvey, of course, was unaware of the ins and outs of the Maxim. But he did know that the man with his finger on the trigger had a poor aim. He had been in full view of the trench for a couple of minutes and hadn't been hit.

The firing stopped as Harvey rode back towards his troop. Maybe the German gunner thought he had scared off the horseman and had begun to change the ammunition drum that hung on the side of the Maxim. The sudden sound of galloping hooves caused him to look up aghast.

Harvey had wheeled his horse round and was now charging the machine-gun position. The German fumbled with the gun as he realized what was happening. It was a frantic race for time. When he next looked up it was to see the Canadian leap from his horse, revolver in hand, and come sprinting towards him. The Maxim on its bipod wasn't a cumbersome weapon in the hands of the three-man crew who normally operated it. How the gunner must have wished he had a full crew now.

Harvey hurdled the wire and he was now near enough for the German to see the shape of his handsome, clean-shaven face. If the machine-gunner reached for his own revolver in the seconds before Harvey jumped into the trench he was too late. His clumsiness had cost him his life.

With the machine-gun captured and the German dead, the last obstacle to capture of the village had been removed. Seeley called Harvey's feat of arms 'remarkable' and recommended him for a Victoria Cross. He was awarded a

DSO by Field Marshal Sir Douglas Haig and wore the ribbon for a fortnight. Then he learned it had been upgraded to a VC. The citation ran:

> 'During an attack by his regiment on a village, a party of the enemy ran forward to a wired trench just in front of the village, and opened rapid fire and machine-gun fire at a very close range, causing heavy casualties in the leading troop. At this critical moment, when the enemy showed no intention whatever of retiring, and fire was still intense, Lt Harvey, who was in command of the leading troops, ran forward well ahead of his men and dashed at the trench, skilfully manned, jumped the wire, shot the machine-gunner and captured the gun. His most courageous act undoubtedly had a decisive effect on the success of the operations.'

Harvey was the first Canadian cavalryman to be awarded the Victoria Cross.

The rest of 1917 followed a similar frustrating path to that of 1916 for the Strathcona's. During the opening stages of the Battle of Arras in April they were in the front line near St Quentin, but they were not called upon to attack the Germans. Nor were they asked to enter the Passchendaele abattoir, despite rumours among the men that they would be used. A visit from Seeley to the battlefield soon put an end to the tittle-tattle. 'I saw at once,' he wrote later, 'that all hope of action was gone. There had been heavy rain, and Flanders was beginning to resemble a quagmire ... so we left the stricken field and marched south.'

South was Cambrai, where the Strathcona's supported the first large tank attack of the war. However, it wasn't until the beginning of the year, nearly twelve months after the fighting at Guyencourt, that Harvey was given another chance to have a crack at the Germans.

On 21 March the German army launched their spring offensive on the Western Front that they hoped would break the Allies before the arrival of significant numbers of American troops. The gamble by Ludendorff, the German commander, ultimately failed, though it required several months of hard fighting before he admitted defeat. Initially the Germans caught the Allies by surprise, advancing out of the early morning fog on 21 March, and killing or capturing thousands of British and French soldiers.

At 8.30 on the morning of 30 March, the Germans were advancing towards

Amiens. Seeley was ordered to cross the rivers Noye and Avre with the Canadian Cavalry Brigade and 'engage and endeavour to delay the enemy'. The Brigade, comprising the Dragoons, Strathcona's, Fort Garry Horse and a machine-gun squadron, crossed the rivers and advanced towards Moreuil wood.

The wood was not yet in leaf. It was dense and triangular in shape, and stretched down from the crest of a low ridge. Seeley knew it contained a large nest of Germans, but he wasn't sure how many. He ordered one squadron* of Dragoons to the right of the wood to capture its south-east corner and two squadrons to the left to seize the north-east corner. He then instructed one squadron of Strathcona's to gallop right round the north-east edge of the wood and surprise those Germans who were moving up to reinforce their compatriots. Once they had taken care of that task, they were to help the Dragoons secure the south-east corner. Seeley finished his briefing by instructing the two remaining squadrons of the Strathcona's to attack the wood at its southernmost point, and to fight their way through until they linked up with their comrades in the south-east corner.

The Germans in the wood were the 101st Grenadiers, hard men who liked a fight. They hadn't been expecting an attack – after all, it was they who had been advancing for the last nine days – but they offered stubborn resistance when the Canadians began their assault. Seeley later reported that: 'Desperate hand to hand fighting ensued, the horsemen engaged Grenadiers at first with their pistols and, when these were discharged, taking to their swords and falling upon the Saxons, cutting and thrusting.' Harvey wasn't one of the men hacking his way through the wood. He was in 'C' squadron, whose job was to skirt the north-eastern edge of Moreuil wood and attack the reinforcements. Harvey was ordered by Lt Flowerdew to take his troop and make good the north-east corner of the wood.

When the troop was 200 yards from the edge of the wood they encountered a superior force of Germans. Harvey and his men dismounted and returned fire. Alerted by the sound of battle, Flowerdew and his three remaining troops rode to the assistance of Harvey. The two men conferred and Harvey suggested his troop advance and flush the Germans from the

* A cavalry squadron at full strength numbered 150 men – although this figure often fluctuated depending on casualties – commanded usually by a major.

wood, while Flowerdew took his men round the back of the wood and finished them off when they emerged from the trees. Flowerdew agreed. The two officers shook hands and parted company. Harvey led his men into the wood and pushed the Germans back at the point of their sabres. Flowerdew, meanwhile, had ridden round behind the wood on to some slightly higher ground in anticipation of an easy kill. Instead he saw a large force of the enemy, about 300 in number, most of whom were the reinforcements for the Grenadiers.

Three troops of Strathcona's would normally number around 110 horsemen, making a fight with a force three times greater unwise. But the regiment had been depleted by sickness and shelling. Flowerdew had with him only seventy-five men. They gazed down upon the enemy moving towards the wood. Then they looked at their officer, waiting for his command. What would he signal?

Flowerdew thrust his sabre into the air. 'It's a charge, boys,' he yelled, 'it's a charge!', and galloped down towards the Germans. Trumpeter Longley put his bugle to his lips to sound the charge but a bullet took off the top of his head before the first notes sounded. Before his body had fallen to the ground the rest of the troops were charging towards the Germans with their sabres raised.

The Germans opened fire and shot many horses from under their riders. But those they missed rode into their ranks and caused hideous wounds with their sabres. The encounter was brief, but bloody. All Trooper Dale could remember later was 'the shouting of men, the moans of the wounded, the pitiful crying of the wounded and dying horses'. The horsemen that had survived the initial charge broke through the two lines of Germans and turned back towards the wood.

As they did so Harvey and his men emerged from the trees and started to lay down a fire in support of their mates. Having broken through the German line, the survivors wheeled round and charged once more. The savagery of the fighting now resembled a medieval battle as the Germans tried to pull the Canadians from their horses. Those that were dragged from their mounts were clubbed to death as they writhed on the ground. Other Germans jabbed at the cavalrymen with their bayonets. A sergeant, Tom MacKay, fought off several attackers but the flesh on his legs was all but stripped off. The medical officer who attended to him later counted fifty-nine wounds on one leg alone.

But the Strathcona's put to the sword several Germans, and they gradually began to fall back in the face of the hand-to-hand fighting and the fire from Harvey's men.

It was during this time that Flowerdew was shot off his horse. Harvey went to his rescue and dragged him to cover with the help of Lt Harrower, who was shot in the foot during the rescue. After putting Flowerdew in the hands of stretcher-bearers, Harvey and his men forced the remaining Germans out of the north-east corner of the wood. At around midday the entire wood was cleared of the enemy. The only remaining threat came from the artillery but Harvey, his energy undiminished by the fierce fighting of the preceding hours, located the batteries and reported their position to the British gunners, who promptly eliminated the threat. Later three battalions of the British 8th Infantry Division moved up and relieved the Canadians.

The Strathcona's had gone into Moreuil wood with 373 horsemen. Forty-five had been killed and another 120 wounded. Harvey was one of the latter. He suffered gunshot wounds as he flushed out the Germans from the wood. For his part in the battle, Harvey was awarded the Military Cross, which was gazetted in June:

> 'For conspicuous gallantry and devotion to duty. In the attack, by his fearless leading, he overcame the resistance of the enemy, although the latter were in greatly superior numbers. He engaged many of the enemy single-handed, and although wounded and suffering from a considerable loss of blood, continued to fight his way forward until he effected a junction with another mounted party, thus contributing in a great degree to the success of the attack. He commanded his men with magnificent gallantry, skill and determination.'

Lt Gordon Flowerdew died from his wounds the following day, unaware that he had been recommended for the Victoria Cross (it was awarded). Of the seventy-five men he had led against the Germans, twenty-four were killed in action, a further fourteen succumbed to their wounds and thirty-seven were wounded. Only fourteen came through in one piece.

The Battle of Moreuil wood was just one in a series of fierce clashes in the spring of 1918 that played a crucial part in deciding the outcome of the war. The British and Dominion forces, as well as the French, offered sterner resistance than the Germans expected. They stood their ground and the decisive breakthrough that the German High Command believed they could achieve never materialized. The arrival of the Americans augmented the Allies' defences and in the summer of 1918 the Germans themselves were pushed back when the Allies launched the Battle of Amiens on 8 August. The Strathcona's were in the vanguard of the attack, galloping through the holes created in the enemy's defences by the British tanks. By late October 1918 they were still in the business of pursuing retreating Germans, this time near Le Cateau, east of Cambrai.

Harvey returned to Canada in 1919. During the next two decades he maintained his links with the Strathcona's. In 1938 he sailed to England to attend a senior officers' training course at Sheerness. When he returned to Canada in May 1939 it was to assume command of the regiment as Lieutenant-Colonel.

Shortly after the outbreak of the Second World War Harvey was promoted to Brigadier. He was a popular and efficient commanding officer, but in 1943 he created something of a furore in the national press when he let it be known he didn't think much of the quality of men being produced by Canada. He called them 'selfish and lacking in Canadian ideals'. The letters pages of the newspapers carried numerous responses to Harvey's obloquy, most of them from parents of serving soldiers, and nearly all of them criticizing his insensitivity.

Harvey may have regretted his words in hindsight. They certainly wouldn't have gone down well with his only son, Dennis, who was in Europe with the Royal Winnipeg Rifles. Brigadier Harvey went to Britain in 1944 for a tour of the Canadian army, so perhaps father and son met up at some point for a good-natured debate about the comments. It would have been good if they had, because in February 1945 Dennis was killed near Nijmegen during the Battle of the Rhineland.

Harvey retired from the army later that year. He and his wife turned their attentions to horses. They travelled widely in Australia, New Zealand and Britain, attending horse shows whenever they could. On the occasions they returned to the British Isles for a holiday, the pair would make sure their visit coincided with the Grand National, the Derby or the Dublin Horse Show.

The Harveys' hectic lifestyle kept them young. In 1960 Harvey, then seventy-two, received a letter from the National Army Museum asking him for details of how he won his Victoria Cross. He began his reply by apologizing for his delay in responding: 'Sorry for not having answered your letter before. I was away on a hunting trip up north.'

What little information the curator of the museum had on Harvey had clearly been gleaned from Brigadier Seeley's accounts of the Strathcona's in the First World War, entitled *Adventure* and *My Horse Warrior*. Harvey told the curator he had also read and enjoyed the books, 'but [I] must say that Seeley was inclined (to put it mildly) to exaggerate'.

Harvey, who was Colonel of the Strathcona's from 1958 to 1966, died on 21 August 1980 aged ninety-one. He was buried with full military honours in the Union Cemetery, Fort Macleod, four days later. His wife died in 1989 and was buried alongside her husband of sixty-six years.

The Wanderers remains an unassuming and unpretentious club. Since the sport turned professional in 1995 it has slipped into the background of Irish rugby, languishing in the second division and in the shadow of more successful clubs such as Shannon and Cork Constitution. Yet of the four Victoria Crosses awarded to international rugby players, three have been bestowed upon former members of the club. If any Wanderers fan was ever found in a Dublin bar claiming to support the 'Bravest Club in the World', it wouldn't be the beer talking.

CHAPTER THIRTEEN

Arnold Jackson

A rnold Jackson, an Oxford undergraduate, trained for the Olympic 1,500 metres race in 1912 on Guinness and burgundy. Yet he strode away with the gold medal, beating the world record holder in the final. In 1914 he joined the Rifle Brigade and, having fought on the Somme, at Arras and in the mud of Ypres, he became the youngest brigadier in the British Army.

'The average young man of today aged something under thirty, whether he be a social butterfly or a junior clerk, is a stupid, conceited creature. Few men are much good until they are thirty.'

The *Daily Mirror*'s editorial in July 1912 was intended to tell the male youth of Britain a few home truths. It had had enough of the kind of indolent fops who had besmirched the Eton v Harrow cricket match at Lord's. The paper's cricket correspondent had been horrified to see 'scores of tired, young men who evidently found it "too much fag" to look on at the game … aimlessly in twos and threes, they shuffled – one couldn't call it walking – about the ground. Most of them looked bored beyond expression with their sur-roundings.' When the man from the *Mirror* eavesdropped on their con-versation he heard heresy. For they talked not of the cricket, but about ' … the way in which women do their hair nowadays'.

Young men in 1912, to borrow a contemporary phrase, were in crisis. Older generations looked at them initially with a mix of condescension and pity. In their era men had been made by war and adventure. They had fought in Abyssinia, Sudan and South Africa and were all the better for it. But the stirring times of the Victorian era had been supplanted by the Edwardian beau monde.

The pity turned to scorn, however, when Britain's standing on the sports field began to decline. The sports field was, after all, the battlefield of the twentieth century and national prestige was at stake, particularly during the Olympics. Losing to Australia at cricket or New Zealand at rugby was one thing; they were part of the Empire and regarded with much the same fondness as an errant younger brother. But the Olympics was the one time when Britain came face to face with traditional enemies such as France, Germany, Italy and that arrogant parvenu, America. In the 1908 Games in London, Britain had won twice as many gold medals as the United States (56 to 23) but, worryingly, the Americans had taken the bulk of the track and field golds, including the 800m, 1,500m, high jump and long jump.

In 1912 the USA won ten individual gold medals in athletics. Britain took one. 'We have been made a laughing stock,' raged the *Athletic News*. 'The results of the games at Stockholm go to show that we have not the men; that in a world's race for supremacy we are veritable amateurs.' The paper had received a letter from Mr W Beach Thomas, ex-president of the Oxford University Athletics Club. What he had to say damaged British pride every bit as deeply as the news of defeats at Isandhlwana and Khartoum. The British team, he said, 'accepted defeat as if the Olympic Games were a competition of parlour tricks in a provincial drawing room'. He had spent much of the Games sitting in the stand alongside an American gentleman who was 'astounded at the want of spirit in the English team'. It had come to this, Britons being patronized by Americans.

The British press, however, displaying a bellicosity sadly absent from the sports field, launched a counter-attack with *The Times* leading, astride its trusty charger called Sportsmanship. 'In conversation the question arises of whether the Games do any good in promoting good will. I have not heard any confident answer in the affirmative. And, while it is a delicate subject, it seems necessary to say that this, it has to be feared, is chiefly the fault of the

Americans ... we all know how much irritation and annoyance the American claques have caused on former occasions, and it is at least arguable whether, if the other countries had followed the example of the US from the beginning, the Olympic Games would not before this have become impossible.'

Perversely, the anguished introspection of the newspapers blinded them to the one British track success. Arnold Jackson had won the 1,500 metres, leaving in his trail a cluster of Americans. The *Sporting Life*, mysteriously, gave his triumph only a cursory six lines. The lead story was the victory in the 5,000 metres of Finland's Hannes Kolehmainen, who edged out by a yard the Frenchman Jean Bouin. Not that the twenty-one-year-old Jackson would have been peeved by such a snub. He wouldn't have noticed. He was probably still in a Stockholm bar celebrating. Unfortunately when on 13 July 1912 the *Daily Mirror* chastised a group of British athletes for having 'been seen outside cafés' – when they should have been training – the paper didn't name the accused. It would have been safe to assume Jackson was one of them.

The kindest word one could use to describe Jacker's attitude to training is 'relaxed'. He arrived in Stockholm in a foul mood, muttering all the way down the gangplank about the iniquities of having to cut short a fishing holiday to compete in the Olympic Games. When anyone tried to give Jackson advice on nutrition he peered at them quizzically, as if he were a Martian who had walked into the Bear Inn, his local pub in Oxford, and asked for a pint of mild. Jackson's fluid intake when he was in training included a bottle of Guinness for lunch and a couple of glasses of burgundy with his supper.

When he wasn't sampling the delights of a Pinot Noir, Jackson combined his running with a degree at Oxford University. He won the Varsity mile in March 1912 in a time of 4 min 21.4secs. The victory did enough in the eyes of the selectors to warrant a place in the British Olympic squad to run the 1,500 metres. He wasn't even required to attend the Olympic trial in May, where he might have found the competition a bit stiffer. There were so many entrants in the 1,500 metres that three heats were run, all vying for the six other places. W Cottrill won in 4min 8.8sec and among the other qualifiers was Philip Baker, a Cambridge student and later Lord Philip Noel-Baker, Labour statesman and Nobel Peace Prize recipient in 1959.

The Vth Olympiad boasted record numbers of competitors. There were

2,547 entrants from twenty-eight countries. Yet, despite the proliferation of athletes, the number of sports was fourteen, seven down on the 1908 Games. This was at the insistence of Baron Pierre de Coubertin, the founding father of the modern Olympic movement. He had disapproved of the London Games, as he made plain in a speech to the Stockholm organizers prior to the 1912 Games:

> 'The next Olympiads must not have such a character, they must not be so comprehensive. There was altogether too much in London. The Games must be kept more purely athletic; they must be more dignified, more discreet; more in accordance with classic and artistic requirements.'

The first round for the 1,500 metres was on Tuesday 9 July. Jackson reportedly spent the preceding twenty hours in bed, having felt a trifle 'stale' on his arrival from his fishing trip. Qualification for the following day's final was simple – the first two runners to cross the line in each of the seven heats would be in the final. Jackson was in the fourth heat, along with John Paul Jones and Anderson, two of the nine American runners. Jones led for most of the race but Jackson ran past him with 150 metres remaining and the American, holding off a late burst from the South African, Victor, took the second qualification spot in 4min 12.4secs, two seconds slower than Jackson's time.

The only other Briton to make the final was Baker. The line-up for the final reflected the strength of American middle-distance running. Of the fourteen finalists, half were from the USA, three were Swedish, two were British and there was a German and a Frenchman.

Jackson had retired to his bed following the exertions of his heat, and doubtless drifted off to sleep dreaming of pike, salmon and less strenuous times. The American squad was staying on board the ship that had brought them to Stockholm. That night, as they strolled round the deck and thought ahead to tomorrow's final, they allowed themselves to be splashed with complacency from the swell of confidence that encircled the squad. Who could blame them? Abe Kiviat, the fastest qualifier in 4:05.4, was also the world 1,500 metre record-holder with 3:55.8. Mel Sheppard was the reigning champion and John Paul Jones held the world record for the mile.

Jackson's personal best prior to the Games had been the 4:21.4 he ran in the 1912 Varsity match. One of his Oxford and Brasenose College team-mates in that competition had been an American by the name of F F Russell. Before the Vth Olympiad he had considered writing a letter to the American coach warning him of Jackson. He never 'got around to it'. He was as confident of success as the American runners. What Russell did do, however, was challenge 'Jacker' to a bet: 'I casually offered to make a small wager on the USA against the world in any single event. He instantly offered to take me up on the 1,500 meter [*sic*].'

When the final of the 1,500 metres got underway it was the Frenchman, Arnaud, who led the field for the first two laps. The Americans were grouped in the middle of the field, while Jackson and Baker brought up the rear. The pace increased after 700 metres – enough for the German to drop out of contention – but it wasn't until the bell that the Americans made their move. Kiviat glided up to take the lead from a spent Arnaud. Close on his heels came two of his compatriots, Jones and Taber.

One of the Swedes, Wide, found another gear with 250 metres to go and moved up to within a couple of yards of the Americans. Jackson was in seventh place but, seeing the Swede go, the tall British runner sprinted wide on to the shoulder of the leading group. Coming into the home straight the Americans, joined by Sheppard, had shaken off Wide and assumed the battle for medals was among themselves.

With 50 metres to go, Kiviat kicked away from his compatriots, and several dozen Americans in the plum-red brick Stockholm stadium rose to their feet to cheer his win. Then, suddenly, they became aware of the lanky figure of Jackson on Kiviat's outside, eating up the ground with gigantic strides. He drew level with the American, and then continued past him, breasting the tape three metres ahead of the world record-holder in a new British and Olympic record time of 3min 56.8sec.

Kiviat and Taber, the bronze medallist, slumped to the ground in misery. Jackson was in a similar state, according to the *Athletic News*: 'He was all out and took a time to recover. But what a race this tall boy had run! What will he do in the future? He took part in neither trials nor [AAA] Championships. He had conserved his energies, and wisely, for this race.'

In September Jackson returned to Brasenose College and Oxford. The effulgence of the city in those dreamy years before the First World War was captured by Max Beerbohm in his book, *Zuleika Dobson*. 'There is nothing in England to be matched with what lurks in the vapours of these meadows, and in the shadows of these spires – that mysterious, ineluctible spirit of Oxford. Oxford! The very sight of the word printed, or sound of it spoken, is fraught for me with most actual magic.'

For many of Oxford's students these years were the high point of their lives. To them the University seemed suffused with a tranquillity that would never end. They were the chosen few – intellectually and socially superior to their contemporaries. One of their number, Osbert Sitwell, observed that: 'The world was a ripe peach and we were eating it.' Jackson, with his gold medal glinting off the sun that 'rose over Wadham and set over Worcester', stood out, even among contemporaries such as Harold Macmillan and Vincent Massey. The Brasenose magazine, the *Brazen Nose*, called Jackson 'the outstanding athlete of his generation. He rowed and played football and hockey for the college as a matter of course.'

In 1914 he completed a hat-trick of Varsity mile triumphs and became president of the Oxford University Athletics Club. He also took a four-man squad to America at the behest of the University of Pennsylvania. It had invited Oxford to send a team to compete in the 1914 Penn Relays, an annual event that had previously been the preserve of American colleges.

The invitation was ostensibly a token of friendship, a hand of goodwill that reached out across the Atlantic from one great institution to another. But there was an ulterior motive. The Americans wanted to avenge their defeat in Stockholm. Why, after all, had only milers been invited when the Relays featured a multitude of disciplines?

Jackson assembled his strongest team: David Gaussen, a twenty-one-year-old Englishman, G M Sproule, an Australian from Melbourne, and Norman Taber, an American and the man who had finished third behind Jackson in Stockholm. Taber had arrived at St John's College the previous year on a Rhodes Scholarship, but Jackson had no qualms about taking him back across the water.

They sailed from Southampton on 8 April, appropriately aboard the *Olympic*. Four days later, while Jackson was probably forgoing a run around deck for a burgundy, the *Philadelphia Inquirer* was billing the race as a battle for the supremacy of world middle-distance running: 'This race has attracted more attention than any single event that has ever been held in this country, and as a result it will be watched with the keenest interest, not only here, but also at all athletic centres throughout the world. Whether America wins or not, the coming race is considered by foreign critics as a very decisive one, in showing the superiority either of the English or American distance men. The event has assumed real international importance.'

Jackson remained blissfully unaware of the Relays' prestige until the *Olympic* docked in New York on Saturday 18 April. One can imagine the horror with which Jackson, an unassuming and sanguine Englishman, viewed the swarm of American journalists on the quayside from the deck of the ship. A few days later the *Athletic News* was able to report with unbridled glee – and not a little pride – the failure of the Americans to pin down their man: 'There has been one amusing side to the visit of the OUAC team to the States, and that is the manner in which A N S Jackson managed to shake off the reporters, who, of course, came out in shoals to meet him off the boat. The American newsman usually manages to make copy out of the most reticent of individuals, but the Oxonian seems to have proved a very hard nut to crack.'

On the Monday Jackson's squad had their first training run for two weeks. Afterwards he conceded defeat in his bid to avoid the press. 'We have received a hearty welcome everywhere,' Jacker told the *Philadelphia Inquirer*. 'We ran this morning on Franklin's Field. I am glad to reach Philadelphia, for a little more entertaining and we would have had to worry much about the race.'

Jackson admitted that he had been rather taken aback to find so much interest: 'We had no idea what a big event this is. It is like the Olympic Games.' Even as Jackson was speaking, 'Coxey', the assistant ground keeper, had his shoulder pressed to the door of the track room, 'in order to keep out the troublesome persons who were anxious to talk to the English team'.

The Oxonians spent the rest of the week training and acclimatizing to the conditions. On Friday 24 April, the day before the race, they rested and took in some of the sights of Philadelphia. Meanwhile, inside the feverish offices of the *Philadelphia Inquirer*, the enthusiasm of the athletics correspondent was beginning to border on the obsessional: '[Jackson] stands over six feet in height and swings a pair of legs measuring 40 inches. He is of slender build, but withal strong and muscular. His speed is well known ... his greatest speed is shown on the last quarter, when he works his wonderfully strong and lengthy legs in rapid fire style. It is in making that long sprint that he takes his longest strides. Measurements taken on Franklin's Field ... show that he covers something more than eight feet every time his foot hits the ground ... during the first quarter of his mile, when he puts forth comparatively little effort, his stride does not measure seven feet. But when he warms up to his work ... he increases his stride to about seven feet and then when he starts on the last lap and lets out with full steam eight feet does not quite measure the distance between his heel and toe.'

The Pennsylvania public fed on such ebullience and 20,000 spectators filed into Franklin's Field the next day. They were betrayed by the weather, which was wet throughout, but their fortitude was rewarded by a rousing finale to the day in the four-by-one mile relay.

Sproule, Oxford's Australian, ran the first mile and at the changeover he was five yards behind Cornell University and the hosts, Pennsylvania University. The young Gaussen took on the baton and Cornell were soon dropped as Oxford and Penn strode clear of the remaining ten runners.

Gaussen got his nose in front during the last lap and slipped the baton to Taber. The American, anxious to impress his compatriots, shot off too quickly and suffered for his impetuosity in the last 200 metres. Madeira, the Penn runner, raced past Taber in the home straight and Jackson, impassive as he stood waiting on the track, was 15 metres down on Wallace McCurdy when he received the baton.

Jackson had reeled in McCurdy after the first 400 metres. For the next 1,000 metres the American could hear the squelch of Jackson's spikes on the sodden cinder track as the Englishman stalked him for two and a half laps. Then, with 200 metres to go, Jackson kicked and passed McCurdy on his outside. The Penn athlete responded and pulled himself level as they entered the home straight. For 40 metres the pair ran shoulder to shoulder until Jackson, his willpower suppressing his burning lungs, found from somewhere a reserve of energy and hurled himself across the finishing line a yard ahead of McCurdy.

McCurdy collapsed to the ground gasping for air. Jackson lurched across the track into the arms of Vivian Nickall, Penn's English rowing coach. Hundreds of spectators charged on to the track and carried Jackson and McCurdy shoulder high, appreciative of the magnificent race they had witnessed.

The American journalists, however, were less magnanimous. Piqued that Jackson had won once more, their churlishness discredited both themselves and American athletics. The *Philadelphia Inquirer* described the English quartet as 'over-rated', while Jackson 'was not quite himself ... [he] could not have been too sure of himself for he made no attempt to take the lead or set the pace'. No mention was made of the 15 metres he had made up on McCurdy.

But it was the comments of George B Underwood in the *New York Press* that raised the dander of the British press. He maintained that Jackson had been beaten on the line and that victory belonged to Penn. This was too much for the *Athletic News*: 'It is accordingly amusing to read Underwood's ignorant comments on the "erroneous decision" on the Yankee four being as "glorious in defeat as it would have been had the officials adjudged them victors". It is typical ... of the American journalists who pour out arrant nonsense to satisfy the cravings of *clienteles* as narrow-minded as themselves.'

When Jackson returned to England in May he had only three months before the lamps of Europe flickered and died. The world, however, for Jackson was still a ripe peach during the hot summer months of 1914. He looked forward to a career as a barrister and a trip to Berlin in 1916 to defend his Olympic 1,500 metres crown.

Jackson would never have the chance to defend his title. In the summer of 1916, instead of running against Germans, he was killing them. Jackson was in uniform a short time after the declaration of war in August. He had enlisted in the Royal North Lancashire Regiment but by the end of September had been attached to the 13th Battalion, Rifle Brigade, otherwise known as the 'Black Buttoned Bastards'.

The Rifle Brigade wore black buttons on their khaki tunics and the rest of their name came from the opinion of them held by many other regiments. They considered themselves a cut above the rest of the infantry, and on the sports field they were nigh on untouchable. Not many regiments could boast an Olympic 1,500 metre champion. But they also had the strongest rugby battalion in the brigade, thanks in no small part to a group of twenty South Africans who had sailed to enlist from Port Elizabeth. There was also in their ranks a contingent of semi-professional footballers from Stockton and at least a dozen professional golfers.

Jackson and his battalion had arrived in France in July 1915 under the command of fifty-two-year-old Colonel Charles Retor-Pinney, an officer with thirty years' experience. Twice Pretor-Pinney had retired, but twice he had returned to the Active List. The men loved him. He was one of those officers who wouldn't ask his boys to do anything he wasn't prepared to do himself.

On 5 July 1916, in the first week of the Battle of the Somme, the battalion moved up towards the front line. As they marched they sang their favourite song, one that they hoped would reach the ears of the King's Royal Rifle Corps, the rival regiment they considered markedly inferior.

> The Rifle Brigade is going away
> To leave the girls in the family way
> The King's Royal Rifles are left behind
> They've two and six a week to find.

The following evening they were in the town of Albert. Knowing they were destined for a 'show' against the Germans, the battalion took the last opportunity to fatten themselves before the slaughter. While the officers dined at the best restaurant in town, the men spent the night on the beer. A group broke into a boarded-up café and drank the place dry. 'If we're going to die for the French,' the soldiers told each other on such occasions, 'then the least they can do is stand us a drink.'

On 7 July they moved into the old frontline trench. Two days later they marched up to the new British front line, to the left of Contalmaison and directly in front of the village of Pozières. Dawn pulled back the covers on the 10 July to reveal a glorious summer's day. The men had little to do during the day except listen to the sounds of battle to their right as the 8th and 9th Green Howards captured Contalmaison village. At 8pm Pretor-Pinney received his orders: the battalion would lead an attack against a heavily fortified German trenchline in front of Pozières at 8.45pm. They would be supported by an artillery barrage, and the 25th and 23rd Divisions would launch flanking attacks at the same time. In addition, Pretor-Pinney was assured, a battalion of Royal Fusiliers would follow up behind in close support of his riflemen.

The battalion had been training two years for this moment. Now it had arrived the carapace of courage that had taken some of the men this far began to crack. 'Some men funked it, of course,' remembered Corporal Joe Hoyles. 'They went over the top all right, they had to or they'd have got my bayonet up their arse. But you could tell from their faces that a lot of people dreaded it.'

At 8.45pm the battalion clambered out of their trenches and advanced towards the German trench, 800 metres away. It was four years to the day since Jackson had won his Olympic title. On that day he had covered a similar distance in around two minutes. Conditions weren't so favourable this time. 'I can still hear the bullets zipping up,' said Corporal Bob Thompson, years later, 'like a lot of bees, and tufts of dirt, thrown up in front of you where the Jerries were shooting. You could see them going zzzp … zzzp, like a lot of bees.'

Even amid the diabolical din of battle, it took Pretor-Pinney just a few seconds to realize that there was no supporting artillery barrage. He glanced to his left, then his right, and saw nothing but a dipping sun lambent with red and orange that seemed to set the skyline ablaze. Unfortunately it wasn't silhouetting men of the 23rd and 25th divisions supporting their flanks. The Germans, admiring the pluck of the British for launching an attack without support, set aside their respect and clambered on to the rim of the trench to get a better sight of the attackers. It was like shooting ducks at a fairground.

As Pretor-Pinney dived into a shellhole to confer with his second in command, a breathless runner slithered down alongside him. Gasping for air, he handed the colonel a piece of paper – 'ATTACK CANCELLED'. The message had reached the artillerymen and the 23rd and 25th divisions. It had even made it to the Royal Fusiliers. But the lead battalion hadn't received it.

Too flabbergasted to lose his temper, Pretor-Pinney ordered the battalion to retire. But several men, the best of the battalion, were out of earshot, having fought their way demonically into the third line of German defences, a fort constructed around a small chalk quarry. One of these was Bob Thompson. He was looking for a place to set up his Lewis gun when he heard a commotion to his rear: 'Sergeant Holford came running across along the trench beneath us and he shouted, "The thing's cancelled! We've got to make our way back."'

It was now just before 10pm. Dusk was falling as the men scrambled away from the hell of battle, but the devil, grinning from ear to ear, barred their exit. A barrage suddenly opened up and the riflemen found themselves in its epicentre. Those that weren't torn apart by the shells were stippled with bits of their less fortunate comrades as the shells decimated the battalion. Then the realization dawned that the barrage was coming from their own artillery.

In the failing light the British soldiers in Contalmaison had seen the fighting and guessed the Germans had launched a counter-attack. They asked the artillery to send down a barrage on the advancing Germans. But the men they could see weren't advancing, and they weren't Germans. They were the retiring 13th Battalion, the Rifle Brigade. Or what was left of them.

The survivors stumbled, reeled, crawled back to the safety of their trenches. Jackson was among them. Four hundred officers and men hadn't been so lucky. The battalion no longer existed in numerical terms. Pretor-Pinney was one of the wounded. But the greatest pain he felt was the realization that his men had been the victims of an unpardonable blunder. When his adjutant found him in a casualty clearing station four days after the fiasco, the veteran campaigner, the epitome of the Victorian army officer, was sobbing quietly. 'What a mess they've made of my battalion,' he murmured, 'what a mess they've made of it.'

By April 1917 Pretor-Pinney was back at the helm and the men felt all the better for it. Jackson was now a major and one of the few surviving officers from the original battalion that had landed in France two years previously.

The catastrophe of the Somme had led to a reshuffling of the British and French packs. Lloyd George had replaced Asquith as Prime Minister at the end of 1916, while in France General Nivelle superseded Joffre as the supreme commander on the Western Front. Lloyd George blamed Field Marshal Haig for the bloody mess on the Somme and when Nivelle proposed a new offensive on the Aisne, Lloyd George accepted, placing the leadership of the British forces under the control of the Frenchman. Haig, however, protested and a compromise was reached whereby Haig could protest to London if he felt British troops were imperilled.

On 9 April, a week before the French launched their offensive in Aisne, British and Canadian troops attacked the German Hindenburg Line at Arras. The battle began with a barrage delivered by 2,800 guns across an eleven and a half mile front. The initial results were encouraging for the British, who showed signs of having learnt the lessons of the Somme. Vimy Ridge, one of the few high positions on the Flanders plain, was captured by Canadian troops and on 14 April Haig called a halt to the battle, as all eyes turned south to the

Aisne, where Nivelle and the French attacked two days later. The offensive failed and so on 23 April Haig recommenced the offensive around Arras.

The 13th Battalion, the Rifle Brigade, had played no part in the initial stages of the battle but second time around they were in the vanguard of the attack. They advanced at 4.45am on 23 April, but soon sustained heavy casualties in the face of a savage German artillery barrage. Pretor-Pinney,* once again leading from the front, was badly wounded by a shell fragment and command fell upon Capt the Hon R W Morgan-Grenville. As he made his way back to battalion HQ he too became a casualty and Captain Boyle assumed temporary command.

Somewhere out in no man's land was Major Jackson. When he emerged from the miasma of battle a few hours later he took command of the battalion. Jackson's first job was to gather up the survivors from the initial assault. The battalion war diary noted that, 'the Bttn had become somewhat disorganized and all that could be found was four officers and 120 Ors … the Bttn was organized for the advance. D Coy, the strongest Coy, were ordered to move out into shellholes in front of the Black Line [the River Scape] and form a first wave. The remainder of the other two Coys to form a second wave. The Bttn moved forward, the enemy barraging heavily the right flank which had some casualties. The Bttn lined the sunken road … and dug themselves in … at 12.30pm Major Jackson went up to reconnoitre the position.'

The battalion took the village of Gavrelle and for the next five days consolidated their position despite continuous shelling from the Germans. On 24 April they sent over forty gas shells and the fumes were blown by the wind into the sunken road where Jackson had established his HQ. They donned their gas helmets and had recourse to them several more times before they were relieved on 30 April.

Lt L S Chamberlin fought at Arras with Jackson and wrote an account of the battle in 1932. 'At 1pm, after three hours of absolute hell, I saw dear old "Jacker" … after seeing the men into the cellars in this grand place, we went off for a clean up and feed to our billets. We had a splendid evening and dinner at the only good estaminet, and so to bed.'

On 24 April, the day after he had assumed command of the battalion, Jackson had been wounded, according to the battalion war diary. Even

---

* He died of his wounds five days later and is buried at Aubigny Communal Cemetery.

though he didn't seek the opinion of the medical officer until 3 May, the wound – undisclosed by the war diary – was serious enough to keep him out of the front line until 5 June. Just over a fortnight later, Jackson was presented with a DSO, and bar, by Commander General Sir H S Horne at a ceremony in Fruges. There is no citation to accompany the first DSO but, judging by its date, it was awarded for Jackson's conduct during the early stages of the fighting at Arras. The second DSO, as the citation disclosed, was bestowed on him for his work in defending Gavrelle.

'For conspicuous gallantry during lengthy operations when he assumed command of the battalion and, although wounded on two separate occasions, was able to carry out most valuable work. By his skill and courage he offered a splendid example to all ranks with him.'

With the death of Pretor-Pinney, the men had lost their most respected officer. Not that many of the present battalion could remember his avuncular brand of leadership. There were few of the old stagers left in the battalion by the autumn of 1917, and in October another link with the past was severed when Jackson was transferred to the 13th Battalion, the King's Royal Rifle Corps. To lose Major 'Jacker' was bad enough, but it seemed to the men of the Rifle Brigade that the brass hats were playing a cruel joke by putting him in charge of their detested rivals.

To reach his new battalion, Jackson had to wade through the mud of the Passchendaele battlefield. As he slithered his way along the duckboards Jackson entered a place that was like a penance in purgatory. One RFC officer who spent a day in the trenches near Passchendaele, looking up his old battalion, wrote later that, 'The terrors of Ypres were told by the fireside. Running up to their armpits in mud … men with the look in their eyes that borders on insanity.'

A few days later the battalion was living in the Hedgestreet Tunnels on Observatory Ridge. Jackson wrote in the war diary that: 'These tunnels are in places very wet and muddy and afford little opportunity of rest and comfort to the men. The weather is still bad and the soakage heavy.'

By the beginning of November the battalion was in the front lines. The conditions the men had to endure remained engraved upon their souls for the rest of their lives. There had been many horrific battles in the war, but

Passchendaele was the fault line that scarred the psyche of the British nation. On one side stood the people back at home, cosy in their belief that the war was still a glorious crusade. Facing them across the divide were the soldiers who had lived through Passchendaele. How could they ever make their wives and mothers understand what it had been like? Most of them never tried – they walled up the torment in the backs of their minds and tried to fit back into civilization.

On 8 November, Haig's chief of staff visited the battlefield for the first time. What he saw made him weep. 'Good God,' he cried. 'Did we really send men to fight in that?' The officer next to him, a veteran of the battle, smiled sardonically. 'Oh, it's worse further up.'

A few days later, Jackson wrote in the war diary: 'Owing to the situation of advanced posts in waterlogged shellholes, and the lack of shelter, special measures were necessary for ameliorating conditions for the men and for the prevention of trench feet, etc. It had been found possible through army channels, to arrange a daily "ration" of dry socks for all in need of them, and there was liberal issue of gum boots. The experiment was tried of getting hot food to the forward positions in tins carried in valises, and packed with hay and straw.'

At the end of the month the battalion marched away from Passchendaele and into the Divisional Area near Scherpenberg. By late 1917 the incompetence of the generals was matched only by the resilience of the soldiers. The battalion Christmas lunch, although postponed until New Year's Eve, was a triumph of resourcefulness. How the men acquired the two pigs, Jackson didn't know. He didn't care. They had earned a good feast. Jackson described the lunch in the war diary:

> 'Men's dinner at 12.45pm. Officers waited on the men. The dinner was a huge success. Two pigs purchased by the battalion, and killed by the MO, Christmas puddings, cigarettes and cigars being outstanding factors. The dinner was followed by an excellent concert given by the "Barn Owls" at 3.30pm.'

The first two months of 1918 offered a blissful respite for the 13th Battalion, the King's Royal Rifle Corps. On 5 March they moved into the front line in Polderhoek in Flanders. Jackson, recently promoted to Lt-Col, would have told the men to be on their guard. He knew all about the niceties of trench warfare. They were the same for both sides. Courtesy demanded that when new neighbours moved into the trenches opposite, it was polite to pop over and say hello. Jackson himself was an acknowledged master of the trench raid. Philip Noel-Baker said after the war that '... he was a specialist in trench raids – raids of extraordinary daring in conception, backed by lightning responses to any enemy resistance or surprise'.

The Germans came early on the morning of 9 March. Jackson wrote his account of the assault in the battalion war diary that evening:

> 'The enemy started a bombardment of our trench system at 7.30am ... the commencement was gradual and not out of the ordinary, but from 10am onwards it increased in intensity. At 12 noon approx, Joppa dugout was staved in and nearly all officers wounded or seriously shaken ... on receipt of this information I ordered Major Russell and Second Lieutenant Marshall to proceed forthwith to the front line.'

The Germans were eventually beaten back. Russell and Marshall were awarded the Military Cross, Jackson received a third DSO. The citation, published in the *London Gazette* on 13 May, read:

> 'For conspicuous gallantry and devotion to duty. His battalion was subjected to an intense bombardment throughout a whole day, which caused many casualties and cut off all communication by wire with the frontline companies. He handled the situation with such skill and initiative that when the enemy attacked towards evening the casualties caused by the bombardment had been evacuated and replaced by reinforcements and communication with the front line had been re-established. It was entirely due to his powers of command and the splendid spirit with which he inspired his men that the attack on the greater part of his front was repulsed and the enemy, though they penetrated into parts of the front line, were counter-attacked and held at bay until the arrival of reinforcements. By his skilful dispositions he materially assisted the counter-attack which drove the enemy back with heavy losses and completely re-established the position.'

May was a merry month for the battalion, thanks largely to the efficacy of their commanding officer. Since he had taken charge, Jackson had achieved heroic status among his men. He had just turned twenty-seven, yet here he was, a Lt-Col, holder of three DSOs and mentioned in despatches six times. With his hand on the tiller, the battalion knew they were heading in the right direction. They were also having a spot of fun along the way, something they couldn't have imagined six months earlier at Passchendaele. On 29 May the battalion held their sports day. The battalion war diarist's exuberance bubbled over into colourful prose: 'Sports were a great success of which part is due to the side shows. "The Lady of the London" [a fortune teller at previous sideshows] was not able to be engaged but one was imported from Paris. She told fortunes with almost the same accuracy as the Lady of London, but was considerably more daring, as while a relay race between officers and Sgts was in progress she rushed out and joined in with Charlie Chaplin causing much laughter. A very gallant fellow stood in an enclosure and had tennis balls thrown at him in an attempt to knock his hat off. Whether it was glued on or not one cannot tell, but it seldom came off.'

Jackson's good cheer was echoed among thousands of Allied soldiers on the Western Front in June 1918. A massive German offensive had been launched against them on 21 March but the attack had been contained and American soldiers continued to arrive in their thousands. The feeling in the British trenches was that the war had swung decisively their way. Just as Jackson had sensed Wallace McCurdy had nothing left to offer on Franklin's Field four years earlier, he now sensed the Germans had shot their bolt, while he still had one last effort left in him.

Shortly after 4am on 8 August the Allies' counter-offensive began. The Battle of Amiens, an Anglo-French attack, achieved rapid gains. By late afternoon the Australian Corps had advanced twelve km. The German commander, Ludendorff, described it as 'the black day of the German Army'.

But the Allies soon encountered large pockets of German resistance. On 21 August the King's Royal Rifle Corps, part of the British Third Army, took part in what later became known as the Second Battle of Albert. Jackson's orders to the battalion were brief and lucid. They must '… make absolutely certain of making good the objectives … at Zero [hour] the three front companies will advance with two platoons in the front line roughly occupying a frontage of 200 yards. One platoon in support and one in reserve. The advance will be preceded by a creeping barrage of shrapnel, HE, Smoke and MG travelling at a rate of 25 yards a minute and by tanks.'

An account of the opening few minutes of the battle was left in the KRRC war diary. Its author – not Jackson – chose to remain anonymous, but he left behind a grandiose description of the attack that was far removed from the normal prosaic accounts found in battalion diaries:

> 'As the fateful hour approached each moment became more intense. The tanks working into positions seemed to our straining ears to be making a hideous noise, and the covering fire provided by MG fire alone, did not seem really enough to drown it. Every minute we expected the counter preparation. Louder sounded the noise of the tanks, but all was silent on the other side. Did they suspect, and what would be our luck? was asked by many a man waiting the moment when he might go forward. The minutes went pass [sic] quickly. Zero minus five minutes and not a shell from the enemy! Had they actually gone back? Whizz! Crash!! and down it came a magnificent barrage, full and beautifully placed. Surely nothing could possibly live in such a rain of fire. Zero plus five minutes and our men began to move forward. Still no sign of the tanks. It was an anxious moment for wire unperfectly cut might easily hold up the attack. However, the attack was launched and there it was. At Zero plus eight minutes our tank was seen to follow and what became of our supporting tanks has not yet been discovered.'

The battalion, along with the rest of the Third Army, paused in the afternoon having made a small but significant advance against stubborn defenders. The Germans launched a series of counter-attacks on 22 August and through into the early hours of 23 August. The war diary noted that at 4am: 'The m-g fire was particularly heavy and nothing could get through its arc of fire. As this fire directly enfiladed the line of our advance we began to feel a little anxious.'

A fresh British push was launched at 11am that morning and this time the decisive breakthrough was achieved. The German Second Army was soon in full retreat. 'Several hundred prisoners and many machine-guns were captured,' the war diary noted that evening. There was a further entry, however, in the diary that evening that spoiled an otherwise excellent day. 'The commanding officer, Lt-Col A N S Jackson, DSO, was wounded by HE [high explosive], a piece of the shell entering the right forearm. Major Johns took over command of the battalion.'

The battalion war diary neglected to record the length of Jackson's recuperation. But when he returned it was as the youngest (acting) Brigadier in the British army at twenty-seven, commanding the 111th Infantry Brigade, 37th Division. At the beginning of October the *London Gazette* carried the announcement of Jackson's fourth DSO, awarded for his actions in late August:

> 'For conspicuous gallantry and brilliant leadership. During an attack by our troops, Lt-Col Jackson advanced with the leading wave of his battalion and was among the first men to reach the railway embankment. The machine-gun fire against them was intense, but the gallant leading of this officer gave such impetus to the assault that the enemy's main line of resistance was broken. He was subsequently wounded during the work of consolidation.'

Some time in the next few weeks Jackson's luck ran out. He was severely wounded in the leg, although little is known of the circumstances behind the incident. It might have happened during the Sambre offensive, the last major attack of the Allies on the Western Front. The KRRC were heavily involved in the fighting that began on 4 November on the French/Belgian border. The 13th Battalion had the misfortune to encounter an exceptionally stout-hearted company of Germans in the village of Louvignies. They were eventually dispossessed, but only after some diabolical struggles amid the ruins of the village. The war diary recorded that: 'Several individual contests took place in cellars. One NCO of "B" Coy fought with three Huns in a cellar and killed the lot. His weapon was a small hand axe which he was carrying for cutting his way through hedges and so the good work went on!'

A week later the armistice was signed. 'Contrary to expectations,' ran the entry in the KRRC's war diary, 'the news was very quietly received.'

Jackson's war had brought him seventeen medals, including the four Distinguished Service Orders. He received one from Field Marshal Sir Douglas Haig, who personally thanked and congratulated him. Jackson informed Haig that he followed him to Brasenose College. 'I'm glad I didn't know that beforehand,' Haig guffawed, 'it would have looked like nepotism.' Jackson laughed with his Field Marshal. If he bore Haig any malice for the degradations he had suffered on his behalf, Jackson kept it well concealed beneath his smiling demeanour.

The two of them were the supporting cast in a poem that appeared in the Brasenose College magazine in 1919 condemning the weakened beer that had been foisted upon the students. While one suspects it would have met with the approval of Jackson, Haig would probably not have received it so favourably.

> Can men find courage in this bastard brew?
> Why, even 'Jacker' must have been content
> With fewer bars! There might have been but Two,
> If nought but this had been his nutriment
> Since earliest youth! And is not 'Haig' enough
> To prove what Brasenose Ale can do?
> Not this poor stuff!!

The leg wound that Jackson received in the death throes of the war left him lame for the rest of his life. It would have been ungracious to grumble. So many of his Oxford peers had been killed, including David Gaussen,* who had ran such a splendid second leg in the Penn Relay triumph.

Jackson thanked his good fortune and embarked upon a new life. In 1919 he was a member of the British delegation at the Paris Peace Conference, a role for which he was subsequently awarded a CBE. The same year he changed his name from Jackson to Strode-Jackson, appending one of his middle names to his original surname.

In 1921 Strode-Jackson emigrated to the USA with Dora Berryman, an American he had married three years earlier. His industriousness in his adopted country was astonishing; he became president of the J C Eno Fruit Salts Corporation; was a director of several other organizations; the director of the first Kentucky Derby Festival in 1935; a colonel on the staff of the

* Second Lieutenant David Gaussen, Bedfordshire Regiment, was killed in action on 31 July 1916, aged twenty-three, during the battle of the Somme.

Governor of Kentucky; a member of the regional Rhodes Scholarship Committee, and a Justice of the Peace.

But such responsibility hadn't blunted his playfulness. In his capacity as a JP he was once called upon to perform a civil marriage between a Protestant groom and a Catholic bride. Shortly before the service began he was asked by the bride's family if he could introduce some Latin into the proceedings for the benefit of the Catholics among the witnesses. Strode-Jackson smiled benignly and said 'of course'. The only Latin he knew, however, was the Brasenose College grace. That would have to do. At a suitably solemn moment he recited the grace, repeating it for effect. Afterwards the bride thanked Strode-Jackson and asked him the origins of the Latin text. He smiled benignly once more: 'I will not tell you its origin, but its meaning is that you should be very grateful for what you are about to receive.'

When the Second World War began the Strode-Jacksons were living in Connecticut. He worked for the US government in their anti-sabotage department during the war, but also frequently drove down to the New York docks to greet the convoys that arrived from Britain. His hospitality became legendary among the sailors who all hoped for an invitation back to Strode-Jackson's place in Spinney-Mill Brooke, where the old English Brigadier plied his guests with whisky and his charming wife served up plentiful helpings of good food.

In the early 1950s Strode-Jackson was back in England – in a pub characteristically – when an American sailor approached his friend at the bar: 'Is that gentleman's name Strode-Jackson?' he asked. When the friend replied in the affirmative, the American beamed broadly. 'I knew it. During the war I landed from a convoy one day at New York and he met us, and I was one of the five whom he took to his home and royally entertained for three days.' The sailor went over to Strode-Jackson and reacquainted himself. The two spent the rest of the night deep in both conversation and beer.

Despite his frequent forays back to England, Strode-Jackson was content to remain in America. He and Dora were an admired and respected couple in the Connecticut community and since 1945 he had held American citizenship. But in 1963 his wife died. Strode-Jackson, now seventy-two, decided he would like to see out his days in the country that had shaped him.

He moved back to England and bought a house in Oxford. The place had changed a lot in the forty-nine years since he had left Brasenose in that serene summer of 1914. He paid frequent visits to his old haunts, arousing the curiosity of the students who wondered who this elderly gent was, tottering along on his walking stick. None could have guessed that the wizened old man was in the opinion of the college magazine 'the Brasenose man of the century'.

In October 1972 he attended the Brasenose Gaudy – a dinner held every ten years for former college members. The college magazine reported that he 'still retained traces of his former magnificent physique, he seemed to dominate the High Table from the invalid chair to which he had been confined since suffering a stroke two years earlier'.

Strode-Jackson died on 13 November 1972, at the age of eighty-one. He was laid to rest at Wolvercote beside his parents. His passing further reduced the survivors of that doomed generation of young Oxonians who had been beguiled into thinking the world in 1913 was a 'ripe peach'. Their dissipation had been ridiculed by older generations and the *Daily Mirror*, in its cruel edition of July 1912, had said that 'Few men are much good until they are thirty'.

By the time he was twenty-seven, Arnold Nugent Strode-Jackson was the reigning Olympic 1,500 metres champion, he had won four DSOs, been mentioned in despatches six times and was the youngest Brigadier in the British Army. But a great many other of his Oxford contemporaries never got the chance to disprove the paper's assumption.

CHAPTER FOURTEEN

Pieter
van der Bijl

*P*ieter van der Bijl had a Test match baptism of fire when England's *Ken Farnes peppered him for hour after hour with bouncers during the series of 1938–9, but this was child's play compared to the battles which followed against Rommel's Afrika Korps in the Libyan desert. Lieutenant van der Bijl's courage and bravery on patrols into enemy territory led to the award of a Military Cross.*

The morning of 21 March 1942 was like any other for the men of the Duke of Edinburgh's Own Rifles in North Africa. The arid terrain shimmered under a sun that was still rising from its nocturnal slumber. The soldiers of the 'Dukes', as they liked to be known, washed, shaved, cursed and cooked breakfast. This particular morning, however, there wasn't the usual banter. Some of the men even passed on the food. Two of them, in fact, were feeling decidedly fragile.

The previous day Erral Penny had turned twenty-one. He had been treated to a few beers by the commander of the armoured car that he had driven with such skill for the last few months. Lieutenant Pieter van der Bijl was thirteen years his senior. In some ways he was like a father figure to Penny. At other times he had the air of the big brother looking to have a bit of fun at the expense of his younger sibling.

There had been the unmistakable glint of mischief in the eyes of van der Bijl as he poured the first glass for Private Penny. They were soon joined by the rest of their squadron and the carousing continued long into the night.

The Dukes were South Africans. Most came from the Cape and all had rushed to enlist when their country declared war on Germany on 6 September 1939. They were typical of the colonial soldier who gave such sterling service to Britain in both world wars. Tough, resourceful and dependable, the South Africans also knew how to enjoy themselves whenever the opportunity presented itself.

On the morning of 21 March, however, fighting was the last thing on the minds of Private Penny and Lieutenant van der Bijl. Their hangovers were the sort that led men to take the pledge. What they would have given for a day of rest, lying in the shade and pulling each other's legs as they picked over the bones of the night's merrymaking. Instead, van der Bijl and Penny, and the two other members of their armoured car, were detailed to provide an escort for the Cape Town Highlanders as they marched into position for an attack against Rommel's Afrika Corps.

The armoured cars led the Highlanders forward towards a crest of a ridge, beyond which lay the German positions. This was where the two parted company. The Dukes' orders were to stay behind the ridge as the infantry attacked over the crest and down towards the German positions roughly 3,000 yards distant.

The German gunners surveyed the South African infantry as they advanced across the desert. Just a few thousand yards away on top of the ridge the men of the Dukes shielded their eyes from the burning Egyptian sun and peered towards the enemy positions. Earlier feelings of apprehension began to recede as the Highlanders made good progress. There was no movement from the German positions. Perhaps they had had the good sense to withdraw?

The leading wave of Highlanders was only a few hundred yards from the enemy line when the first shells exploded in their midst. Private Penny was an experienced campaigner in desert warfare. Perhaps he had ushered in his birthday with one too many beers, but in the last twelve months he had seen sights that no man deserved to witness, least of all one so young. He might even have become a little indurate. But his memory was branded in the next few harrowing minutes by the hot iron of war. 'There must have been about sixty or seventy German guns and they lambasted these poor bastards with every rotten variety of fire you could think of mortars and 88mm airbursts did most of the damage. From 3,000 yards back on our ridge we could see the Highlanders crumpling down, dropping down, and then, having kept up that fire for ten minutes, the Germans stopped as suddenly as they had started.'

The Highlanders had been all but obliterated. Few had escaped unscathed. A number, six, seven at the most, were alive, but badly wounded. 'They started crawling like animals towards a bush that offered the only protection,' remembers Penny.

From up on their ridge the Dukes gazed down upon a scene that was like Botticelli's depiction of Dante's Ninth Pit of Hell. The German gunners were pleased with their handiwork. Now they sat and waited to see if the soldiers in the armoured cars would be brave, or foolish, enough to try and rescue the handful of wounded men cowering behind the bush.

Van der Bijl and Penny looked at one another. The idea of driving across 2,000 yards of exposed terrain towards a solitary bush while a couple of hundred German artillerymen looked on wasn't, remembers Penny, a 'particularly attractive' proposition. In fact, 'to drive down there into the face of this great fire was bordering on lunacy'. Yet they went. Just one armoured car. Commanded by van der Bijl, driven by Erral Penny, with Allan Bell as the radio operator and Dennis Melville working the Vickers.

It's the minutiae soldiers often remember about war. For Penny it was the sound of birdsong, an accompanying requiem, as they drove over the top of the escarpment ridge and down into the hollow. At any time they expected to hear the roar of an armour-piercing shell – like an express train hurtling through a station – but they heard nothing. It took them only a couple of minutes to reach the bush, but it had felt like hours. Penny reversed up and they jumped out and began lifting the wounded through the double doors at the back of the car. 'We packed these poor buggers in like sardines in a can,' recalls Penny. 'There's not a lot of room in the back of an armoured car and they were lying one on top of each other but efforts had been made to save them and they appreciated that.'

They slammed shut the doors and clambered back inside the car. As they did Penny turned to his commander: 'I knew they wouldn't fire on us,' he said. 'They knew we were coming to save the wounded.' Van der Bijl didn't reply; it might have been that he didn't share the optimism of his youthful driver.

The first shell dropped a few feet short of the armoured car and the explosion startled Penny. 'I got such a bloody fright that I jammed my foot on the accelerator and the car rushed forward.' The agonized howls from the wounded acted as a brake and Penny immediately took his foot off the pedal. 'Thank God I did. For the next round landed a few metres in front of us and if I hadn't taken my foot off the accelerator we would have been right in the middle of it.'

The ride back to the top of the escarpment was 'colourful', according to Penny, who drove with such skill that the enemy artillery was unable to draw a bead on the little car zig-zagging across the desert, like a scarab beetle scurrying away from the clutches of a scorpion.

Van der Bijl might sometimes have despaired at the impetuosity of Penny but now he offered up a prayer of thanks for a driver who could control his vehicle with such dexterity. They made it back in one piece and deposited the wounded into the hands of the medical officer. Then van der Bijl led his squadron west in the moonlight, towards base and a brew, and uninterrupted sleep.

The first they knew about the minefield was when the left-hand side of the second car in the column was torn open by an explosion. Miraculously no one was badly hurt. Van der Bijl yelled 'Mines!' down the turret and, as if on cue, the front wheel of their car was blown 100 yards to their right. 'It was quite a shock to the constitution,' says Penny, in the understated manner that was the norm for the men of the Dukes. Fortunately for the soldiers in the two lead cars the rest of the squadron had yet to enter the minefield. They drove off to fetch the Royal Engineers, leaving van der Bijl and his crew to spend the night in the wrecked car.

When van der Bijl eventually made it back to base, his whole being demanded sleep. As he pulled the blanket up over his bruised and battered body he probably tried to remember if he had ever been so persecuted. Only one other occasion sprung to mind and that had been three years earlier in South Africa.

It was hard to believe it was only three years. It felt a lot longer to van der Bijl. For two of those years he had been fighting with the Dukes, first in northern Kenya and Abyssinia against the Italians, and then in North Africa against Rommel's Afrika Corps. It seemed like an age since he had made his Test debut for South Africa against Wally Hammond's England at the Wanderers in Johannesburg in December 1938.

Van der Bijl had been chosen for the series because he offered the selectors application and determination. As an opening batsman he was more artisan than artist, crafting his innings with diligence and an impeccable technique.

The first two Tests of the series were drawn. Van der Bijl took one match to adjust to the pace of Test cricket – scoring 4 and 38 in Johannesburg – before he made 37 and 87 in the second Test at Newlands, Cape Town. That match started in 1938 and finished in 1939, although it was all over within five days. The fifth Test, however, at Kingsmead in Durban in March, seemed to the players to last an eternity.

England went into the match leading 1–0 in the series thanks to an innings victory in the third Test. Van der Bijl had scored 28 and 13 in that game, and he had made 31 in the fourth Test that finished in a draw, although had it not been for the Johannesburg rain South Africa might well have levelled the series.

The pressure was on van der Bijl when he arrived in Durban. He had shown promise in his previous innings but he needed to be more pertinacious at the crease. The selectors wanted him to turn his solid starts into something more prolific. But it was easy for the selectors to pontificate from the comfort of the stand; they didn't have to walk out into the middle and face Ken Farnes.

Farnes opened the England bowling attack. In the first four Tests he had taken only eleven wickets, suffering like the other seamers in the series from over-prepared wickets that favoured the batsmen. But where he couldn't get wickets, his 6ft 5in frame could get bounce, and he had no compunction about sending down a barrage of short-pitched deliveries that reared up off the bone-dry wickets. For the batsmen it was nothing short of terrifying. They had to rely on just their courage. No helmets, no thigh pads, no arm guards, no sightscreens and no restriction per (eight-ball) over on how many bouncers Farnes could bowl.

Off the field Farnes* was a charming chap, but on it he could be a right

* Pilot Officer Farnes was killed on active service in October 1941, aged thirty.

bastard. And he seemed to have it in for van der Bijl. It was nothing personal. The tall, easy-going South African with the innate sense of fair play wasn't the sort of man to bring out the devil in people. But he was a frustrating batsman to bowl to because his composure seemed to be bomb-proof. The two knew each other well. The first time van der Bijl had felt the rush of wind in his hair from a Farnes bouncer was in the 1932 Varsity match. Van der Bijl had gone up to Oxford as a Rhodes Scholar in 1930 after graduating from Cape Town University, and had probably wished he hadn't when he faced the Cambridge quickie at Lord's. Farnes took five wickets in the Oxford innings, including van der Bijl, who was out for seven, and another future South African batsman, Alan Melville, for three.

Van der Bijl in 1939, however, was a more obdurate opponent than the one Farnes had bowled to seven years earlier. By his own admission, van der Bijl had made the most of his time at Oxford, socially and in sport, but he was determined not to buckle before Farnes in Durban.

The fifth Test started on Friday 3 March with Melville and van der Bijl opening the batting for South Africa. It was just like old times as Farnes ripped into them but the pair navigated their way to lunch unbeaten. They shared an opening stand of 131 before Melville went for 78. Eric Rowan was out a short while before the end of play but the home side closed on 229 for two. Van der Bijl was unbeaten on 105. Farnes returned to the team hotel and seethed. Having slept on the problem of van der Bijl, he woke on the Saturday determined to bounce him out.

The first session of the second day was cricket at its most bitter. Once Bruce Mitchell had gone early for 11, Dudley Nourse and van der Bijl found themselves in the eye of a storm of short-pitched deliveries. Only 17 runs were scored in the first hour, but van der Bijl took twice as many hits to his body. Nourse, at the non-striker's end, wrote later that: 'He took the simple and painful course of allowing Farnes' deliveries to hit him on the hip or body rather than risk the possibility of deflecting one where eager hands were awaiting a catch at short leg. In expectancy they waited, but in vain; van der Bijl was risking personal injury rather than his wicket. By this time he must have been in considerable pain because he had endured such treatment from Farnes.'

One English fielder who knew exactly what van der Bijl was going through was Len Hutton. The previous summer he had batted against Farnes in a

Gentlemen v Players match at Lord's. It had been the most disturbing experience of his cricketing life: 'He pitched just short of a length,' he recalled, 'and he had the height and pace to make the ball rear spitefully and alarmingly at head height. I find it impossible to think bodyline could have been more frightening and intimidating.'

Van der Bijl had wrapped himself in towels before going out to bat but they afforded little protection. The bouncers kept coming and the South African kept taking them, although, said Nourse, 'never once did van der Bijl wince as the ball hit his body, though he did often rub his side'.

Farnes had begun by now to warm to his task. Nourse remembered that two or three times van der Bijl politely asked the Englishman to refrain from the short stuff, 'whereupon Farnes would grin at him and deliver another in the same spot'.

It was compulsive if grim viewing, and it was enlightening for many South Africans. Just about the first word anyone ever used to describe van der Bijl was 'gentleman'. He was a former Rhodes scholar and a schoolmaster at Bishops School. His genial and gentle nature, and unimpeachable integrity, made him the ideal man in whom to entrust the education of one's child. But score a century in a Test match? A lot of people said he didn't possess the fighting qualities required of a South African batsmen, as though his affable exterior was somehow incompatible with the inner toughness needed to thrive in international sport. Perhaps they didn't know that at Oxford he had also won a blue for boxing.

Manners, however, meant a lot to van der Bijl and he took them with him everywhere he went, even when he was batting against a competitor as unforgiving as Farnes. Throughout his ordeal at Kingsmead, said Nourse, van der Bijl was 'a soul of patience and forbearance ... [he] lost his equanimity on one occasion when he quite crossly said with an obvious touch of annoyance in his voice: "Will you stop it now, please, Ken?" That was the strongest protest I heard him utter.'

Van der Bijl was eventually out for 125, bowled by Reg Perks. He had scored his maiden Test century, faced down Farnes and proved that he had the temperament for a sport that could be as brutal as it was beautiful. The remaining South African batsmen built on the foundations laid down by van der Bijl. By the time their last wicket fell an hour before the close of play on day three they had scored 530. It was of no concern that they had taken so long to compile the runs. It had been agreed before the Test started that the match would be played to a finish, unfettered by time.

England were all out for 316 in their first innings, giving South Africa a lead of 214. When day five finished the home side had extended their advantage to 407 with seven wickets in hand. Van der Bijl had enjoyed another productive day with the bat, and Farnes had given him a few more bruises to add to his already impressive collection. He fell for 97, just three short of becoming the first South African to score two centuries in the same Test match.

The pitch was now as gentle as the breeze that gave the players a little respite from the searing Durban sun. South Africa continued to make hay with the bat, scoring 481 in their second innings. England had time for one ball before the sixth day ended with the tourists chasing 696 to win. At the end of day seven, Friday 10 March as some players needed reminding, England had reduced the deficit by 253 for the loss of Len Hutton. The wicket was so bland that Bill Edrich, who had scored 20 runs in the previous four Tests, was unbeaten on 107.

Rain washed out play on Saturday and Sunday was a rest day. They reconvened on the Monday for the ninth day of play. The joke, unlike the wicket, was beginning to wear thin. Nourse recalled that by now, 'The usual witticisms were replaced by ironic laughter. Most of the joy seemed to have gone out of the game and we played merely because we were compelled to complete a contract we had started.'

South Africa managed to prise two Englishmen from the crease during the course of the day. Gibb went for 120 and Edrich finally fell on 219. That brought to the crease Wally Hammond and Eddie Paynter, who took England to 496 for three at the close of play on Monday. They still needed 200 to win. Victory was within their grasp, but the sands of time were running through their fingers. Their boat left Cape Town on the Friday but they had to catch the 8.05pm train from Durban if they were to cover the 1,000 miles in time. Someone mooted the idea of catching a plane on Wednesday but the MCC had little faith in the safety of air travel and refused. No, the match would have to be completed on Tuesday.

South Africa came out on day ten determined to restrict England's run-making opportunities. Norman Gordon spent much of the first session bowling at leg stump to try. But he refused to adopt the tactics of Farnes and instead toiled away in sweltering conditions. 'Running in to bowl my trousers felt like they had been glued to my legs because of all the sweat.' Gordon bowled 92.2 overs in the match and took just one wicket. But it was a vital one, Paynter in the second innings, to break the partnership with Hammond.

The weather began to deteriorate and Hammond increased the tempo, batting like a man who had a train to catch – which indeed he had. Twice the players were forced off through rain and shortly after Hammond was stumped for 140, a downpour pushed the teams back into the pavilion. This one, however, wasn't as short as the others. It seemed even the weather had tired of the match. Shortly after tea on day ten the South African Cricket Association Board issued a statement:

> 'In consultation with both captains, [we] have agreed that the match should be abandoned, the Board recognizing that the MCC team would otherwise not have the requisite number of hours in Cape Town before sailing.'

England, with five wickets remaining, were just 42 runs short of victory. England departed for their train, South Africa for their beds. The statisticians thumbed through the books to see if there had ever been a match like it. Dudley Nourse didn't care if there had, just that there must never be a repetition of the ten-day Test: 'I hope never again to have to figure in a match of that description. It is soul-searing to players and spectators alike.'

The match broke sixteen cricketing records. They included the longest first-class match at 43 hours and 16 minutes; the highest number of aggregate runs in a match (1,981); the record number of balls bowled by one man (766 by England's Hedley Verity); and van der Bijl's century, compiled in seven hours and 18 minutes, was the longest Test innings played by a South African. The 'Timeless Test', as it came to be known, had entered cricket folklore.

Van der Bijl returned to Cape Town a couple of days later and headed down to the Olympic Club for a well-earned pint among friends. When he entered they were playing billiards. 'Pieter, old chap,' one of them said, glancing up from the table, 'where have you been?'

The Olympic Club was a sanctuary for van der Bijl. It was a club frequented by old boys of Bishops School, in search of a pint and a bit of a gossip. Often the conversation didn't stretch to much more than cricket, rugby and girls. But throughout the South African winter of 1939 the talk turned increasingly to the ambitions of Adolf Hitler.

As war became inevitable many of the men from the Olympic enlisted in one of Cape Town's local regiments, the Duke of Edinburgh's Own Rifles. Second Lieutenant van der Bijl embarked with the Dukes on 20 May 1940 and was with them when they earned their first battle honour at El Wak, on the northern frontier of Kenya, against the Italians in December that year.

The war in East Africa continued until 18 May 1941 when the Italian army surrendered unconditionally. Prime Minister Jan Smuts cabled his congratulations:

> 'South Africa has been thrilled by the news of the surrender ... The whole of the Abyssinian campaign will take a high place in the annals of warfare and an illustrious chapter to African and South African history.'

The Dukes used Smuts' homage as a fig leaf of validation to cover a night of wild celebration. A party was thrown in the sumptuous hotel that had been the HQ for the Italian chief of staff. Present were not just the South Africans, but several high-ranking British officers and a number of Italian generals, invited by their captors for a final hurrah before they were removed to a prisoner of war camp.

Van der Bijl was among the throng that drank the night away in such incongruous surroundings. For the past few months he had slept under the stars and luxuries such as showers and good food had been nothing more than a pipe dream. Pat O'Sullivan, also present, remembers that van der Bijl, 'participated to the full' in the party. At some point in the evening (no one was sober enough to give a precise time) van der Bijl disappeared and returned with a fire extinguisher. His targets were the Italian officers whom he considered too foppish for soldiers. 'Unfortunately for him, however,' says O'Sullivan, 'in his then advanced state of unsteady aim his attention was drawn also to some of the British officers who were outstanding in their own military uniforms and very differently attired by comparison to the South African "battle-dress" of his friends.' Maybe the accents of the British officers brought back memories of Kingsmead and short-pitched deliveries.

The British officers came off worse than the Italians. It could have caused a diplomatic incident but van der Bijl melted into the darkness and no steps were taken to identify the culprit. 'Perhaps the British officers, in the spirit of the event and the tremendous party, simply turned a blind eye to the incident,' says O'Sullivan, 'or perhaps they could not see who was responsible due to the camouflage provided by the full flood of foam directed against them.'

Word soon spread of van der Bijl's commando attack and he rose a notch further in the estimation of his men. Pricking the balloon of British bombast was nearly as much fun as fighting the Italians.

The Dukes were now battle-hardened, but they knew there were less malleable and more determined foes to fight than the Italians. The war in East Africa had been a good grounding for the regiment; the men now knew what it was like to come under fire for the first time and while they weren't fully inured to the sounds, sights and smells of war, they had a far greater sense of the reality of battle.

East Africa for the Dukes, if one may be permitted a cricketing analogy, had been like facing a gentle medium-pace bowler; when they embarked for Egypt to fight the Germans, they were up against the opposition's strike bowler.

The Dukes arrived in Egypt in June 1941. They established their base at the small village of Mersa Matruh on the Mediterranean coast; small it may have been, but it was strategically important because it was an important railhead and harbour. It was also the place where the Allies planned to hold the Germans if they broke through the frontline defences.

It was a miserable time for the Dukes. Mersa Matruh was raided frequently by enemy aircraft because of its strategic position and the men spent much of the time digging slit trenches – or funk-holes as the British called them – for cover. But all the while they were being trained in new battle tactics: co-operation with armour, dispersion, signals, supply systems and the maintenance of vehicles. Smuts hit the nail on the head when he said: 'We are once more launched upon a warfare of mobility, of surprises, of tricks or ruses … There is no front. It is a wild war dance between the armies.'

It was with such methods in mind that the Dukes began to launch a series of 'hard-hitting packets' (HHPs). An HHP was a strong patrolling force comprising a company of infantry, two troops of armoured cars, a troop of 25-pounders and a troop of anti-tank guns. Such a force was too unwieldy for the South Africans who, unlike their British counterparts, had a greater licence to improvise. They stripped down their HHPs to the bare minimum, a column of armoured cars equipped with Vickers machine-guns, with or without the support of a single 25-pounder. The HHPs would slip behind enemy lines to reconnoitre and, whenever the opportunity arose, cause trouble by shooting up any stray vehicles and bringing back Germans for interrogation. Sometimes they were gone for a few hours, other times for two or three days, travelling up to 150 miles from base. It required boldness, initiative and nerve, and Pieter van der Bijl was the acknowledged expert at leading the patrols.

Where van der Bijl led, Penny drove. The pair worked well together, even though Penny was the subordinate and thirteen years his junior. 'The gap of years disappeared,' says Penny, 'and I'm enormously flattered that it did … [but] the desert war was very exciting, bloody noisy and not without concomitant danger, and the people with whom you go through such experiences inevitably become closer because you're no good on your own; you've got to be a member of a pack, and the more you work together the more closely you are committed to one another.'

Van der Bijl's previous driver had been damaged during a raid by the Luftwaffe in a place christened Stuka Valley by the Dukes. Penny was volunteered by van der Bijl to become his driver because of his knowledge of automobiles. 'I knew of him earlier,' says Penny, 'because he was such a huge brute that you couldn't ignore him.'

Penny addressed his officer as 'Pieter, sir', but familiarity didn't breed contempt. 'He was a man of outstanding moral integrity,' recalls Penny, 'and a gentleman to his fingertips … until he got drunk and then he was very noisy! I remember one time in Egypt, the morning after a good party, when Pieter climbed into the turret still six sheets to the wind and in his stupor imagined that he was his father, who had been a steward at the jockey club. Imitating his father, and the way he used to describe the horses at the start of a race, Pieter adopted the same tactics and began describing the armoured cars: "Now here's a lovely-looking filly, wonderful reputation although doubts remain about her stamina", and so on. He became more and more enthusiastic until he toppled out of the turret.'

But such revelry was the exception not the norm, as it had to be in such an unforgiving campaign, where the Dukes worked cheek by jowl with the Long Range Desert Group. Van der Bijl set himself exacting standards and he expected the same from his men, a fact still remembered by Penny. 'The two armoured car squadrons worked alternate days and on more than one occasion when it was our rest day Pieter would announce, "Come on, chaps, I feel belligerent, let's go out on patrol". There was no need for it, but that was Pieter's way.'

Van der Bijl and crew, hitherto engrossed in their own operations against the Germans, now became caught up in the bigger picture. In November 1941 the Allies launched a major offensive called 'Crusader', the purpose of which was to relieve Tobruk in Libya and destroy the Axis forces. The first objective was achieved but the Germans were more tenacious than the Italians.

In January 1942 Rommel and his Afrika Korps counter-attacked and captured the town of Benghazi, five weeks after losing it. The Dukes were sent to reinforce the Libyan area of Gazala where they formed a defensive line and were ordered to contain Rommel 'at all costs'. The two armies faced each other across the Libyan desert, circling one another like two heavyweight boxers, sending out the occasional probing jab but neither confident enough to come forward looking for the knockout blow. The Dukes' probing was carried out through a number of two-man patrols – volunteers only – who would penetrate German lines and gather as much information as possible on troop movements and defences. It was for one of these patrols that van der Bijl was awarded the Military Cross.

The Brigadier had asked for volunteers to go into enemy territory and bring back a prisoner for interrogation. He wasn't at all surprised when van der Bijl and Penny presented themselves for the task. At 2am the next morning they set out west and walked for two or three hours before going to ground as dawn broke.

For the rest of the day they remained secreted in three-foot-high gorse. Occasionally they would whisper to one another but most of the time they simply perspired. They wore their winter battledress, the one which had been widely approved of when it was issued the previous November. The blouse and trousers were in wool serge, ideal for protection against the bitter desert nights. It wasn't so comfortable under a relentless midday sun.

The desert comes alive when darkness falls. Insects, animals and reptiles emerge from their burrows and go in search of supper. Penny and van der Bijl also decided that now was the time to catch a German. As they prepared to move off they heard the sound of voices. It was pitch-black but they estimated the voices were about 200 yards in front of them. 'We moved towards the noises,' recalls Penny, 'and I had the Mills bombs all ready to throw. We were wearing our heavy desert boots, which had very thick rubber soles, and when you walked on desert stones they made a sort of clinking noise.'

The pair inched forward, pausing every few seconds, and listening. They could barely see each other, let alone the Germans. It was shaping up to be another bitterly cold desert night, but Penny could feel the rivulets of sweat running down his back. They stopped and remained motionless for what seemed an age. Just a few feet away an unknown number of Germans were doing exactly the same. It was the ultimate game of blind man's bluff. 'We realized that we were in the middle of these bloody Jerries,' chuckles Penny, at the memory. 'They couldn't see us and we couldn't see them. They were armed and we were armed. It was a most disconcerting and disorientating situation. We stood there for a couple of minutes and then Pieter took my arm and we crept away, as quietly as we could.'

They headed north-west and walked for about eight miles until the safety curtain of night began to be raised by dawn. Fortunately they stumbled into a wadi, a depression in the desert that to a pair of tired South Africans was an ideal place in which to lie up till nightfall. The wadi was about 200 yards across and in its centre was a solitary bush. It wasn't a big bush, maybe 20ft in height with a tangle of loose branches that didn't suggest comfort. 'But when you're being pursued,' says Penny, 'you are like an animal, you look for cover in which to hide.' The two pushed their way into the bush and lay down to sleep. 'It was so cold,' remembers Penny, 'that we hugged one another, and for me to hug another man it needs something quite unusual!'

Penny woke a few hours later to find van der Bijl gone. He clambered out of the bush and saw him 50 yards away on top of an old ant heap scanning the horizon with his binoculars. Penny wondered what he was doing. There was nothing to see, except a rough track that came down through the wadi, past the side of the bush. Penny had just started to climb back into the bush when he heard the sound of vehicles. In rapid succession, six trucks crammed with Germans appeared at the top of the wadi. They must have been parked out of sight just over the lip of the wadi. The co-drivers of each car were searching the sky for signs of the RAF. If they had looked down they would have seen a pair of massive British army boots poking out from behind a tiny scrub. 'Pieter had heard them as quickly as I had,' recalls Penny, 'and he had thrown himself down on to the ground but his bloody great boots were sticking up. I thought to myself, "What am I going to do?" I had two guns and a handful of grenades, but there were a lot of Germans in the vehicles. I was sure they were going to spot Pieter, sure as God made little apples.'

As well as the dirt track that led down into the wadi and past the bush, there was also a track that ran past the old ant hill and round the side of the depression. The Germans took the latter. Somehow they had failed to spot a 6ft 4in South African with size thirteen boots just a few feet in front of them.

They staggered back to their unit twenty-four hours later, without a prisoner but able to give a detailed account of the enemy's activity. 'Private Penny's outing deserves the highest praise,' van der Bijl added. 'More than once it was his plan that we adopted.' Van der Bijl was promoted to captain and awarded a Military Cross, although the medal was as much for his conduct throughout the campaign in North Africa as it was for the incursion into enemy territory. The citation finished by saying that:

> 'As armoured car platoon commander he daily went out on patrol and at all times under fire showed leadership and courage of the very highest order. Whenever any dangerous job was to be done Captain van der Bijl begged to be allowed to tackle it, and his consideration for others was an inspiration to his men, who would follow him anywhere. Not content with his daily patrol work, he went out at night to reconnoitre enemy positions so as to be able to direct his daily patrols more effectively. This officer has been one of the greatest sources of inspiration in the battalion. His great cheerfulness under any conditions and his outstanding devotion to duty have been an example of inestimable value to all ranks.'

For the next few months the Dukes remained in the desert, sparring with the Germans, and contending with enervating temperatures well in excess of 100 degrees. But at the end of May 1942 Rommel and his Afrika Korps punched through the Allied lines and grabbed the prize locality of Bir

Hacheim.

The Allies clung on grimly, beaten back against the ropes by the German onslaught, and looking as if their knees would buckle at any moment. The Luftwaffe desisted for a few hours from dropping bombs upon the heads of the Dukes and instead jettisoned thousands of leaflets, calling on the South Africans to surrender and join the fight against British imperialism. The Dukes gratefully gathered up the bundles of papers. The toilet paper shortage was at an end.

On 14 June van der Bijl and the rest of the Dukes withdrew in what became known as the 'Gazala Gallop'. The nadir came for the Allies a week later when they threw in the towel at Tobruk and Rommel accepted the surrender of 30,000 soldiers, a third of whom were South Africans. Rommel, his tail up, pressed his attack on the night of 23-4 June, confident that the Allies' will had broken. He was wrong. Tobruk was to be for Rommel what 21 March 1918 had been to his compatriot on the Western Front, Ludendorff. He became intoxicated by his rapid success and underestimated the spirit of his foe.

General Auchinleck took over command of the Eighth Army and ordered the Gazala Gallop to stop at the El Alamein line. The outcome of the Battle of El Alamein has been passed down to successive generations. Winston Churchill called the victory 'the turning of the hinge of fate' in the war. Field Marshal Lord Montgomery, architect of the triumph, said that success had gone to 'the highest bidder in courage, skill and self-sacrifice'. The Dukes, though they occupied forward posts when the battle began on 23 October, were kept in reserve during the next twelve days of fighting that led, over the course of the following few weeks, to the full-scale retreat of the German army and the end of the desert war. But the Dukes in North Africa had enhanced their reputation for bravery and dependability first gained on the Kenya border twenty-nine months earlier. At the beginning of 1943 the regiment arrived back in South Africa to wide acclaim

Van der Bijl showed indecent haste in pulling on his whites once he arrived home. In March he captained a First Division XI against a Rest of South Africa XI at the Old Wanderers. It was a step back in time for van der Bijl as he led a team that included Bruce Mitchell, the Rowan brothers and his old mucker from Oxford, Tuppy Owen-Smith.

Van der Bijl's leadership qualities had caught the eyes of more than just the organizers of a wartime cricket match. When the Dukes arrived back in South

Africa they were reorganized and Captain van der Bijl was appointed the regiment's commanding officer. He was promoted to Lieutenant-Colonel, leapfrogging the rank of major, and at the end of 1943 he led his men into Italy. It was a short-lived appointment. Van der Bijl was badly injured in an accident and was invalided back to South Africa, disconsolate at having to part with the men he had fought alongside for nearly three years.

The injuries were severe enough to end his cricket career but van der Bijl accepted the news with the same equanimity that he had displayed against Farnes. Besides, he had other things to keep himself busy now, such as his wife, Betty, whom he had met during the war.

The war had crippled van der Bijl physically but his great moral strength was undiminished. He was appointed headmaster of Bishops junior school in 1950 and instilled in his boys the qualities he exemplified: courage, integrity, humility and compassion. He practised what he preached during the 1950s, joining a series of marches to protest against the Nationalist Government's decision to take away the vote from the Coloureds.

The van der Bijls had three children, the youngest of whom, Vintcent, grew into one of the finest cricketers never to play for South Africa. He was selected for his country in 1969 but a few weeks later the world banished South Africa from the sporting arena because of the government policy of apartheid. That he never saw his son play for South Africa hurt van der Bijl, but he had no doubt the boycott was justified.

Van der Bijl retired from Bishops in 1970, ending an association with the school that had begun in 1934. Three years later, one warm February morning, he began to feel unwell as he made himself a cup of tea. He lay down on the floor and suffered a heart attack. It was as peaceful an end as an old soldier could wish for. He was sixty-five.

Lord Moran, who served as a medical officer in the First World War and later became Winston Churchill's physician, wrote that war has no power to transform, it merely exaggerates the good and evil that are in us all. 'Man's fate in battle is worked out before war begins,' he wrote. 'For his acts in war are dictated not by courage, nor by fear, but by conscience ... the man whose quick conscience is the secret of his success in battle has the same clear-cut feelings about right and wrong before war makes them obvious to all. If you know a man in peace, you know him in war.'

Pieter van der Bijl was the embodiment of Moran's conviction.

CHAPTER FIFTEEN

Bill Edrich

Bill *Edrich salvaged a terrible start to his Test career with an innings of 219 in the 'timeless Test' of 1939, just in time to go to war as a bomber pilot. After the war he enjoyed one of the greatest of all seasons in 1947 with his Middlesex 'twin' Denis Compton, and gained a reputation for living life to the full, an attitude that brought him into conflict with the MCC.*

Bill Edrich sat before Sir Pelham Warner like a naughty schoolboy facing his headmaster. 'We've had this report from Bob Wyatt,' said Warner, President of the MCC, nodding to a file that lay before the committee. He didn't need to say anything else. Edrich could guess the gist of Wyatt's statement. Warner shifted uncomfortably on his chair. This was difficult for him. He had an enormous amount of respect for the man perched in front of him. Nevertheless it had to be done. One couldn't allow an England batsman to return to the team hotel sozzled just a few hours before he went out to bat against the West Indies. Warner asked Edrich to withdraw his name from the list of prospective players to tour Australia that winter. Edrich refused. He was perfectly fit, so there was no reason for him to rule himself out of contention. Warner's phlegmatic exterior belied the admiration he felt for Edrich's steadfastness.

However, it left him, under pressure from the tour captain, Freddie Brown, with no alternative but to omit him from the squad as punishment for what was considered an unacceptable breach of discipline. Edrich rose, thanked the gentlemen for their time, and walked out of Lord's and the England cricket side. It was the summer of 1950. He wouldn't return for another three years. As he stormed through the Grace Gates, what nettled Edrich most was the pettiness of it all. Some people were so hidebound by tradition and convention they had allowed themselves to become obsessed by a silly bloody game. As if there weren't more important things in life.

Edrich hailed a cab and climbed inside. He sat and brooded as he sped away from St John's Wood. Perhaps his mind drifted back nine years to a summer's morning and a few hours so petrifying that the memory of them lingered still, as persistently as a black cloud hanging over Lord's on a July afternoon. If some of those committee men had been with him aboard his Blenheim bomber then perhaps, just perhaps, they would understand why he was on a mission to wring every last drop of enjoyment from life. He was living not just for himself, but also for all the boys who didn't get much of a chance to enjoy life's pleasures.

The target for 107 Squadron that warm summer's morning in 1941 was a fighter base on the island of Sylt, off the north-western coast of Germany. Bomber Command had tried to play down the concerns of the crews by assuring them that the base's defences would be under strength as the attack was timed for Sunday lunchtime, when the enemy would be sipping a beer and chewing on a Wiener schnitzel.

In the last minutes before the crews began to taxi down the runway, two of the nine Blenheim bombers were found to be unairworthy. It was not a good omen. There were 800 miles to be covered before they reached their target and for all that time they would have to fly below 50ft to avoid radar detection. Radio silence was also a requisite of daylight low-level flying, one of the hardest aspects of any mission for Edrich, a naturally ebullient individual. It denied him the chance of enjoying a natter with Ernie Hope, his Lancastrian wireless operator and rear-gunner, and Vic Phipps, his navigator.

Low-level daylight flying was an unwelcome and hazardous task for a bomber pilot in the Second World War. The one thing that could be said for it was at least it spared the crews the freezing temperatures that gnawed away at airmen thousands of feet higher. Even at high noon in midsummer there could be thirty degrees of frost at 20,000ft; at the same height in winter there could be twice as much. Edrich guarded against such temperatures by wearing his England cricket jumper underneath his RAF flying suit.

The seven Blenheims reached their target bang on time and discovered British intelligence had been inaccurate. The German anti-aircraft crews were not at lunch. 'The water between the island and the mainland looked like a film shot of a naval battle,' recalled Edrich. 'It was crowded with ships who were firing everything they had – at us! Plumes of water from bursting shells were lifting higher than our planes, and in no time three of our formation were lost. With that we had to split up, so that we never reached our target. In fact, we ran back across the island and dropped our bombs indis-criminately, but in that shooting gallery there was no time for the gallantries of war – whatever they may be.'

The four remaining Blenheims turned tail. The drone of the Blenheim engine was accompanied by the trepidation of the airmen as they scanned the skies for German fighters. With Sylt 90 miles to the rear and no sign of being bounced by enemy planes, Edrich gave the strictly unofficial order for his crew to light cigarettes. 'Although forbidden by regulations, this was the usual procedure in a bomber once it was considered the danger was past,' he later explained. 'My navigator was just handing me a lighted cigarette when Ernie Hope's voice came over the intercom: "Snappers".' Edrich looked back to the port side and in the distance he could see four specks. 'The party was not yet over.'

As the four Messerschmitt 109s homed in on the bombers they split into pairs, two attacking starboard while the others went round to port. Like all good hunters they were familiar with how their prey would react when threatened. RAF bomber tactics against enemy fighters were to turn into the attack, giving the enemy less chance to fire than when they were following. The German tactics, said Edrich, meant that 'we could not turn into the attack against both sections together'.

The ensuing air battle lasted twenty minutes. 'Twenty minutes of air battle is a hell of a long time,' Edrich wrote a few years later, 'like two or three lifetimes rolled into one.' All four Blenheims suffered grave damage as the Messerschmitts raked them with fire time and again, but by some freak of fortune none was shot down. 'By the end of the encounter there was not a gun firing among the Blenheims, all of them being jammed or out of ammunition.'

Three of the Messerschmitts had broken off the attack – probably through lack of ammunition – but one of the Germans came round once more. Maybe he had guessed the Blenheims hadn't a cartridge left among them. The Luftwaffe pilot singled out Edrich's plane and closed in. 'We were sitting ducks,' Edrich recalled, as he and his crew waited for the bullets to rip through the fuselage. 'He closed to point blank range – about 30 yards – and then nothing happened!' As the Messerschmitt overtook the Blenheim, Edrich looked up straight into the face of the German. He bore the look of the cheated hangman, furious with the faulty trapdoor. 'His look of exasperation was unmistakable,' wrote Edrich, '[but] with a shrug of his shoulders he turned away.'

They limped back to their base in Driffield, Yorkshire, unhurt but all badly shaken by the experience. As Edrich hobbled across the tarmac he reflected on his continued good fortune. Twelve missions flown but how long would his luck last? He was understandably nervous about the next, unlucky thirteen, so he decided to ask his commanding officer, Lawrence Petley, if he could take the leave that was due him before his next sortie. Petley agreed, as Edrich thought he would. The two shared a mutual respect; Petley, a keen club cricketer, was tickled pink to have an England star in his squadron – he had even given him permission on a couple of occasions to fly to RAF Hendon so he could take part in one-day matches at Lord's; while in turn Petley's courage and leadership qualities were appreciated by Edrich.

Edrich spent his leave at a local beauty spot. He tried to unwind but an air of melancholy hung over him. On the way back to Driffield he bought a newspaper to see if it contained an account of the raid on Bremen by his squadron. 'As I read the names of the crews who were missing, it became fairly obvious that the squadron had been hit hard again.' Listed among the missing was Petley.*

The death of Petley didn't put an end to the cricket matches. For Edrich and a host of other airmen cricket was the valve through which their stress and fear could temporarily escape. For much of the summer of 1941 the squadron was based in Norfolk, Edrich's native county, and not too far from Massingham Hall. A match was organized one Saturday between 107

* Wing Commander Lawrence Petley is buried at Becklingen, 50 miles north of Hanover.

Squadron and a Massingham XI. Edrich was down to play but a call came to attack some shipping on the Dutch coast. He described it as 'hard-pounding at close quarters'. His brother, Brian, who also served in the RAF and played cricket for Kent, elaborated: 'The Blenheims attacked the ships by coming straight at them, just lifting over the top, and then releasing their bombs into the sides of the vessels. At the speed they came in – around 250mph – they were fairly easy targets.'

The German convoy took a pasting but two of the Blenheims were shot down. Edrich recalled that when they arrived back at base just after midday, 'it was necessary to rearrange the squadron side for the afternoon match, and bring in some reserves in place of the men who were now at the bottom of the North Sea'.

Edrich wrote about the incongruity of the match, just a few years later, and one suspects it was afternoons such as these that shaped his subsequent attitude to life and cricket.

> 'There were the big elms throwing grave shadows on the English grass, the wild roses in the hedges, the lazy caw of a rook passing overhead … and the quiet sound of bat and ball … Every now and then would come the old, accustomed cry – OWZATT? – and then one's mind would flicker off to the briefing, and to joking with a pal whose broken body was now washing in the long, cold tides, and one saw again his machine cartwheeeling down, flaming from nose to tail; and then a ball would roll fast along the green English turf and in the distance the village clock would strike and the mellow echoes would ring through the lazy air of that perfect summer afternoon.'

In the minds of Bomber Command the scale of losses sustained by the crews was proportional to the damage inflicted on the morale of the Germans. When Hitler ordered the invasion of Russia on 21 June 1941 it was decided to start attacking the very heart of the German industrial heartland to disrupt the essential resources needed to maintain a war machine in Western and Eastern Europe.

The targets selected were the Cologne power stations of Knapsack and Quadrath. The crews practised the raid over a disused power station in Bedfordshire, simulating the attack but without releasing the four 250lb bombs they would drop over the target proper.

When the fifty-four Blenheims actually set off on the morning of 12 August 1941, they were divided up into three formations with each one of these subdivided into three boxes of six Blenheims. Edrich, because he had recently been promoted from Pilot Officer to acting Squadron Leader, commanded one of the boxes.

They covered the 750 miles to the target at a height of 100 feet. As the Blenheims screamed over the Dutch countryside, the men and women working the fields looked up and waved. The formations came in low over Knapsack, at a height of between 200 and 800 feet, and bombed and machine-gunned the power station. At Quadrath the bombs were released from the height of the chimneys. It was stunningly audacious and when news reached Bomber Command there was a feeling of immense glee that they had successfully carried out so brazen an attack.

For the airmen the sentiments weren't quite as euphoric. For hours Edrich and the other pilots milled around the airfield, reliving the raid and peering east, hoping to see a speck on the horizon that would loom ever bigger until it could be confirmed as another returning Blenheim. But by late afternoon there was a grim acceptance that twelve of their number would never come home.

A total of two DSOs (Distinguished Service Order), ten DFCs (Distinguished Flying Cross) and three DFMs (Distinguished Flying Medals) were awarded. Edrich was put forward for a DFC. The recommendation ran:

'This officer had the difficult task of bringing his formation in to attack the main power station immediately after the leading box had attacked. This needed fine judgement as it was imperative that the target should be bombed from as low an altitude as possible. He had to delay his attack in order to avoid his formation being destroyed by explosions from the delay action bombs of the previous boxes. This required coolness and courage … Squadron Leader Edrich led his formation in at exactly the right height and time, all aircraft dropping the bombs in the centre of the target area. By carrying out his orders with the greatest exactitude and determination, he must be given credit for a large part of the success of the attack.'

'Drink raises morale in a bomber squadron,' Lord Moran remembered being told by a pilot. 'He meant that after a raid where the losses have been particularly heavy "drinking with the boys" in some local pub over a game of darts keeps them from going off alone.'

Edrich didn't drink to excess during his time with Bomber Command, but he was acquainted with 107 Squadron's mess. Alcohol was a temporary escape from the terrors of low-level daylight bombing missions. It would be used either to toast a successful sortie or to blot out the death of a fellow pilot. As Edrich admitted in after years: 'In four months in 1941 I experienced the heights and depths of emotion – supreme elation, like the effects of a good wine, and profound remorse at losing so many fine friends.'

Denis Compton, Edrich's cricketing 'twin', attributed his post-war drinking to his RAF days: 'He would obviously need a few beers to restore himself between operations. And this becomes a customary habit if you do it for a long time in such circumstances.'

Edrich's drinking didn't cause any problems within the RAF. In 1943 he was sent to the Staff College at Camberley and in the run-up to the invasion of France in 1944 he was working in the RAF Group Operations Room. But within the confines of the RAF he was among like-minded people. They appreciated how quickly life could be snuffed out and they shared Edrich's desire to live for the moment because one never knew what was round the corner. There was fear and exhilaration in equal measure for the men who saw active service during the Second World War. As in all wars, those who served and those who did not were never quite able to meet on common ground thereafter. When Edrich returned to civilian life his behaviour was incomprehensible to those who had never come under fire. One exception was his England team-mate, Trevor Bailey, who said of Edrich: 'He believed life was for living, not existing. Now was the vital time and he was never unduly concerned about the morrow … [he] went his own way expecting to be judged only by his performances on the field.'

His performances with the bat for Middlesex, once he had been demobilized at the end of 1945, took time to get off the ground, labouring like a Blenheim bomber struggling to clear the runway because of a heavy bomb-load. The 1946 season was one of the wettest on record and Edrich toiled for small reward under the drizzle of May and early June. His form improved, however, in the second half of the season and he finished with 1,890 runs at an average of 49.73. For the first and only time in his career, Edrich's feats with the ball surpassed his talents with the bat. The moistness in the air aided his particular brand of swing bowling and he finished with 68 wickets at 18 runs apiece. In his solitary Test appearance of the summer, against India at the Oval, he took four for 68 in the only innings of the match completed before the rains came.

The deluge denied Edrich the chance to prove to the selectors they had been wrong to leave him out of the first two Tests. It had been seven years since his last innings for England and he might have begun to think he wouldn't make the cut for the tour to Australia. But Edrich was among the names announced by the MCC in September.

The tourists sailed on the *Stirling Castle* and one can imagine the look of horror on Edrich's face when he discovered the ship's bar was 'dry'; only a Messerschmitt pilot had seen such a look before. Fortunately for Edrich the metaphorical Spitfires arrived off the starboard side to bale him out of his predicament. They appeared in the shape of 200 war brides, sailing to Australia to be reunited with the servicemen they had married during the war. Edrich beamed from ear to ear as he watched them swan up the gangplank. For if there was one thing Edrich appreciated more than a good beer, it was a pretty woman.

Edrich was on his second marriage when he toured Australia in 1946–7 and while there was no suggestion of impropriety aboard the *Stirling Castle*, it wouldn't have prevented him from window-shopping.

Edrich tied the knot five times in total and he loved all his wives in his own inimitable way. His eye for the ladies was nearly as sharp as that for the new ball. Edrich first married when he was twenty and he was still at it forty-seven years later, exchanging vows with Mary in 1983. The feature, however, of all his marriages was the lack of animosity when they drifted apart. Jessy remembered the 'happy ... wild and hilarious times'. Valerie, whom he married in 1960 and who even weaned Edrich off alcohol for a year, said after his death: 'He was a good man ... given the chance I would still marry him.' His sister, Ena Taylor, said of her brother: 'He was quite hopeless – you had to laugh – he couldn't resist a woman ... [but] he could never open himself up to be with one woman for any length of time because it became too mundane.'

Perhaps a few weeks off the booze revitalized Edrich because in Australia he enjoyed his most productive spell to date as an England batsman. The home side won the series 3–0 but Edrich triumphed personally, putting behind him his pre-war failures for his country. He scored 462 runs at an average of 46.20 and, although he scored a century in the second Test at Melbourne, perhaps his most remarkable innings was the 16 he squeezed from a wicked strip in the first Test at Brisbane. He was peppered with lifting deliveries from Ray Lindwall and Keith Miller, but *Wisden*'s correspondent described it as 'one of the most skilful batting displays I have ever seen'. Len Hutton wrote in his autobiography that when Edrich returned to the pavilion he looked as if 'he had gone ten rounds with Muhammad Ali'. It was bodyline in all but name.

The first Test was also marred by umpiring controversy, igniting a fuse that burned slowly throughout the series and only failed to explode because of the discipline of the English tourists. During Australia's first innings Bradman edged a ball to Jack Ikin at second slip when he was on 28. 'We waited for Bradman to leave,' remembered Edrich, 'but he stared down at the ground with a black frown, and Ikin appealed in an incredulous voice, OWZATT?' The umpire gave him not out and Bradman went on to make 187.

Edrich wasn't so fortunate in the third Test when he played a ball from Ray Lindwall on to his pads when he had made 89. The inside edge was heard by the English team in the pavilion and by the journalists in the press box. They were as stunned as Edrich when the umpire adjudged him lbw: 'For a part of a second I stood there wondering what they were talking about,' said Edrich. 'According to the rules the umpire is always right; but it was a mistake.'

The 1947 season back in England will for ever hold a special place in the affection of those who remember it, as John Arlott did, as a 'legendary time of gallant cricket, played in the glory of sunlight'. England was gradually recovering from the wartime austerity that had cast a pall of gloom over the country the previous year, although when South Africa arrived for their tour they were shocked to discover rationing still in place two years after the end of the war. Their health deteriorated as a result but what really suffered most was their morale, and it was the 'Terrible Twins' who were largely responsible.

Denis Compton and Bill Edrich had first met in 1934 when they joined the MCC ground staff. It was the beginning of a friendship that remained as strong fifty years later as it had throughout the intervening years. 'In all our long association together,' reflected Edrich, 'we had only one difference of opinion and that was over a run we had embarked on. I can't recall the rights and wrongs of this case but I do remember the summing up of Gubby Allen. He said, "When Denis and Bill are batting together and one calls the other for a run, it's merely a basis for negotiation".'

Six times in the summer of 1947 Compton and Edrich compiled partnerships of 200 plus, twice in Test matches against South Africa. The tourists' captain, Dudley Nourse, was moved to write after the tour: 'As individuals we liked and admired Edrich and Compton ... as a pair together at the wicket they strained our friendship to the limit. There was a wholesale massacre of our bowling on a grand-size scale.'

Edrich scored 870 runs against South Africa for club and country that summer; Compton weighed in with 1,187. That was just a fraction of their overall total as they finally guided Middlesex to the County Championship. Edrich finished the season with 3,539 runs at an average of 80.43. His twin scored 3,816. Both tallies surpassed the previous record aggregate of Tom Hayward (3,518 runs) established in 1906.

The pinnacle of their season was scaled against South Africa in the second Test at Lord's. The pair put on 370 for the third wicket before Edrich was bowled for 189. 'It was,' wrote *The Times*, 'a splendid innings by a splendid cricketer, who is always well and truly in the game ... his innings was as near as could be immaculate.' Compton was eventually out for 208. *The Times* struggled to remember a blemish during a masterly innings. 'He was once beaten by a leg-break from Mann, but these rare mistakes serve only to emphasize the perfection of their craftmanship.'

Edrich tormented the South Africans with more than just his bat. He took 16 wickets in the four matches he played but it was the last Test series in which he contributed significantly with the ball. A shoulder injury he sustained in August restricted his efforts and in future Tests he was brought on only for occasional spells.

Edrich batted in 1947 as he did throughout his career, with pugnacity, courage and panache. His batting was really just an extension of his life. Basil Easterbrook once wrote that: 'To see him come through the gates at Lord's and walk out to the middle was to see the personification of self-confidence and aggressiveness. He walked with chest thrust out like the human fighting cock he was, but as light on his feet as a girl going to her first dancing class.'

Like a lot of short batsmen – he was 5ft 6in – Edrich loved to hook and pull. He had an exquisite eye and Trevor Bailey knew of no cricketer who watched the ball as closely. But it was his courage that contemporaries remembered best. Twice he was badly injured while batting. The first time was in 1938 when he was flattened by a delivery from Ken Farnes while batting for the Players v the Gentlemen at Lord's. The second occasion was sixteen years later when he faced a young Northamptonshire bowler called Frank Tyson, yet to acquire the sobriquet 'Typhoon'. Edrich didn't know much about this twenty-four-year-old pace bowler; he knew even less about the first ball he received that shattered his cheekbone. 'He went down in a welter of blood,' remembered Tyson. He was carted off to hospital but the next morning Edrich reappeared at the ground and began to pad up. Compton and David Montague, the physio, begged him to report sick: 'David,' he said sternly, 'If I could fly bombers over Germany in the war, I can go out and bat against Frank Tyson.'

Tyson stood at the Nursery end, tossing the ball from hand to hand and watching Edrich approach the wicket. 'He looked like a war casualty. His jaw was in a sling … his face was more black and blue than pink, and his eyes were almost closed by the massive facial bruising.' As Edrich took guard, the young fast bowler looked across to his captain, Denis Brookes, and received a nod. First-class cricket, said Tyson later, 'is no place for sentiment'. Edrich was probably expecting a bouncer first-up and Tyson didn't disappoint. 'But, believe it or not,' Tyson added, 'Bill tried to hook it.' He went on to make 20 before edging one to slip.

With Edrich's penchant for fast bowling it was only natural that Ray Lindwall was a favourite opponent. When Lindwall toured England with Australia in 1948, however, he came out on top in their duel, taking the wicket of Edrich four times and finishing the series with 27 wickets in total. Edrich had endured a dismal start to the series, scoring just 38 runs in his first four innings. His form picked up in the third Test, where he scored 32 and 53, but the fourth Test at Leeds was the match where he showed his old class. He scored a century in the first innings, and 54 in the second during a thrilling partnership of 103 with Compton.

Australia needed to score 404 in less than six hours if they were to nick an improbable victory. They did it with seven wickets remaining. It was a dire England performance in the field, and one of those fingered by the press bearing responsiblity for a dismally substandard display was Jim Laker. He finished with match figures of three wickets for 206 runs on a helpful wicket. His time against Australia would come eight years later. Edrich, on the other hand, looked forward to gaining revenge when England toured down under in 1950–51.

When the 1950 season started Edrich was fairly confident of making the tour to Australia. He had enjoyed a good series the previous summer against New Zealand, scoring 324 runs in six innings at an average of 54. His socializing showed no signs of abating but it was doing no one any harm and he looked a good bet for the tour. Then came Old Trafford.

In 1950 the West Indies were in England for the first time since 1939. With them were two unknown spinners, Alf Valentine and Sonny Ramadhin. It was Valentine who got Edrich for seven in the first innings of the first Test at Manchester. Godfrey Evans rescued England from a parlous situation with his maiden Test century. Edrich thought it only proper to throw a party to celebrate Evans' knock. 'Now I have always liked a party,' he later wistfully recorded, 'to me it has always seemed part of the social atmosphere of cricket. And this was a pretty good party.'

A rather tired and emotional Edrich stumbled up to his room at an hour when most Test batsmen should have been tucked up in bed. He was later unable to recall the events with much clarity, although he did concede there might have been 'a spot of noise' as he attempted to locate his room. 'I awoke the fellow in the next room – Bob Wyatt, chairman of selectors and a man with a more puritan outlook on the social life of cricket than myself.'

Nothing was said the next morning and when Edrich scored an unbeaten 56 to help England finish the day on 104 for four, he presumed his high jinks had been overlooked. It wasn't, after all, the first occasion Edrich had stumbled into the milkman on his return to the team hotel. Indeed, his most famous innings for England had been played on the back of a first-class night of revelry.

When Edrich had arrived at the party hosted by Tuppy Owen-Smith, the former South African cricketer, on the evening of 9 March 1939, he was unsure whether to have a drink or not. England and South Africa had just finished day six of the final Test at Durban. Len Hutton and Paul Gibb, England's openers, had faced one ball before the close of play, and there was a strong possibility Edrich would have to bat the next day. He eyed up the bottles of champagne, then thought of his previous scores in the series: 4, 10, 0, 6, 1. He had promised himself he would remain dry during the Test matches, and he had. Fat lot of good it had done him. Things can't get any worse, he probably told himself. He picked up a glass and caught the eye of the waiter.

Edrich was put to bed by his team-mates in the early hours of Friday morning. The first person he met at breakfast was his captain, Wally Hammond. 'I'm going to put you in first wicket down,' said Hammond. 'This is your last chance in this Test series. You can make runs, if you try,' he added, 'but don't be afraid to go for the ball.'

Hutton and Gibb put on 78 for the first wicket, before Hutton was bowled by Mitchell. As Edrich walked out to bat he knew he was batting for his Test life. Since he had made his debut against Australia in June the previous year he had scored 88 runs in eleven innings. There were murmurs of 'good luck' from the other England players and Reg Perks, the fast bowler, shoved something into Edrich's glove. It was a tiny white elephant. 'It'll change your luck, Bill,' he winked.

As Edrich walked to the wicket several of the South African players were grinning. Pieter van der Bijl clapped politely but most found it amusing that England had promoted Edrich up the order. Norman Gordon, the only player from the series still alive at the turn of the century, recalled the reaction of his team-mates. 'We were all very surprised when he walked out to bat. But to be honest we were surprised he was in the team at all because he had been so out of form in the previous Tests. I was fielding close to the bat on the leg side and I thought to myself, "This won't take long, I'll soon get him". And I did. I caught him when he popped one up off the bowling of Langton. But by then he had scored 219.'

Edrich cracked his first ball from Mitchell for four. He hit a further seven fours on his way to his half-century. At the close of play he was unbeaten on 107. Saturday was rained off but the rest did him good. On Monday he completed his double century in six hours and thirty-five minutes. At tea he had made 215. As he sat in the pavilion waiting for the resumption of play he heard the pop of a champagne cork. Edrich turned round to see A J Holmes, the tour manager, pouring him a glass. 'I hear you've been training on this stuff,' he grinned. 'You'd better have some now.'

Edrich celebrated his knock in customary fashion and was joined by team-mates and opponents alike. Gordon tagged along for the ride. 'There was a great atmosphere throughout the series,' he remembered, 'and I actually went out socially with Bill a few times. It's fair to say he was a bit wild, but he was also a very nice chap and modest, too. I'm pleased he wasn't around in modern cricket because I don't think we would have seen much of him; he would have spent most of his time sitting out matches for disciplinary reasons!'

The punitive measures imposed on Edrich after the Old Trafford incident in 1950 excluded him from series against Australia, South Africa and India, but he refused to compromise himself and step into the ready-made clothes in which conformists like to dress. His streak of individuality continued to underpin his existence. Never was this more clearly seen than during his annual trips to Yorkshire for the Scarborough Festival, an event that he referred to as 'one long party'. Trevor Bailey recalled that: 'The one concession he was prepared to make to the strain of playing nine days' cricket with the absolute minimum of sleep was to stand somewhat deeper than usual at slip. On one occasion I suggested to the captain that Bill should come up a few yards to save the single.'

The English selectors might have expected Edrich's form to fall away without the stimulus of Test cricket. If so, it was another indication that they couldn't fathom their man. His form for Middlesex throughout his wilder-ness years was marked by a consistent excellence and in 1953 he enjoyed his most prolific season for six years, scoring 2,557 runs at an average of 47.35. In 1953, Bob Wyatt and Freddie Brown redeemed their earlier churlishness by recalling Edrich to the England side for the third Test of the home series against Australia.

The Ashes had been in Australian hands since 1934 and few people held out much hope of success this time around. It seemed to most fans that England had a bigger mountain to climb than Edmund Hillary and Tenzing Norgay who, as the Australians arrived for the start of their tour, were establishing base camp at the foot of Everest.

The first two Tests were drawn and Edrich got the call for the third at Old Trafford, which also ended in stalemate. He was now thirty-seven and Ray Lindwall, the Australian fast bowler he had first encountered seven years earlier, was in his thirty-second year. Age had not withered either, as was demonstrated in the fourth Test at Headingley. 'He [Compton] and Edrich withstood hostile bowling from Lindwall, Miller and Archer,' reported *Wisden*. 'They were subjected to a series of bumpers but stayed together to add 77 runs in two and a quarter hours.' In spite of a battling 64 from Edrich the Test went the way of the previous three.

It all came down to the fifth and final Test at the Oval. England gained the upper hand after the first innings, dismissing the tourists for 275 and scoring 306 themselves. Edrich made 21 but it was a precious knock; a show of defiance in the face of the Australian intimidation. Rex Alston, senior commentator with the BBC, said 'the moral value to England's cause of his innings was out of all proportion to the number of runs scored'. Edrich's bellicosity inspired his team-mates and they skittled Australia for 162 in their second innings. England needed just 132 to win the Test and the series, and to regain the Ashes after nineteen years.

Hutton went cheaply for 17, and at the end of the third day England were 38 for one. Edrich was unbeaten on 15 and May on six. Around 25,000 fans crammed into the Oval the next day to see if England could do it. Hillary and Tenzing had climbed their way into history. Could England make it a sensational double to hand to the new sovereign, Queen Elizabeth?

May had made 37 before he was out; that brought Compton to the wicket. They had first played together in 1934, the same year Australia took the Ashes out of England. If they could hit the winning runs there would be a pleasant symmetry to the whole affair.

Cricket correspondent Jim Swanton reported that Lindwall 'kept up a ceaseless, fast and accurate attack … Edrich and Compton had to watch with all their eyes and wits.' Edrich now was in his element, back on centre stage playing the part of the battling gallant. Rex Alston reported that he 'was safe … if in doubt, ask the Australian bowlers. They just did not know how to get either of them out. If a fast bowler dropped one short … Edrich hooked him savagely for four.'

Edrich had made 55 when Compton hit the winning runs, the sound of the ball clattering against the advertising hoarding below the gasometer the starting gun that sent the crowd streaming on to the Oval turf. 'Back in the dressing room,' wrote Edrich later, 'Denis said: "We'll have a quiet beer together on this. This is the happiest day in my life." Quiet beer, what a laugh! The champagne flowed in that Oval pavilion like rain in an English August.'

Edrich played five more matches for England before his Test career came to an end against Australia in 1955. In his thirty-nine Tests he had scored 2,440 runs at an average of exactly 40.

Along the way he had upset one or two of the 'blazers' in the committee room but no lasting harm had been done. It was difficult to harbour a grudge against Edrich for longer than the time it took him to slap the malcontent on the back and offer him a beer. Edrich, wrote the respected sports writer Ian Wooldridge, 'epitomised the particularly British breed of incurable scallywag …but there was a bottom line to his roistering. You had to be there before the start of play, next day. Then, hung over or otherwise, you had to fight.'

Edrich continued to play Minor Counties cricket for Norfolk until 1971 when he retired, thirty-nine years after his first game for the county. In later years he dabbled in financial consultancy and maintained his links with Middlesex CCC.

He died on 23 April 1986, St George's Day, appropriately enough for a man who considered it a stroke of fortune to have been born an Englishman. Five years later the MCC decided it would rename two stands at Lord's after Denis Compton and Bill Edrich. At the lunch interval of a one-day international between England and the West Indies in 1991, Compton and Justin Edrich, one of Bill's two sons, walked out into the middle of the ground for the unveiling ceremony. As the crowd rose to their feet in appreciation, Compton shook his head in amazement. 'How,' he muttered, 'could there be two such stands without a bar between them?'

CHAPTER SIXTEEN

Blair Mayne

B lair Mayne toured South Africa with the British Lions in 1938 and gained a reputation as a softly-spoken Irishman who never let down his team-mates on the rugby field. Yet he also revealed another side to his personality during the tour; it was the aggressive and wild streak that would be used to such deadly effect during the Second World War. Mayne was one of the founding fathers of the SAS in 1941 and is arguably the greatest soldier in the regiment's history.

Blair Mayne was a keen gardener. He was proud of his rose bushes and he enjoyed seeing the progress of the tropical shrubs he cultivated. He had other passions, too. He was an avid reader of poetry, and if he wasn't reciting a sonnet to himself when he took his beloved collie for a walk, he was whistling the tune of an Irish folk song. If one had chanced upon Mayne walking his dog in the lush countryside near his home in Northern Ireland, one would have been struck by his shy and unassuming manner, and the gentle Irish brogue that was sometimes inaudible above the rush of water from the trout stream he often wandered alongside.

In the years after the Second World War Mayne would come to the stream and brood. Perhaps he threw stones into the water, watching the ever decreasing circles of the ripples. It was a metaphor for his own life in his final years. Gradually the circles for Mayne diminished until, encircled by one solitary pool of loneliness, he died in circumstances not befitting such a prodigious warlord.

Because despite Mayne's fondness for the arts and for horticulture and for dogs, his greatest love was for war. In the annals of military warfare few have surpassed the deeds of Blair Mayne. He was a soldier fit to stand comparison with the greatest warriors of history, from Charlemagne to Richard I to Geronimo. He killed easily, and without compunction – one comrade in the SAS remembered how he would go on raids in search of 'some good killing' – yet to his own men he was as compassionate and considerate as he was merciless and brutal to the enemy. If he wasn't devising new methods to kill Germans he was writing letters to the mothers of the men who served under him, reassuring them that their sons were doing just grand. This contradiction in his personality only added to the mystique that hung around his colossal frame. No one who knew him, except probably his own mother on whom he doted, really got inside the mind of Blair Mayne. All they did know was that they were glad they were on his side.

The men who sailed with Mayne to South Africa aboard the *Stirling Castle* in May 1938 knew little about the 6ft 3in, twenty-three-year-old Irishman who had made his debut for his country the previous year. The other members of the British Lions touring party found him pleasant company, even though he was unusually quiet for a second row forward. They had heard through the grapevine that he was reading law at Queen's University, but Mayne himself was too modest to tell them he was Irish Universities heavyweight boxing champion or that he came from a prosperous middle-class family in the rolling countryside of County Down. 'He was a very quiet chap,' recalls Vivian Jenkins, the vice-captain of the tour. 'He was a bit of a loner in one way, but he was immensely popular on tour. At first glance you would think he wouldn't hurt a fly, but we soon discovered that when he got steamed up, he would do anything.'

South Africa suited Blair Mayne. He liked the people whom he viewed as similar to himself; polite and correct on the surface but resourceful, rugged and uncompromising underneath. This was certainly true of their rugby players, who had a habit of intimidating their British and Irish counterparts on the field. Mayne, however, was every bit as hardy as the Springbok players. One former South African international, Duggie Morkel, said of the Irishman's performances on tour: 'He is the finest all-round forward I have ever seen and he is magnificently built for the part. In staying power he has to be seen to be believed.' The Springbok captain in 1938, Danie Craven, echoed Morkel's words, describing Mayne as a 'tough, hard-working and strong forward who could take everything that came his way'.

Mayne played in nineteen of the twenty-four matches in South Africa, including the three Tests. The first Test at Ellis Park in Johannesburg went the way of the home side 26–12, a performance rated by Craven many years later as one of the great Springbok displays. Mayne, said one South African paper, 'was outstanding in a pack which gamely and untiringly stood up to the tremendous task'. Jenkins kicked a penalty from within his own half to reduce the Lions' deficit and the length of the kick impressed even Mayne: 'About the only time I ever heard Blair speak on a rugby pitch was after I had kicked that penalty,' recalls Jenkins. 'As we ran back to await the kick-off he said in that soft voice of his, "good kick". That was some compliment coming from a man like Blair.'

The second Test was played in Port Elizabeth in sweltering conditions that sapped the stamina of both teams. South Africa won 19–3 but it was the Lions' forwards who finished the stronger in temperatures that touched 100 degrees. Mayne was still trying to blast a way through the Springbok defence in the closing minutes, his shock of red hair matted in sweat and his lobster-red legs pumping furiously as he ran the ball at the home side. Alongside Mayne, screaming for the ball, was the Welsh hooker, William Travers, known to his mates as 'Bunner'.

Mayne and Travers came from contrasting backgrounds. Mayne was the educated and reserved trainee solicitor from a comfortable middle-class family in Ireland. Travers was a coal trimmer from Newport, occasionally obstreperous but always, in the words of Jenkins, 'very, very funny'. Both, however, had volcanic temperaments and when they erupted the molten lava that spewed forth could engulf everything in its path. Haydn Tanner, who played with Travers for Wales and on the 1938 Lions tour, remembers that when Ireland played Wales in 1937 – Mayne's first cap – the pair, 'kicked lumps out of each other … there was no mercy. It really was some sight when they squared up to one another.'

In South Africa they stood foursquare together, on and off the pitch.

Jenkins remembers an occasion in Kimberley when the pair were sitting at a bar enjoying a few drinks and a chat: 'This chap came up to them and said, "Have a drink with me". Bill, who could be quite abrupt, said, "No thank you, I've got one". And this chap walks off saying "Aw, bloody roinecks".* Bill sprang to his feet and told him if he repeated that word there would be trouble. "Well you are bloody roinecks, aren't you?" he said. And with that Bill gave him one, and I've never forgotten the phrase he used afterwards: "Viv," he told me, "he split like a bloody tomato."'

Mayne was an archetypal roineck. His fair complexion wasn't suited to the South African climate and he soon became fed up with the sniggering from some of the tanned locals. In Durban he and Travers decided to do something about it. While the rest of the squad dressed in white tie and tails and attended a dinner at a Country Club, Mayne and Travers went down to Durban docks. 'For some reason that I was never quite sure of,' says Jenkins, 'we had been given these big, thick fishermen's jumpers earlier in the tour from one of our hosts. Bunner and Blair put them on and went down to the docks. They sat and chatted and waited for some dockers to call them "roinecks". Inevitably they did before long and they were soon getting stuck in to them. Of course, they flattened them all – they were both hard men – and they came back having had a great time.'

The captain of the tour was Sam Walker, a prop forward and an Ulsterman, who tolerated the excesses of Mayne and Travers. Mayne, in turn, says Jenkins, respected Walker because he led by example. 'There were three or four wild boys on that tour,' recalls Tanner, 'but they would always toe the line if Sam or Jock Hartley, the manager, told them they had overstepped the mark.'

Jenkins endorses that view although he says there was one time when Mayne took the law into his own hands and cocked a snoot at the tour authority. The tourists had arrived at their Pietmaritzburg hotel after a game, only to discover that they had been allocated the dingiest rooms because the best ones had been reserved for the locals attending the post-match dance in the hotel that evening. 'Blair wasn't happy,' chuckles Jenkins at the memory. 'So he decided to stage a one-man protest.'

* A derogatory term used by Afrikaners that stems from the Boer War when British soldiers often suffered red necks from the hot sun when marching.

Jenkins was hanging up his tie and tails in the rickety wardrobe in the corner of his room when he heard a commotion coming from the next room. 'It was Blair. He proceeded to break everything in the room, the bed, the wardrobe, the drawers, he broke the whole bloody lot, and then piled it in a heap in the middle. I might have been vice-captain of the tour, but I kept very quiet because there was no way I was getting involved. The manager of the hotel, who was braver than me – or more stupid – banged on Blair's door and demanded to know what was going on. Blair opened it and stood there in the doorway, glaring down at the manager. "What do you want?" he growled. The manager said he had come to investigate the noise, whereupon Blair said, "This is my room, clear off." He slammed the door and continued to smash up the place.'

The hotel manager ran gibbering to the Lions management. The next morning Mayne was ticked off by Jock Hartley in the garden of the hotel, while from the windows above the rest of the squad peered down like curious schoolboys. Mayne took his dressing down badly. In his opinion he had been justified because the squad had been treated with contempt by the hotel. When the players assembled later that day to take the coach to Durban, he was missing. Hartley and Walker conferred and decided that Mayne, while prone to bouts of indiscipline, would never let down his team-mates. They were confident that he would appear in Durban in time for the match against Natal three days later.

Mayne turned up at the Lions' hotel – and this one fortunately met with his approval – on the day of the match and helped his side to a 15–11 win. 'Mayne was the outstanding forward,' wrote one South African newspaper, 'and he worked very hard throughout.'

He remained tight-lipped about his desertion but Jenkins later discovered what had happened: 'The story I heard was that Blair stormed off and got talking to a farmer in a bar. The two of them had a few drinks and then decided to go on a bit of a thrash. They had ridden on horseback to a village where a dance was being held. They rode straight into the hall, across the dance floor and then back out again, chased by several irate villagers.'

Mayne played in the third Test at Cape Town where the Lions won 21–16. In the dressing room beforehand, Walker had exhorted his men to give their all in the pursuit of victory, 'even if it means leaving Newlands in an ambulance'. It was the sort of battle cry that appealed to Mayne and he was described by one reporter as 'again outstanding in the open and magnificent in defence'.

To some of the older spectators Mayne reminded them of another wild Irishman who had toured South Africa years earlier. There was, they told one another, a touch of the Tom Crean about Mayne, even if he wasn't quite as quick and as skilful as the man they had watched … when was it? 1896? It seemed like only yesterday.

Mayne and Crean shared many characteristics, leaving aside their rugby talent, but there were also a number of differences in their personalities that would probably have hindered a firm friendship being formed.

They were both naturally pugnacious and courageous, traits that often concealed the compassionate streak underneath. But Crean was an extrovert who enjoyed being the centre of attention. Mayne loathed any form of self-publicity. One of the men who fought with him during the war never knew he had played for the British Lions until someone told him years later.

The pair would have enjoyed having a drink together, although the initial intelligent conversation would quickly have turned to blather as they warmed to their task. After a few beers the two would probably have parted company at the bar; Crean would have looked for a pretty woman with whom he could flirt, while Mayne would have become increasingly maudlin, resolutely refusing to make small talk with a species he found unfathomable and slightly daunting. Vivian Jenkins remembers for Mayne the only disagreeable aspect of the tour was the social obligations: 'He didn't like going to dances because he wasn't a womanizer. It was a shame because he was magnificent-looking and a number of the young women found him very attractive.'

The tourists arrived back in Southampton at the beginning of October 1938, just a couple of days after Neville Chamberlain had stepped off the plane from Germany, waving a piece of paper and confidently declaring 'Peace in Our Time'. Mayne had more pressing issues than the proclamations of the Prime Minister. He had to rush back to Queen's and prepare for the final year of his law degree.

He also moved clubs and joined Malone, captaining them to the final of the Ulster Cup. He managed his time well at the start of 1939, attending lectures in between playing for Ireland in the Five Nations and joining a territorial anti-aircraft regiment in February. The next month Hitler seized

Czechoslovakia, but Mayne barely looked up from his revision notes as he swotted for his Finals. By the time he had passed his exams and joined a solicitors' firm in Belfast, Britain was issuing a final ultimatum to Germany to respect Poland's borders. Hitler, as disdainful of the threat as Mayne had been of the hotel manager's, marched into Poland and the world was at war.

At the same time that Mayne was battling with an alarming amount of paperwork in his new job, a twenty-four-year-old Scotsman was travelling through America having spent several weeks climbing in the Rocky Mountains. David Stirling, short of cash and in need of some relaxation, decided to spend a few days gambling in Las Vegas to raise sufficient funds for his passage back to Scotland, whenever that might be. A few days later he heard that Britain had declared war on Germany. Fortunately he had come out on top in Vegas and he used his winnings to catch a flight back home.

Stirling volunteered for the Commandos and in the spring of 1941 sailed for North Africa where he took part in three raids against coastal communications. All three were deemed a failure by Middle East Headquarters (MEHQ) and the concept of a Commando force began to lose its appeal in the eyes of the top brass.

Stirling, however, was adamant in his own mind that small numbers of men infiltrating German lines and attacking specific targets could be devastatingly effective; but they had to be well co-ordinated, something the nascent commandos hadn't been. Stirling wrote a memo entitled 'A Special Service Unit' and then bluffed his way into MEHQ. Once inside he barged his way in to the office of General Ritchie, Deputy Chief of Staff, and one of the few men in HQ who wasn't, in the words of Stirling, a member of the 'Freemasons of Mediocrity', the cabal of senior officers who were wont to veto any proposal they viewed as too risky or unconventional.

Within a few days of meeting Ritchie, Stirling had been promoted to captain and given permission to recruit six officers and sixty other ranks for the purpose of attacking German airfields and transport lines. What was this new unit to be called? he asked MEHQ. Someone suggested the Special Air Service Brigade. Stirling agreed. He didn't much care what the unit was called just so long as it could fight the enemy.

Stirling had no problem finding volunteers for the ranks of the SAS but he was fastidious in his choice of officers. They had to be exceptional men. One of the first he recruited was an Irishman called Eoin McGonigal. Stirling asked him if he knew of any other suitable men for what he had in mind. McGonigal said he did. He was friendly with a young Irish officer who had volunteered for the Commandos and had been mentioned in despatches for his part in an action at Litani River against the Vichy French earlier in the year. Stirling asked where he could find this man. He's in jail, replied McGonigal, awaiting a court martial for striking a senior officer.

Blair Mayne had quickly adapted to life as a prisoner. A few months cooped up in a solicitor's office had prepared him for the confinement. He was lying on his bed singing to himself when Stirling appeared and introduced himself to Mayne. 'My name's Blair, not Paddy,' he scowled. Stirling, recalling that first meeting, said: 'He was suspicious of me from the start ... I probably appeared to him as a young whippersnapper who could well have been out just to impress the MEHQ brass.' Stirling outlined his plans for the SAS. When he finished he asked Mayne if he had any questions. 'He was very quiet and he spoke in that gentle Ulster brogue which could charm the faeries,' Stirling reflected. 'I can't see any prospects of real fighting in this scheme of yours,' Mayne said sceptically. 'There aren't any,' replied Stirling. 'Except against the enemy.' Mayne glowered at the man opposite him, and then began to laugh. 'All right. If you can get me out of here I'll come along.' Mayne extended his hand but Stirling didn't take it. Instead, he returned the Irishman's earlier glower. 'There's one more thing. This is one commanding officer you never hit and I want your promise on that.' Mayne grinned. 'You have it.'

Stirling pulled the necessary strings to open Mayne's cell door and he joined the SAS with all charges dropped. The physical training proved no problem for Mayne and he soon exhibited all the signs of being to the desert born. His navigational skills, initiative and ingenuity were exceptional, even in the company of men who were all brilliant soldiers.

Johnny Cooper, who joined the SAS in 1941 aged only eighteen, is one of the handful of 'Originals' of the regiment still alive. He remembers that Mayne 'gave the appearance of a gentle giant, but he wouldn't suffer fools gladly. If a soldier wasn't doing his job properly he wouldn't stand by and tolerate inefficiency.' During one of the route marches a young lad called Chesworth whinged incessantly until Mayne's patience snapped. He grabbed Chesworth by the collar and with one hand dangled him over the edge of a cliff: 'Any more from you,' he said, his voice as soft as his face was hard, 'and that's your lot.'

By the beginning of November 1941 the SAS was coming together as Stirling had envisaged. The weaklings had been weeded out and each man was now skilled in all aspects of desert warfare, from parachuting to navigation to sabotage. Their first opportunity to put into practice what they had learned came in mid-November when they were tasked with raiding a series of airfields on the eve of the launch of the Allies' 'Crusader' offensive against the Germans.

The mission was an unmitigated disaster. It coincided with the worst hurricane to strike North Africa in thirty years and not one of the five raiding parties met with any success. Indeed, of the sixty-two raiders who had parachuted into enemy territory, only twenty-two returned safely. Mayne made it back but one of the men with him, Bob Bennett, recalled that as they trudged back to base, 'Paddy* was tight-lipped and silent. He was so choked up with disappointment that I couldn't get a word out of him.' Mayne's depression deepened when he discovered that Eoin McGonigal, a friend since his schooldays, had been killed during the raid. 'I am tired of this country,' he wrote to his brother, 'especially since Eoin landed a loser.'

Stirling was as disconsolate as his fellow officer. What irked him most was that the failure would bring a smile to the faces of the pen-pushers within MEHQ, who had doubted the wisdom of the SAS from the start and who would now call for it be disbanded. Stirling, however, was determined to prove to these staff officers, whom he described at the time as 'fossilized', that innovation was the secret to success against Rommel's Afrika Korps.

Fortunately for Stirling the senior command kept faith with the SAS. In late November it was agreed that he and his men should establish a new base at the Jalo oasis, well behind enemy lines, but an ideal spot from which to attack the German airfields that lay north-west. On 8 December two raiding parties led by Mayne and Stirling left Jalo to attack the airfields at Sirte and Tamit.

Stirling was again unlucky. There was no hurricane this time, just a minefield and two nervous Italian sentries who began shouting at the shadows they spotted crouched on the edge of the minefield. Stirling ordered

---

* Most of the men in the regiment called him Paddy, although perhaps not to his face, and he is still remembered by the survivors as Paddy Mayne.

his men to retire. As they made their way dejectedly back to the rendezvous, Cooper remembered seeing the sky to the east 'illuminated by a succession of flashes which suggested that Paddy had had happy hunting at Tamit'.

Mayne had enjoyed a field day at Tamit. He hadn't had such a *craic* since the thrash with the South African farmer at the village dance. He had led three men onto the airfield without being challenged. The first thing they stumbled upon was a hut from inside which they could hear voices. Mayne later wrote an account of what followed:

> 'I kicked open the door and stood there with my Colt 45, the others at my side with a Tommy-gun and another automatic. The Germans stared at us. We were a peculiar and frightening sight, bearded, unkempt hair. For what seemed an age we just stood there looking at each other in complete silence. I said: "Good evening". At that a young German arose and moved slowly backwards. I shot him … I turned and fired at another some six feet away. He was standing beside the wall as he sagged … the room was by now in pandemonium so we left, throwing hand grenades to add to the confusion.'

The explosions from the grenades lit up the airfield like a Yuletide tree and brought a smile to the faces of the four SAS soldiers. They were, recorded Mayne, 'as grateful as children on Christmas morning [as] we moved from plane to plane, placing our bombs in the cockpit or petrol tanks'.

As they began to beat a retreat from the airfield, their bombs counting down on a thirty-minute fuse, they realized one Messerschmitt had been overlooked. Bob Bennett looked on with a mixture of mirth and incredulity as Mayne 'climbed up to the cockpit and demolished it with his bare hands'. Mayne himself remembered that, with a 'sharp tug, then a heave, I had ripped out the dashboard for a souvenir'.

Stirling was cock-a-hoop when he discovered Mayne's party had destroyed twenty-four planes. This would silence the freemasons. It would also disturb the enemy, and the annihilation of the guardroom would sow in the minds of the Axis forces seeds of fear, something of which Mayne was only too aware. 'The dozen or so enemy that we had killed or wounded,' he said later, referring to the attack on the hut at Tamit, 'did not matter much numerically. But we hoped to create a feeling of insecurity and anxiety.'

A fortnight later Mayne revisited Tamit. Before they set out the regiment's medical officer, Malcolm James, wished him good luck, 'to which he replied by saying he thought there should be some "good killing"'.

Mayne's return to Tamit was as successful as it was audacious. He and his men destroyed twenty-seven aircraft and left behind a confused and frightened contingent of Italians who fired randomly into the darkness, hoping to hit the raiders they knew had outwitted them once again. The SAS men reached the rendezvous without hitch, only to learn that another raiding party, led by Jock Lewes, hadn't been so fortunate. They had been attacked by German fighters and Lewes was dead. It was the end of one of the most respected and capable officers in the SAS.

Lewes' passing presented Stirling with a problem. He had planned to put him in charge of training recruits. Now he needed someone else. Who? Stirling looked around their camp and spotted Mayne lounging in the shadow of a jeep, reading one of his ubiquitous *Penguin* paperbacks and occasionally dipping his hand into a bag of dates. He had just finished Mottram's *The Spanish Farm* and had recommended it to James, the medical officer. James acted on Mayne's advice, as most men did. 'There was something very rugged and forceful about Paddy's leadership,' James recalled after the war. 'Although he lived and slept with the men, queued up behind as he waited his turn for food, and ate with them, no one would dare overstep the mark and become too familiar.'

Stirling appointed Mayne training officer. Not only did he have the right leadership skills but he was a proven warrior whose skill in battle might just rub off on some of the new recruits. He also possessed, according to Stirling, 'the knack of touching exactly the right chord in each of his men; these were things he never had to think about. They were just there, waiting to come out.'

When Stirling informed Mayne of his decision the Irishman went 'icy cold'. His blue-grey eyes narrowed and Stirling could feel his gaze cutting into him as though it was a thrust from a bayonet. He accused his commanding officer of removing him from the front line because he was jealous of his success. This was untrue, but Mayne wasn't thinking straight. He was too distraught at the thought of training new recruits instead of killing Germans. Stirling, however, soon came to realize that his rationale in selecting Mayne had been flawed.

With no prospect of action Mayne became morose and resentful. He rarely left his tent in the training camp and he took no interest in how the new recruits were shaping up. When Stirling returned after several weeks behind enemy lines he was shocked by what he found. 'I realized at once what a dreadful mistake I had made in committing this superb soldier to a training and administrative role ... he spoke in monosyllables and didn't even look me in the eye. He was not the Mayne of a few weeks earlier.'

For the first time Stirling caught a rare glimpse inside the mind of Mayne. Until then he had been as unable as everyone else to slip through the defences that Mayne had erected around himself. It became clear to Stirling that administration stupefied and frustrated the Irishman. Mayne, realized Stirling, had a 'subconscious need to create'. He had first stumbled across this facet of his personality when he had told Mayne about his own failure to become an artist before the war. 'Paddy was by then quite drunk and pretty maudlin, but he suddenly came to life and I realized that here was a man suffering from an equal ... frustration.' War, however, had provided Mayne with the outlet to express himself, however perverse that might sound amid all the destruction he caused. To Mayne, the war he waged against the Germans was an art, and when he planned and executed an operation, he was creating in just the same way as a composer or a writer. Colonel David Lloyd Owen, who served with Mayne in the desert, recalled that he had 'an aggressive and ingenious brain which was always seeking new ways to harry the enemy ... he was a born leader and he could flourish under the powers that he could exercise.'

The 6ft 6in Stirling was a big man in every sense. He apologized to Mayne and admitted he had made an error of judgement. Within a few days he was back with his boys, with a smile as broad as the one that had greeted the news of his first cap for Ireland five years earlier.

The rest of the men were delighted to have him back. Paddy was different from them, that much they knew. Desert warfare had its fair share of excitement but it could also be horribly dangerous and frightening. Mayne, however, seemed to thrive on it. 'This sort of fighting was in his blood,' recalled James.'There was no give or take about his method of warfare, and he was out to kill when the opportunity presented itself. There was no question of sparing an enemy – this was war, and war meant killing.'

Johnny Cooper maintains sixty years later that Mayne was fearless. 'I never saw him scared, he just hadn't the same sort of fear that the rest of us had. He didn't have a problem about his own safety – although he cared deeply about the rest of us – and it seemed that he accepted death as part of the job and if it happened, well, it happened.'

Mayne's composure almost certainly saved the lives of his men one night in June 1942. The previous evening Stirling had enjoyed a good night's hunting at Benina airfield. Upon his return he ribbed Mayne over his comparative lack of success at the aerodrome at Berkha. Mayne, a mischievous glint in his eye, impugned Stirling's tally of destroyed planes, goading him into suggesting they revisit Benina for verification. Stirling cheerily accepted the dare.

The pair borrowed a Chevrolet truck and, with five others including Cooper, set off into the heart of enemy territory. The Germans by now had become thoroughly fed up with the activities of the SAS, led by the man they had nicknamed 'The Phantom Major'. Stirling assumed they would have little trouble retracing their steps but this time the Germans had set up a roadblock in case the Phantom attempted to ghost through their lines once more. Mayne was at the wheel of the truck when they ran into a heavily armed roadblock. 'This is it,' Cooper remembers thinking. 'The barrier extended right across the road in the form of barbed wire on trestles and there was no way to slip round. As far as we could make out from our shielded lights, there were at least twenty Germans in obviously aggressive stance behind machine-guns.'

A sergeant-major approached the driver's seat where Mayne sat with his pistol in his lap. Cooper and the other four men in the back of the truck silently removed the pins from their grenades as the sound of the German's footsteps became louder. He shone a torch into the face of Mayne, who squinted at the intrusion and curled the fingers around his hidden pistol. The sergeant-major demanded the password and was met with a barrage of abuse from Karl Kahane, who leaned forward from the back of the truck and berated the German in his own language. 'How the bloody hell do we know what the bloody password is? We've been fighting the British for six bloody weeks. Now remove the bloody barrier and let us through because we're cold, tired and we want a bloody bath.'

The German was taken aback at the tirade but it seemed to have convinced him the men in truck were his own people. But then he glanced at the driver.

There was something not quite right. He just didn't look German. The sergeant-major took a couple of steps forward and crouched down so he could get a good look at Mayne's face. As he did so he found himself looking down the barrel of a pistol. He glanced beyond the gun, into the face of the man holding it and he saw no fear in the impassive eyes that stared back. Here was a man in complete control of his emotions. Then Mayne smiled. The German stiffened with fright. He turned to his men manning the roadblock and barked out a guttural command. There was the clatter of boots on the dusty road as his men hastily removed the barricade and bade the men in the truck, 'Gute Nacht'.

They returned safely early the next morning, unharmed and exhilarated, if a little bruised from all the bumps they had received courtesy of the cross-country route Mayne had been forced to take to escape a German armoured car that had been alerted by the roadblock.

The encounter at the roadblock was a microcosm of the desert war as a whole in the summer of 1942. Like the Germans confronting the truck, the Afrika Korps had allowed an opportunity for success to slip through their hands when they had failed to capitalize on the capture of Tobruk in June. The phlegmatic Field Marshal Montgomery refused to panic and, from a seemingly hopeless position, the tide gradually turned, culminating in the defeat of the German forces at the seminal battle of El Alamein in October.

The SAS, having been granted regimental status in the autumn of 1942, spent Christmas in a wadi south of Misaurata. For the last couple of months, Mayne's 'A' squadron had been busy attacking German targets around Tobruk. Now was a chance to unwind and enjoy the festive season. Montgomery, in appreciation of Mayne's effort, had sent each man a bottle of whisky and 500 cigarettes. They basked in the sun, at times quiet as they thought of their families back home, but as the whisky began to take effect, they became more garrulous, swapping anecdotes and taking the rise out of one another. Mayne, cradling the bottle of whisky in his gigantic hands, sat back and closed his eyes as he listened to his men sing. Then, remembered James, 'Paddy, with his bushy beard and massive shoulders ... [started] giving way to the mood of the moment and joining in with his strange unmusical singing to each song in turn. But he refused to sing a solo, contenting himself instead with reciting poems and becoming so enrapt with their spirit that, even as he did so, his brogue became marked enough for us to find the verses hard to follow.'

Mayne was still around to celebrate Christmas in 1943 but he was surrounded by few of the original men who had responded to Stirling's call for volunteers eighteen months earlier. Stirling himself was in Colditz, having been captured by the Germans in January. Command of the First Squadron SAS had passed to Mayne, while Stirling's brother, Bill, had taken charge of the Second Squadron.

Both had seen the desert war to its conclusion in May 1943 before embarking for Sicily. Mayne had led his men on to the beaches at Augusta on 12 July, an action for which he was awarded a second Distinguished Service Order to go with the one he had received in 1942 for his work in destroying enemy aircraft.

The Sicily campaign was to be over in thirty-eight days but when the SAS landed on the Italian mainland at the port of Termoli in early October they encountered stubborn German resistance. Mayne's orders were to seize and hold a road junction to the south-east of the town. Pitted against the SAS were a detachment of elite paratroopers. They inflicted heavy losses on the British, killing twenty-one, wounding twenty-four and capturing a further twenty-three. Mayne, however, proved too good for the opposition. As the *Official History of the SAS* recorded: 'Mayne was reported to have conducted a minor war single-handed. He was observed to have killed twelve Germans early in the fighting ... he seemed to have a charmed life but possibly some part of his "luck" was his amazingly quick reaction.'

At the start of 1944 all SAS units were recalled to Britain to prepare for the invasion of France that summer. The regiment established its headquarters in a remote Scottish village called Darvel and Mayne set about recruiting soldiers to replace the dozens who had been lost in Italy. Many of the aspirants arrived with tales of their derring-do in one theatre of war or another. This cut no ice with Mayne. He detested braggarts and he could easily detect when someone was shooting him a line. One of the new arrivals was the Reverend Fraser McLuskey. He remembered that Mayne 'could ask the most discomforting questions in the blandest of manners, and he could cut a person short with hardly a word spoken'. McLuskey had arrived in Darvel early one morning, just as Mayne and Cooper were coming to the end of an all-night drinking session. Cooper was startled to see the padre standing before him when he answered the knock at the door, but Mayne took it all in his stride. '"Well, Johnny, bring in him," he told me,' remembers Cooper. '"Pull him a pint of beer". McLuskey entered and I handed him his pint as ordered. Paddy then said, "It's time for breakfast, Padre", and clutching our tankards we entered the mess dining room, much to the astonishment of the staff.'

McLuskey, himself a shrewd judge of character, was fascinated by Mayne. He found him shy and reserved, except when he went on a drinking spree, but he soon discovered, as he proved his worth to Mayne, that 'he possessed more than his fair share of the wit and charm that come from Ireland'.

For the two months following the invasion of France on 6 June, Mayne remained in England directing operations from the regiment's new HQ in Gloucestershire. Cooper had been one of the first men dropped into occupied France to link up with the resistance and harry the German forces. He would have been glad of Mayne's inspiring presence, but unbeknown to Cooper at the time, his CO was supporting his men from England. 'While I was operating behind German lines,' recalls Cooper, 'Paddy wrote a long letter to my mother in which he told her I was in France and, although I couldn't send letters out, I could receive them when the RAF made a drop of equipment. I can't tell you how much that letter reassured her. And it wasn't just my mum he wrote to, he sent similar letters to the families of all the men in France. It showed a side to Paddy that few people were ever aware of.'

Soon, however, Mayne became bored with the life of commanding officer, perhaps worried that he ran the risk of turning into one of the pen-pushers he despised. At the beginning of August he parachuted into France, ostensibly to step up attacks on the Germans who were streaming north to escape the Allied landings in the south of the country, but also to avoid the banality of administration.

Mayne was awarded a third DSO for the way he organized and inspired his men during the entire month of August as they facilitated the advance of the Allies into German-held territory . The citation ended by saying:

'During the next few weeks he successfully penetrated the German and American lines in a jeep on four occasions in order to lead parties of reinforcements. It was entirely due to Lt-Col Mayne's fine leadership and example and his utter disregard of danger that the unit was able to achieve such striking success.'

Such effusive praise from Mayne's superiors belied the true nature of the relationship between a number of senior British officers and the maverick Irishman. To them he was a surly, unstable and disrespectful rogue who needed to be brought down a peg or two. Mayne, on the other hand, didn't waste his time thinking about officers who wouldn't know a German if he popped up behind the mess bar offering them a gin and tonic.

Cooper remembers one occasion in Italy 'when he punched a brigade major because Paddy discovered that this officer had kept a bag of the boys' mail. But Paddy was demoted and reinstated within a week because he was such a good soldier.'

But there was one way the 'freemasons of mediocrity' could blackball Mayne. They could ensure he was never awarded the Victoria Cross. He received a fourth DSO in April 1945, but everyone who was witness to what Mayne did on that remarkable day swore blind that he deserved a VC. 'It's regimental knowledge,' said Cooper, 'that everyone was a little put out at the failure to award Paddy a VC. But I think without question his reputation for manhandling senior officers worked against him.'

Mayne, still only twenty-nine, spent Christmas 1944 at home in New-townards with his family, reassuring his mother, in between mouthfuls of her delicious home cooking, that talk of his daring exploits was just blarney and his DSOs were more for leadership than heroism.

In March 1945 the SAS was called upon to spearhead the Allied thrust into Germany. They crossed the Rhine and penetrated enemy lines, gathering information and sending it back to the advancing forces coming up behind them. Mayne didn't join his men until the start of April, by which time he was fractious beyond belief having already missed out on three weeks of fighting because he was organizing proceedings from regimental HQ in England. His first task was to field a request from the Fourth Canadian Armoured Division to scout ahead and clear a path so their tanks could advance towards Oldenburg in the north-west corner of Germany.

Mayne briefed his men. Major Bond would lead B Squadron while he took charge of A Squadron. They would advance in their jeeps along parallel roads and rendezvous near Pappenburg. Within an hour Bond was dead, shot by a detachment of SS soldiers concealed in two buildings. The news was radioed to Mayne who arrived a few minutes later in a 'white-hot fury', according to Billy Hull, one of the survivors of the ambush who was now returning fire.

Mayne told the other two men in his jeep to get out. He reached into the back and pulled the Bren gun into the front passenger seat. Clipping a new magazine into his tommy-gun, he turned to Hull and told him to lay down a blanket of covering fire when he moved towards the house. Mayne rammed his foot on the accelerator and roared towards the house. Bullets sent fountains of earth from the gravel track shooting skywards but he had acted too quickly for the Germans to draw a bead on the jeep speeding towards them. It screeched to a halt in front of the doorway, the wheels throwing up a plume of dirt and dust that momentarily obscured Mayne from the Germans as he jumped out and removed the front door from its hinges with his boot. Then his men lost sight of him. For a few nerve-tingling seconds they listened to the distinctive chatter of the tommy-gun, hammering out a deadly tune to the accompaniment of the agonized shrieks of the occupants. Mayne reappeared briefly outside the house. He hurled the tommy-gun to the ground and pulled the Bren from the jeep. Stuffing two fresh magazines into his tunic pocket he disappeared inside the second house. From 100 yards up the road, Hull and the rest of Mayne's men could see his shadowy but huge figure move from room to room, killing anyone he found with bursts from the Bren.

Satisfied that he'd removed the threat, Mayne stepped over the bodies of the ten or so Germans and calmly signalled for his men to join him. Having issued them with their instructions to consolidate the newly-won position, he climbed inside his jeep with another officer operating the twin Vickers machine-gun at the rear of the vehicle. What happened next was described in the citation for his fourth DSO:

'He continued along the road all the time engaging the enemy with fire from his own jeep. Having swept the whole area very thoroughly with close-range fire, he turned his jeep round and drove back again down the road, still in full view of the enemy. By this time they had started to withdraw. Nevertheless they maintained an accurate fire on the road and it appeared almost impossible to extricate the wounded.'

The wounded were a handful of SAS men ambushed in the initial attack that had left Bond dead. They had spent several terrifying minutes sheltering behind their jeep as the Germans attempted to finish them off. In the words of Mayne's citation:

> 'Any attempt at rescuing these men under those conditions appeared virtually suicidal owing to the highly concentrated and accurate fire of the Germans.'

Mayne wasn't a man to run out on the wounded. He pulled up alongside the jeep behind which his injured men were cowering and, under intense fire, lifted them gently one by one into his jeep, telling them softly as he did so that he would soon have them in the hands of the medics. With the wounded removed from the firing line Mayne led the remainder of his men against the Germans and by the end of the day they had opened up a passage for the Canadian tanks that stretched 20 miles into enemy territory. Mayne's citation ended by saying:

> 'From the time of the arrival of Lt-Col Mayne, his cool, determined action, and his complete command of the situation, together with his unsurpassed gallantry, inspired all ranks. Not only did he save the lives of the wounded but he also completely defeated and destroyed the enemy.'

Ten years later, on the night of 15 December 1955, Mayne was again behind the wheel of a vehicle, his foot pressed hard against the accelerator as he drove wildly along an empty road. This time there were no Germans firing at him. The only enemy Mayne faced was himself. As he raced up Mill Street on the outskirts of Newtownards he lost control of his bright red sports car and smashed into a parked lorry. Blair Mayne, DSO and three bars, Croix de Guerre and Légion d'honneur, was dead. Hundreds joined Mayne's funeral cortege when he was laid to rest in the family plot a few days later. But not all mourned his passing so piously. There was the son of a Dublin senator who had been accosted by Mayne in 1952, a drunken fracas which warranted a court appearance and cost him a fine. The police, on both sides of the Irish border, had also had their run-ins with Mayne after one or other of his alcohol-fuelled escapades got a bit out of hand.

Despite his reputation as an occasional hell-raiser, Mayne was an important figure in Northern Ireland. He was Secretary of the Law Society of Belfast, attending conferences around the UK, and he had been selected as second-in-command of a British expedition to the Antarctic, but a back injury sustained in the war forced his withdrawal. He had a solid circle of friends but it seemed to them that Mayne struggled to find some purpose to his life when the war was over. The role of a peacetime officer would have been as boring to Mayne as sitting in a solicitor's office all day. When he drank sometimes he could forget his frustrations and think back to all the good times in the war; the camaraderie, the excitement, the danger. And the fear? Perhaps. None of his friends got close enough to discover if he had ever been truly scared.

One friend remembered that: 'At times it seemed that he really had settled down after the war and could find some fun in peace … [but] there were times, of course, when he became too boisterous and the more timid people in the bar decided to leave.' Vivian Jenkins, who saw him occasionally after the war at rugby internationals, still retains a great affection for his former team-mate: 'What a bloody daft way to die, after all he had been through. But he found it so hard to readjust to civilian life and you can understand it, can't you?'

Unfortunately many were unable to understand Blair Mayne in the post-war years. They viewed him as wild and uncouth, perhaps even uncontrollable, when he had had a few drinks. Some of the other men featured in this book were regarded with similar disdain. They had all fought to defend the conventional way of life enjoyed by their people and yet when they returned from the war they had difficulty in adhering to the rules deemed acceptable by these same people.

Yet society cannot send young men to war without giving something in return. They must show compassion when they come back. And if sometimes these men enjoy a boisterous night in the pub, or a bit of horseplay after a party, and it develops into something that steps outside the bounds of normal propriety, remember what they did for us.

Bibliography

Allen, D R, *Punches on the Page, A Boxing Companion* (Mainstream, 1998)

Alston, R, *Over to Rex Alston* (Frederick Muller, 1953)

Bailey, T, *The Greatest of My Time* (Eyre and Spottiswoode, 1968)

Barker, R, *The Royal Flying Corps in France* (Constable, 1995)

Barker, R, *Ten Great Innings* (Chatto and Windus, 1964)

Barron, B, *Oh When the Saints!* (Northampton: Byline, 1990)

Batchelor, D (ed.), *The Boxing Companion* (Eyre and Spottiswoode, 1964)

Blunden, E, *Undertones of War* (Four Square Books, 1962)

Bose, M, *Keith Miller* (George, Allen and Unwin, 1979)

Brady, M, *The Centre Court Story* (Fireside Press, 1957)

Brown, M, *The Imperial War Museum Book of 1918* (Guild Publishing, 1996)

Brown, M, *The Imperial War Museum Book of the First World War* (Guild Publishing, 1991)

Buchan, C, *A Lifetime in Football* (Phoenix House, 1955)

Buchanan, I, *British Olympians,* (Guinness, 1991)

Capt. Carpenter, A F B,*The Blocking of Zeebrugge* (Herbert Jenkins, 1921)

Carpentier, G, *The Art of Boxing* (George Harrap, 1926)

Carpentier, G, *Carpentier* (Hutchinson, 1955)

Carver, Field Marshal Lord, *The Boer War* (Pan, 1999)

Chesterton, G and Doggart, H, *Oxford v Cambridge Cricket* (Collins Willow, 1989)

Childs, L, *Ladysmith – The Siege* (Leo Cooper, 1999)

Coleman, F, *From Mons to Ypres with French* (Sampson Low, 1916)

Cooper, J, *One of the Originals* (Pan,1991)

Corri, E, *1000 Fights* (C Arthur Pearson, 1919)

Creagh, Sir O'Moore VC and Humphries, EM, *Distinguished Service Order 1886–1923* (Standard Art Book Company, 1924)

Creagh, Sir O'Moore VC and Humphries, EM, *Victoria Cross 1856–1920* (Standard Art Book Company, 1921)

Edrich, WJ, *Cricket Heritage* (Stanley Paul, 1948)

Edrich, WJ, *Round The Wicket* (Frederick Muller Ltd, 1959)

Edwards, S, *Soldier and Sportsman – the life of Edgar Mobbs* (Sheila Edwards,1998)

Evans, H, *Welsh International Matches 1881–2000* (Mainstream, 1999)

Ferguson, N, *The Pity of War* (Penguin, 1998)

Fleming Gibson, G, *The History of the Imperial Light Horse* (GD & Co., 1937)

Forsythe-Jaunch, Colonel W E I (compiler), *The Medical Victoria Crosses* (unpublished)

Frindall, B (ed.), *The Wisden Book of Test Cricket, 1877–1984* (Guild Publishing, 1985)

Frith, D, *By His Own Hand* (Good Books, 1990)

Frith, D, *Slow Men* (George, Allen and Unwin, 1984)

Gliddon, G, *Victoria Crosses of the Somme* (Gliddon Books, 1991)

Gliddon, G, *Victoria Crosses of Arras and Messines* (Gliddon Books, 1994)

Godwin, T, *The Guinness Book of Rugby Facts and Feats* (Guinness Publishing, 1981)

Green, B (ed.), *Wisden Anthology 1900–1949* (Guild Publishing, 1988)

Greenberg, S, *Whitaker's Olympic Almanack* (The Stationary Office, 2000)

Greyvenstein, C (ed.), *Giants of South Africa*

Griffiths, J, *The British Lions* (The Crowood Press, 1990)

Grodzinski, Captain J R, *The Battle of Moreuil Wood* (unpublished account for Lord Strathcona Regt)

Harris, J, *Arsenal Who's Who* (Independent UK Sports Publishers, 1995)

Hill, A, *Bill Edrich* (André Deutsch, 1994)

Hoe, A, *David Stirling* (Warner Books, 1992)

Horne, A, *Macmillan, 1894–1956* (Macmillan, 1988)

Horne, A, *The Price of Glory, Verdun 1916* (Penguin, 1962)

Howat, G, *Plum Warner* (Unwin Hyman, 1987)

Howat, G, *Walter Hammond* (George Allen and Unwin, 1984)

Hutton, L, *Len Hutton, Fifty Years in Cricket* (Star, 1986)

Illingworth, Capt A E and Robeson, Mjr V A H MC, *A History of 24 Squadron RAF* (RAF/Hendon Museum)

James, M, *Born of the Desert* (Greenhill Books, 1991)

Johnson, J, *Grand Slam Australia* (Courtney)

Jones, H A, *The Official History of the War in the Air* (Imperial war museum official book, 1921)

Kendall, A, *Australia's Wimbledon Champions* (ABC, 1995)

Despatches from the Vice-Admiral Roger Keyes, Dover Patrol (Published in the London Gazette, Supplement No 31189, February 19, 1919)

Lambert, B DFC, *Combat Report* (William Kimber and Co Ltd, 1973)

Lewis, C, *Sagittarius Rising* (Greenhill Books, 1993)

Luckin, M W (ed.), *The History of South African Cricket* (Hortor, 1915)

Macdonald, L, *They Called it Passchendaele* (PaperMac, 1978)

Macdonald, L, *Somme* (Papermac, 1983)

McKenzie, C, *The Raid on Zeebrugge* (www.mckenzie.uk.com, 2000)

McKenzie, A G, *The History of the Duke of Edinburgh's Own Rifles* (Galvin and Sales, 1957)

Mare, J, *The History of Air Force Rugby 1919–1999* (The RAF, 1999)

Marrinan, P, *Colonel Paddy* (Pretani Press, 1983)

Martin-Jenkins, C, *The Complete Who's Who of Test Cricketers* (Guild Publishing, 1984)

Meher-Homji, K, *Great Cricketing Families* (Reed Books, 2000)

Meyers, A W, *Memory's Parade* (Methuen, 1932)

Middlebrook, Martin and Mary, *The Somme Battlefields* (Viking, 1991)

Moore, W, *A Wood called Bourlon* (Leo Cooper, 1988)

Moran, Lord, *Anatomy of Courage* (Constable Robinson, 1945)

Maule, R, *The Complete Who's Who of England Rugby Union Internationals* (Breedon Books, 1992)

Nourse, D, *Cricket in the Blood* (Hodder and Stoughton, 1949)

Parker, A C, *Springboks 1871–1970* (Cassell, 1970)

Pawle, G, *R E S Wyatt: Fighting Cricketer* (George Allen and Unwin, 1985)

Pelmear, K, *Rugby Football: An Anthology* (George, Allen and Unwin, 1958)

Pitt, B, *Zeebrugge – St George's Day 1918* (Cassell, 1959)

Ponsonby, Rt Hon Sir Frederick, *The Grenadier Guards in The Great War* (Macmillan, 1920)

Pollock, W, *The Cream of Cricket* (Methuen)

Porter, C W, *Sir Jack Hobbs* (Spellmount, 1988)

Pridham, Major C H B, *The Charm of Cricket Past and Present* (Herbert Jenkins, 1949)

Reyburn, W, *The Lions* (A H and A W Reed, London, 1954)

Roberts, R, *Jack Dempsey* (Robson Books, 1990)

Robinson, D, *Run with the Ball* (London: Collins Willow, 1984)

Sewell, E H D, *Rugby Football Today* (John Murray, 1931)

Sewell, E H D, *The Rugby Football Union Roll of Honour 1919* (RFU publication, 1919)

Smith, R, *Great Days in Test Cricket* (ABC, 1996)

Steel, N/Hart, P, *Defeat at Gallipoli* (Papermac, 1994)

Sweet, R, *Natal 100: Century of Natal Rugby Union*

Taylor, A J P, *The First World War* (Penguin, 1963)

Terrine, J (ed.), *General Jack's Diary* (Cassell, 2000)

Thomas, C, *The History of the British Lions* (Mainstream, 1996)

Uys, I, *For Valour, History of Southern Africa's VC Heroes* (Uys Publishers, Cape Town, 1973)

Uys, I, *VCs of the Anglo-Boer War* (Fortress Financial Group, 2000)

Van Esbeck, E , *100 Years of Irish Rugby* (Gill and Macmillan, 1974)

Ward Price, G, *The Story of the Salonica Army*, (Hodder and Stroughton, 1917)

Warner, P, *Long Innings* (Harrap, 1951)

Warner, P, *The SAS* (Sphere, 1971)

Warner, P, *The Zeebrugge Raid* (William Kimber, 1978)

Webster, Lieutenant-Colonel F A M, *Olympic Cavalcade* (Hutchinson, 1948)

Wellings, EM, *Vintage Cricketers* (George, Allen and Unwin, 1983)

Whitworth, R H, *The Grenadier Guards* (Leo Cooper, 1974)

Winton, J, *The Victoria Cross at Sea* (Joseph, 1978)

Woodcock, J, *One Hundred Greatest Cricketers* (Macmillan, 1998)

Wright, G (ed.), *Wisden Cricketers Almanack 1987* (John Wisden, 1987)

Pope, S/Wheal, E A, *The Macmillan Book of The First World War* (Macmillan, 1995)

Giants of South African Cricket (Don Nelson Enterprises)

Periodicals

Cricket Lore, an article written by Richard Hill, with assistance from Brian Bassano and Mike Spurrier

Cricket – A Weekly Record

Over the Front, (Vol 3, issue 3)

Rugby Football

Rugby World

Index

Acknowledgements

One of the most rewarding aspects of writing *Fields of Glory* has been the chance to meet so many friendly and helpful people, many of whom are related to the men featured in the book. In no particular order, I would like to thank Patricia Moorhead, whose grandfather, Frank, was Tom Crean's brother. She was helpfulness itself in providing details of Tom's life, as well as a portrait reproduced in the following pages.

The entire Lowe family, in particular Cyril's son, Charles, and his son, John, both went out of their way to give me information.

Rosemary Fitch, granddaughter of Admiral Carpenter, and Colin McKenzie, great nephew of Albert McKenzie, both of whom took part in the Zeebrugge Raid, provided me with photos and anecdotes of the raid in which Arthur Harrison lost his life.

Jenny Edwards, niece of Edgar Mobbs, kindly gave me permission to quote from letters sent from her uncle to his family.

In the course of writing the book I was fortunate enough to wangle myself a trip to South Africa, where I shared a few beers with a childhood hero of mine, Vintcent van der Bijl, as we talked about his father. It was a memorable day. Vince pointed me in the direction of several people who knew his father. Thank you Mrs van der Bijl, Paul Dobson, Norman Gordon, Clive van Reynveld, Brian de Kock and Pat O'Sullivan and Chris Enstin and everyone connected with the 'Dukes'.

Others who deserve a mention in despatches are Sunderland FC, Rob Mason, the club's 'oracle', Ian Cook at the Arsenal Museum, Major BT Eastwood, Regimental Archivist of the Grenadier Guards, the Old Malvernians, Bill Adcocks, UK Athletics, Colonel (Retd) Ian McCausland, Regimental Museum, The Royal Green Jackets, the British Olympic Association, Ian Buchanan, author of *British Olympians*, Georgina Ferry, editor of *Oxford Today* magazine, Diana Coke at the Royal Humane Society, Stephen Green at the MCC Library, Mark Mortimer – my military adviser, Terry Marsh of the Old Alleynians, the Magnus family, Constable Publishers for allowing me to quote from Lord Moran's *Anatomy of Courage*, Lionel Leventhal and Greenhill Books for allowing me to quote from *Born of the Desert* by Malcolm James, Hugh Ross, David Harkins, Mark Williams of Lion Street Books in Hay-on-Wye, George Mobbs, Ros Hargreaves at Northampton Saints RFC, Portoroa Royal School, Enniskillen, Audrey Snell at the All England library, Malcolm Pleydell and the untiringly cheerful and helpful staff at the Public Records Office at Kew, the Imperial War Museum, the RAF Museum, Hendon, the *Belfast Telegraph* and the National Maritime Museum, the National Army Museum and, last, but by no means least, Rex King and Jed Smith at the RFU Museum at Twickenham.

Terry Long, of Wanderers RFC, was magnificent in digging out photos of Fred Harvey and Robert Johnston. Cheers, Terry, I look forward to sinking a few pints with you in Dublin. Glen Hunter kindly sent in a fantastic framed photograph of Herby Taylor all the way from South Africa. Elizabeth Boardman, Brasenose College Archivist, and Mary O'Doherty, Royal College of Surgeons in Dublin, were also wonderful in responding to my requests for information on A N S Jackson and Tom Crean respectively. One of my most arduous tasks in researching the book was the trip to the Green Howards Regimental Museum. I had the misfortune to travel on a day when the train service was at its most temperamental and, although it took me nearly as long to reach Richmond, Yorkshire, from London, as it did Cape Town, I made it eventually and was calmed by the hospitality of Richard Leake and Roger Chapman. The museum, by the way, is well worth a visit.

My publishers at Carlton warrant a special mention, particularly Martin Corteel, Deborah Fioravanti, for her diligence in pursuing the photos, and Kerrin Edwards for tolerating my tardiness in sending the finished manuscript. The French postal service, Kerrin, honest…!

I would like to thank Rory Underwood very much for writing the foreword to the book. Thanks are also due to Peter Arnold for his help.

John Kane, Haydn Tanner and Vivian Jenkins all demand my most sincere thanks for their reminiscenes, hospitality and photographs. Three great men.

Talking of hospitality, thanks to the boys – Tim Clifton, Tom Tudor, John Dobson, Julian Crabtree and Tim Northam – for giving me a floor on which to crash on my frequent trips back across the Channel to London. At the time I offered them a mention in the book and a cut of the royalties. One out of two ain't bad!

To Sandy, thank you for your patience and love, sweetheart, and I promise, no more war stories, well, for a while. To mum and dad, I owe you a massive debt of gratitude, not just for proof-reading the book and offering your suggestions, but more importantly, for tolerating my occasional waywardness and never having put pressure on me to conform.

Finally, I would like to thank Erral Penny and John Cooper. You were kind enough to reach into your past and provide me with stories and memories that were a privilege to hear. I know the readers of *Fields of Glory* will feel the same when they read what you did as young men. In a world which has lost the true meaning of the word 'hero', you are its personification.